The American Crow and the Common Raven

NUMBER TEN

The W. L. Moody, Jr., Natural History Series

The American Crow

and the Common Raven

BY LAWRENCE KILHAM

Illustrations by Joan Waltermire

TEXAS A&M UNIVERSITY PRESS : COLLEGE STATION

Library of Congress Cataloging-in-Publication Data

Kilham, Lawrence, 1910–
    The American crow and the common raven / by Lawrence
Kilham ; illustrations by Joan Waltermire. — 1st ed.
    p.   cm.— (The W.L. Moody, Jr., natural history series ; no.
10)
    Bibliography: p.
    Includes index.
    ISBN 0-89096-377-0 cloth; 0-89096-466-1 paper (alk. paper) :
    1. Corvus brachyrhynchos — Behavior.   2. Corvus corax —
Behavior.
3. Birds — Behavior.   I. Title.   II. Series.
QL696.P2367K55   1989
598.8'64 — dc19   88-10174
                                                                      CIP

How many of us have ever got to know a wild animal? I do not mean merely to meet with one once or twice, . . . but to really know it for a long time . . . and to get an insight into life and history.

ERNEST THOMPSON SETON

Contents

Figures

Tables

Preface

This book reports my observations of American Crows (*Corvus brachyrhynchos*) on a cattle ranch in Florida where the crows were unusually tame and on a farm in New Hampshire where they were wary, as they are in most places. My aim has been to make a study of all aspects of crow behavior. As often happens, it seems that our commonest birds are the ones most neglected by researchers. When I began this study in 1981, many of the behaviors I have observed, including cooperative breeding, territoriality, storing of food, copulations, play, foraging, interrelations with other animals, allopreening, and various "uncrowlike" vocalizations that I have recorded, had either not been described or had been described in only minimal detail by previous authors. As far as I am aware, the cooperative breeding of American Crows, hitherto almost entirely neglected by ornithologists, is more highly developed in them than in any other bird north of Mexico.

Many of my observations on corvids have been published in the *Auk, Wilson Bulletin, Condor, Journal of Field Ornithology, Florida Field Naturalist,* and *Canadian Field-Naturalist.* For this book I have added many new observations as well as more complete interpretations of earlier material. The book includes three chapters on Common Ravens (*C. corax*), which I also observed on the farm in New Hampshire. I have supplemented field studies on both species with observations on hand-raised individuals. These were important in giving me a deeper appreciation of these birds than I could have gained from field studies alone. Some of the material on hand-raised crows is reprinted from my book *A Naturalist's Field Guide,* with permission of Stackpole Books, Harrisburg, Pennsylvania.

In seeking to present American Crows and Common Ravens in their entirety as living birds, I decided that a narrative style would be the best way of doing so. Statistics, useful as they are in many fields of biology, are not necessarily so in trying to understand animals (particularly ones as highly developed as crows and ravens) as whole, sentient, consciously thinking beings that share many emotional and other mental attributes with ourselves. Although personal observations predominate in the text, I have included extensive references to the behavior of *Corvus* species throughout the world as well as to other birds that illustrate special points. In giving the contexts of various behaviors, I have recapitulated incidents given in other chapters.

I have spent eight thousand hours over a six-year period studying crows and ravens. The introductory chapter and the epilogue express the views of an amateur on research in animal behavior, the need for a broader approach, and, if only more amateurs could be induced to take up the study of bird behavior, the considerable opportunities that lie open, as I show in this book on the "common" crow, to add to our knowledge of our commonest birds.

Throughout the book I have used the convention "(n = 3)" or some other number to indicate how many times a given phenomenon or behavior was observed. If males were observed doing something three times and females six, I would write that the behavior "was observed in males (n = 3) and females (n = 6)."

My recordings of crow and raven vocalizations were made on a Sony WM D6 Professional Walkman recorder with a Realistic, 33-1062, Ultradirectional Electret microphone. Copies of my recordings have been deposited in the Florida State Museum Bioacoustic Archives, Gainesville, Florida, and are available to other workers.

I thank James H. Hendrie, Sr., and John A. Hendrie for permitting my wife Jane and me to visit their ranch; James N. Layne and Fred E. Lohrer for general assistance while we were staying at the Archbold Biological Station, Lake Placid, Florida; J. W. Hardy of the Florida State Museum, for advice on making sound recordings and providing sonagrams; Jane Chamberlain-Auger for sending me unpublished results of her observations on the cooperative breeding of American Crows on Cape Cod, Massachusetts; and my wife Jane for help in watching nests. I am also obliged to my son Ben for aid in studying crows and particularly ravens in Lyme, New Hampshire, and to Walter Record for permitting me to visit his farm and for giving me much helpful information.

The American Crow and the Common Raven

1. Introduction

Crows are something special. I discovered this when I was eight years old. I had loved animals since I was five, but all that I could get hold of as pets were rabbits and white mice. We lived in Brookline, Massachusetts, on the outskirts of Boston. School was out in 1918 when, walking around the corner of the road where we lived, I met a policeman holding a well-feathered nestling crow. He had picked it up on the sidewalk and, not knowing what to do with it, was happy to give it to me. Nothing could have been more exciting than that crow. The family was about to move to our summer place in the White Mountains of New Hampshire. When we got there, I liberated Joe the crow. Our house was surrounded by woods and fields, and Joe was free to come and go. He chose mostly to stay close to us and became very much one of the family. He followed me on walks and was a wonderful companion until he flew off early in September, to join his own kind, I hoped. In a life devoted to natural history and keeping animals, I have always remembered Joe as an outstanding experience. I have met others who have had crows when they were young. They all glow with enthusiasm at the memory. Crows, and with them I include ravens, seem as though by convergent evolution to have something in their psyches corresponding to something in our own.

A prime consideration in studying a bird is to find just the right place to do so. Finding a group of Red-headed Woodpeckers in an unusually favorable place in Maryland, I decided that here indeed was a bird to concentrate on, to learn all I could about its habits, which I did off and on for twenty years. I did the same for Pileated Woodpeckers when I discovered Sapelo

Getting Started: A Sense of Place

Island, a sea island off the coast of Georgia. All of the places that Jane and I visited over a thirty-year period to study some particular bird, whether Sapelo or the Mayan ruins at Tikal in Guatemala, were not only A-1 from the bird-watching point of view but were beautiful and interesting in themselves, with varied kinds of natural history to watch on the side. I never imagined that I would someday find a place with comparable attractions for studying crows.

Crows are so wary in most places that for years I gave little thought to studying them. But after more than twenty years of studying woodpeckers on early mornings, weekends, and vacations from teaching and doing research on viruses at the Dartmouth Medical School, I was ready for a change. Retired and with more time, I wanted a project that, like the woodpeckers (Kilham 1983), would provide things to discover for years to come.

After several years of trying this and that, Jane and I found ourselves staying at the Archbold Biological Station in southern Florida. My idea was to study the courtship of Red-shouldered Hawks. I have long had an interest in the courtship of birds, and the circling and screaming of Red-shouldereds in spring has seemed to me, since pre-college days, one of the more stirring of bird performances. Florida Red-shouldereds are relatively common, and after some scouting within reasonable distances of the Archbold station, I found that the best place to watch them was at a cattle ranch not far down the road. I was there following a hawk on December 29, 1980, when I lost it. It was a cold, gray day, and I felt discouraged at how little I had found that morning. It was at this low point that a remarkable event occurred. Out of a swamp came an exotic *cu-koo*. What could make such an odd sound? An escapee from a zoo? I walked in the direction of the sound, but I did not have to walk far before finding a crow on a low tree only eight meters above my head. After shaking its head, the crow bowed with bill against its chest, then pulled its head up sharply as it made a clear *cu-koo*. Instead of flying away as I expected, it came even closer. It was obviously tame, and so were others that alighted on branches to have a look at me. They were almost asking to be studied! With a background of fondness for crows, I was not long in making up my mind. Here was an incredible opportunity. At times I think, like Thoreau, that I am lucky beyond what I deserve.

"Each biologist," wrote Agnes Arbor (1954), "should be able to say to himself, like Descartes, that his intention is to build upon a foundation that is all his own." This may seem difficult when one is starting out, but it is the only way likely to be enjoyable. There is no such thing as one scientific method that all must follow (Conant 1964). As Nietzsche said of philosophy, "This is my way. What is yours? As for the way, there is no such thing." Each must find or invent techniques best suited to his or her individual approach.

When I started out as a professional microbiologist or "virus hunter," I wondered how my other love, studying birds on early mornings, evenings, and weekends, would fare. Would my enthusiasm for birds and animals cut in on my pursuit of viruses? I need not have worried. My birds, in a roundabout way, complemented and aided my viruses. When I discovered a new virus or a new aspect of some disease, I had exciting work to do for a number of years, work with no competition. Papers poured forth. When returns began to diminish, I faced a period of lower productivity until I again discovered something. My low virus periods, fortunately, were often high ones for the woodpeckers. Mere numbers of publications, of course, mean nothing in themselves. One really good paper is accomplishment enough for a lifetime. But I find for my own good that writing and observing go hand in hand. Writing is a way of thinking, and by writing about what I see, I am apt to see more. To always have things on hand is good for the morale. In this sense pursuing viruses and birds at the same time was no loss but more entertaining, I think, as well as productive. I have never seen the wit of limiting oneself to narrow interests.

Ornithology is one of the few sciences in which an amateur has a chance of getting something published. How thankful I have been to editors of the *Auk*, the *Wilson Bulletin*, the *Condor*, and other professional journals for accepting articles and notes I have written, each one, however minor, representing something discovered. My bird studies influenced my viruses in more ways than one. I carried my amateur outlook into the laboratory and did work that I liked to do and not, I am afraid, what administrators (who were not researchers) directed.

Preferring to be a free agent, I have always shunned the idea, whether with birds or viruses, of starting with a hypothetical problem and sticking to it. The challenge is to get from the known to the unknown. Almost any problem may set the wheels in motion. But once under way, I know that I can do best by observing all that birds do, taking notes, then reviewing and

Strategy and Tactics

reflecting on them when I get home. Persisting in this pedestrian fashion I find that something always turns up. It is the chance discovery that makes science exciting. As Lorenz (1970) states in a chapter entitled "Companions as Factors in the Bird's Environment," "The factual data upon which all of the following investigations are based are derived almost entirely from chance observation." The chance experiment, he thinks, assures an impartial observer freedom from any initial hypothesis. I have long found such ideas congenial. They echo Louis Pasteur's dictum, enshrined at the Harvard Medical School, where I went for four years, that "chance favors the prepared mind."

Initial Discoveries

I must admit that when I started watching crows much of what I saw was confusing. In studying woodpeckers I was usually watching a single pair with the sexes differing in plumage. With the crows in Florida, I found myself looking at a group of individuals that looked much alike. A few discoveries, however, provided ways of organizing. One was that a cattle drive, a track bordered on either side by wire fences, was a territorial boundary between two groups of seven to nine crows. A second discovery, following shortly thereafter, was that each group consisted of a breeding pair plus auxiliaries. I was to find out later that the latter aided in all phases of nesting. It was exciting to discover that crows were cooperative breeders. I could not find a single paper on the cooperative breeding of American Crows in the literature nor any on their territorial behavior. I was to learn in the next year or two that many aspects of crow behavior had either never been reported or were mentioned in only minimal detail by others. "There has," writes Stokes in *A Guide to the Behavior of Common Birds* (1979), "been amazingly little study of Crows by researchers." The "common" crow, it turned out, was something of a frontier, a bonanza in terms of discoveries lying around, as it were, waiting to be made. My discoveries have not been earthshaking, but that does not bother me. All is process. The fun is in searching, and my search has been to find out how crows live and, as far as possible, what goes on in their minds.

I could not have spent so many years and thousands of hours at a place like the Hendrie ranch had Jane not been there to share my excitements. Yet in the many beautiful and unusual places that we have visited, we have never stayed together when actually watching. Once we arrive at a place, she likes to go the way that appeals to her, and I wander about pursuing things of interest to me. In this way each of us, at the end of a morning, has news for the other. Both of us have long realized the importance of being alone when observing. "My method," writes Lawrence (1986), "requires that I work alone, for a second person invariably distracts me by his or her very presence. This means that I cannot put myself in a fully relaxed, neutral state, which I have found to be a way that works best for me when I am trying to gain the confidence of a wild being."

Whether working with viruses or birds, I like to work with a minimum of apparatus. As Rousseau remarked, "the more ingenious and accurate our instruments, the more unsusceptible and inexpert become our organs: by assembling a heap of machinery about us, we find afterwards none in ourselves." A feature of studying behavior is that all one needs is a pair of field glasses, a notepad, and an open mind. One cannot, or at least I cannot, study bird behavior and be occupied with a complicated piece of apparatus. Observing is a full-time occupation. You have to have your mind on what you are doing. Important bits of behavior—a copulation, a glimpse of a passing predator, or something new and unexpected—can take place in seconds. If one's mind is on a camera, wondering how to get a good picture, one's mind is not on what a bird is doing; being a good photographer is also a full-time occupation.

I have used the camera as an example, but the principle applies to any kind of apparatus. Wanting to record some of the "uncrowlike" vocalizations made by crows in the early breeding season, I bought a tape recorder, light, compact, and easy to use—a model apparatus. Yet when bent on getting the best possible recordings of this or that vocalization, I was dismayed at how much crow behavior I missed. To me, statistics, when used as a "must," are as much of a drag on observations of the kind that I like to make as is the use of a camera or a tape recorder. If one concentrates on producing a statistically sound publication, one may overlook much of what birds are doing. Emphasis will be on covering as many nests or pairs as possible. But in trying to study birds as whole, living entities, noting everything they do, I find that two pairs of woodpeckers or, with crows, two cooperatively breeding groups, is the maximum that I can study effectively. I am committed to this approach and thus feel that simple narration, or an anecdotal style, is the soundest way of presenting how animals live. As Griffin (1984) points out, "We are still over reacting to the disparage-

Working in the Simplest Way

ment of anecdotal data on which Darwin relied . . . these inhibitions have filtered out of the published data base many observations that could become starting points of new research."

Recognition of
Individuals

Recognition of individuals is essential to behavior studies, but
I never cared to do so by banding birds or animals that I have
studied. Color banding birds does not solve all problems.
When I tried following woodpeckers banded by others, after
years of studying unbanded individuals, I found the bands
more of a hindrance than an asset. It took too much time for
a woodpecker to get in the right position for me to see what
bands it wore. By not having my birds banded, I forced myself to look for natural physical or behavioral markers, which
is an exercise that can, in itself, lead to discoveries. By looking carefully at Downy and Hairy Woodpeckers I found that
they all have different patterns of black, white, and red on the
backs of their heads, which is easier to see than bands on legs
(Kilham 1983).

A few scientists, including Snow (1976), Burley (1985), and
Southern and Southern (1985), have reported deleterious effects on birds that have been trapped, handled, or banded. A
dominant male Calfbird that Snow banded was sufficiently
traumatized that, when back on his porch on the following
morning, the bird periodically closed his eyes and was driven
away by one that had been his subordinate. There had evidently
been a fight, for there were forty-two feathers on the ground.
It took the banded male a week to regain his former position.

In studying Jungle Babblers, which are cooperative breeders, Gaston (1977) found that they became accustomed to his
presence and allowed a close approach. But when he caught
one of a group in a mist net, the tameness was destroyed. I
did not want to climb trees to band crows or to look at nests
because I knew that these procedures would badly frighten the
birds. A few false moves and I could be labeled an "enemy of
crows" and thus, in one blow, have destroyed the value of the
ranch as a very special place. Croze (1970), with similar con-
siderations for Carrion Crows, writes that "I did not colour-
ring the crows, since this would have meant catching them on
the field and scaring them badly. I therefore relied on the behaviour of the crows (who sported no distinct markings) to
determine whether or not they were the right pair."

Crows, being essentially all black, present difficulties. But
by scattering corn to each group within its territory every morn-

Figure 1. Seven crows of cooperative breeding group A feeding on corn scattered for them every morning. A pair of Sandhill Cranes fed with them regularly.

ing I could view the ones I was studying at distances of seven to ten meters (Fig. 1) and be able to distinguish adults from yearlings readily. Good (1952) and Dwight (1975) state that yearlings have a brownish and adults a purplish cast to the feathers of back, wings, and tail. This difference, however, is usually not discernible in the field. Of greater value is the finding of Emlen (1936) that while adult crows have rectrices that are generally intact, with truncated ends forming a rounded tail, those of yearlings are frayed, pointed at the ends, and form square tails.

The sexes of breeding pairs in each group were recognizable by behavior: the males were dominant, and the females built nests and incubated the eggs. Further recognition of individuals, as I bring out in later chapters, was by physical markers such as broken or missing wing or tail feathers, bill deformities, vocalizations, and special behaviors.

Importance of Tameness

Animals cannot be expected to act naturally if they are afraid. Of utmost importance in conducting any life-history study is to be sure not to disturb the subjects. If I sat too close to a nest of woodpeckers, I observed one kind of behavior. If I moved back until I could detect no signs of hesitancy or fear, results were different. By preserving the tameness of the crows in Florida Jane and I could walk freely below nests without disturbing their owners. It was not difficult at eight to ten meters to learn when eggs hatched or how many young were being fed. Had I had more years at the ranch, I would have experimented with ways to make them even tamer. One has to get close to birds and animals to understand them fully.

Two Schools of Thought

One cannot write a book such as this without facing the fact that there are two schools of thought regarding animal and bird behavior and that proponents of one are not always tolerant of those of the other. The most widely accepted or behaviorist view is that birds and animals are not much more than mechanical robots and that most everything we need to know about them can be established scientifically, by quantification and statistics.

There is no doubt that many scientific problems have yielded to these approaches. But a successful methodology can become a dogmatic creed. The behaviorists cry "anthropomorphism," "trivial," or "anecdotal" whenever they suspect anyone of interpreting animal behavior in a way outside the accepted view. "As scientists," wrote Olas Murie (1962), "we are extremely timid about assigning to other animals any of the mental or psychological traits of man. One would think that the scientist is the perfect fundamentalist, carefully maintaining a wall between man and other animals." One has to have really lived with animals, either hand-raised individuals or ones in the wild, to realize the strength of the behaviorists' opposition. "We are living in a time," wrote Nobel Prize winner Lorenz (1970), "in which it has become fashionable to assess the exactitude, and the values of any scientific result by the extent to which quantitative methods have taken part in producing it. Now this is one of the dangerous half-truths which fashion is prone to accept." The fallacy is what the philosopher Alfred North Whitehead referred to as "the fallacy of misplaced concreteness." Donald Griffin, professor of biology at Rockefeller University, thinks that scientists should stop considering animals as robots and study them as feeling, consciously thinking entities. "The behavioristic viewpoint," wrote Griffin (1984), "has been accepted implicitly if not explicitly, by ethologists studying animal behavior, so it is not surprising that they learn very little about animal thoughts and feelings." He thinks the viewpoint "should be abandoned not so much because it belittles the value of animals, but because it leads us to a seriously incomplete and misleading picture of reality."

I do quantify some aspects of crow behavior in this book, such as feeding visits to nestlings, where I think quantification especially helpful. Among the more useful courses I took at Harvard, oddly enough, was one in statistics. Although I have never liked mathematics, I enjoyed the course and got a good grade. But I doubt if my instructors knew why I was so pleased. What I realized was that, in the kind of research that I wanted to do, whether with viruses or birds, I would never need to resort to statistics. Furthermore I would not need to be overawed by those who used statistics and quantification with an air of such finality.

There is much that is enjoyable in thinking for oneself and studying birds in one's own way. Few seem to realize that even an ordinary person can make discoveries. The only hitch is, as Polanyi (1959) pointed out, that "you cannot discover or invent anything unless you are convinced that it is there ready to be found. The recognition of this hidden presence is in fact half the battle. It means that you have hit on a real problem and are asking the right questions." This book is mainly an account of my search for the "hidden presence" in crows and ravens. There has been no magic involved. Only the thousands of hours of watching, none of which have been dull.

Part I. BEHAVIOR OF COOPERATIVELY BREEDING CROWS ON A CATTLE RANCH IN FLORIDA

I find studying the behavior of animals in their natural surroundings a fascinating hobby. It allows one to live out of doors and in beautiful scenery; it gives free scope to one's urge to observe and to reflect; and it leads to discoveries. Even the most trivial discovery gives intense delight.

NIKO TINBERGEN

In more ways than one, the Hendrie ranch was a grand place for studying wildlife. Not the least of its attractions was its accessibility, being only short distance down a highway from the Archbold Biological Station. After unlocking the gate, Jane and I had fifteen minutes of driving over a sandy road to reach the crows. But the time was not wasted. We occasionally saw bobcats, gopher tortoises, deer, Florida Scrub Jays, Wild Turkeys, and once a diamondback rattler. On approaching the center of the ranch in early January, after being away for eight months in New Hampshire, I always wondered whether the crows would still be around. Parking the car in its usual place by a pasture gate, I scanned the landscape. How deserted everything looked! Had something happened? "Crowsy, crowsy, here crowsy," I yelled. Then within seconds Jane and I heard the welcome sound of *caws* coming from all directions. It was as if we had been away only overnight instead of eight months. The crows remembered us! Of the many kinds of birds in the world, I wonder how many are as personable as crows.

One male was particularly tame. Almost every morning on one of our four-month stays at the ranch, he and two or three of his associates, noticing when I scattered corn to a neighboring group, gathered at their boundary waiting for me to come. Morning after morning when I crossed over to walk their section of pasture, the male accompanied me, flying from one cow pie to another just ahead. I talked to him as I went along. Talking to animals that I am fond of, whether dogs or crows, puts me in the kind of rapport I like to have, a feeling of empathy. At the ranch I became just one more animal, like several old horses and five hundred or more head of cattle that the crows accepted as part of their environment.

Another positive feature of the ranch was the ease of walking about on it. At the center, where the crows lived, the grazing of cattle kept the grass short and the groves of live oaks free of undergrowth. The trimmed appearance reminded Jane and me of an English country estate. Since the ranch was eight kilometers square and separated from adjoining lands by swamps and bayheads, the center of it was like an island, a sanctuary that few visited except those running the ranch.

There was an abundance of animals, some wild and some domestic and all interesting to us. In addition to bulls, cows, and calves — mixtures of everything from Brahmans and zebus, to Herefords — there were feral hogs with litters, caracaras, Sandhill Cranes, river otter, and, following heavy rains, hundreds of White Ibis and other waders. While it might seem a distraction to keep an eye on this array of wildlife, it was apparent that the crows did so as well. Some discoveries, ones that excited me the most, came from noting the relations of the crows to various birds and animals.

Florida is a cattle-raising state. If more ranch owners were as enlightened as the Hendries in protecting wildlife and not cutting down all the trees or draining all the swamps, I often thought, what a boon it would be, not only to wildlife but also to those who might wish to study it.

2. Varieties of Foraging

Crows are intelligent, curious, and omnivorous, and the combination leads them to look for food in a wide variety of places.

TREES

It is easy to believe that crows are essentially birds of open fields, for it is usually difficult to see what they are doing when they are among trees. I was surprised in Florida at how much of the crows' foraging was done either in trees or on the ground below. They seemed particularly drawn to cabbage palms. Crows visited them in groups of two to six, with one or two in the top beating on the hard leaf stalks or shaking the leaves by moving about. The remainder walked or stood below with bills pointed up, waiting for whatever might fall. Some jumped to catch prey before it landed. Cabbage palms provide lurking places for a variety of creatures, and beating on leaf stalks was a way of dislodging them. Among the prey knocked down and captured were large insects, spiders, small frogs, and a snake 25 centimeters long.

Knocking on cabbage palms was a standby type of foraging. If other places were barren of food because of rain, cold, or drought, the palms were something to turn to. The crows of one group worked on a small grove of palms near their nest every morning in the drought year of 1985. Additional attractions were dead fronds on the ground that might conceal food. When turning over a big one, a crow might put its head underneath, then shove while flapping its wings.

Trees in the center of the ranch other than cabbage palms were mainly live oaks and bay trees that grew in the wet places known as bayheads. Many times when I thought a crow no more than resting on a limb, it would suddenly fly to a leafy branch to knock prey to the ground or, landing farther up, work its way down a branch while flapping its wings or even hanging upside down. Prey captured in these ways included katydids, wolf spiders, small frogs, and anoles. The ground below groves was covered with leaves that fell in winter. Crows spent much time walking about among them, occasionally finding caterpillars, frogs, small snakes, and other items. One snake was captured in a sally from a low limb.

The oaks were a special resource in the winter of 1982–83 when they bore a crop of acorns. Crows gathered acorns by flying to the top of an oak, filling their antelingual pouches, then flying to a pasture to pound them open, using cow pies and weathered logs as anvils. Acorns remained on oaks until well into January, when crows continued to recover them in small numbers on the ground.

The crows of one group spent much time in a bayhead in the wet winter of 1982–83. They caught frogs there, for I watched a number of them fly out with frogs in their bills. As with the acorns, the crows used cow pies as anvils for pounding and tearing. Clusters of wax myrtle berries, growing along the edges of bayheads and other places, were visited by four or five crows at a time, several crows walking about picking up berries on the ground while others clung to clusters above. On January 15, 1983, when five crows suddenly flew from a wax myrtle, two carried sprigs of leaves and berries in their bills. The only other fruit I saw crows taking were pokeberries.

Pastures

The crows spent much time walking about pastures, either alone or in scattered groups, stopping here and there, but seeming to find little on many occasions. From a distance, however, it is difficult to determine what a crow may be finding. Turning over cow pies was a frequent occupation, especially in the dry years when the pats were hard on top and moist underneath. A usual approach was to seize a cow pie, push it on edge, then let it fall over. A crow might hop, run, or do both in its hurry to reach a cow pie. Skead (1952) noted Black Crows in South Africa making quick approaches to cowpats, apparently to overcome the agility of dung beetles, of which they are especially fond. This could have been true of the crows in Florida. There were fewer cow pies at the ranch in wet years, seemingly because crows, Sandhill Cranes, and others of what I called the "cow pie guild" had an easier time knocking them apart.

The crows exhibited various behaviors when hunting insects. They might stand upright, as if on the lookout, then walk, run, or fly to make a capture. When chasing grasshoppers and flying insects, a crow's course, involving a mixture of running, flying, hopping, jumping to this side or that, was highly erratic.

Feral hogs damaged pastures by rooting up large areas of sod. Crows sometimes stood on the ground by the head of a hog as it rooted, on the lookout for what might turn up. The crows also turned over old sods. I could not determine what they were finding until one morning, when they were close, I saw that they were feeding on small, wiry earthworms.

The crows usually did little digging. On January 1, 1983, however, I noted a few of them jabbing their slightly opened bills into an area of rough grass, pulling up tufts of sod, then finding something beneath. I have also watched crows digging under oaks. While it is difficult to see just how they use their bills, I once had a close view of how they probably do so. I had left a plastic bag containing corn on the grass, and a crow, coming upon it, pecked hard to dig out the corn. Although unable to penetrate the bag, the crow opened its bill wide at the end of each blow, as if to enlarge any opening or weak place that might present itself. I have seen the maneuver used in storing corn, and Jollet (1984) saw Carrion Crows using it in digging for earthworms. Sallies from fence posts were another form of foraging. I occasionally saw crows fly from them to seize a frog, a dragonfly, and once, the egg case of a Polyphemus moth.

The only prey that I ever saw a crow catch in flight over a pasture was a young cotton rat. The crow was flying above tall grass when it suddenly banked, then dropped on its prey in the manner of a Northern Harrier.

FLOODED FIELDS

Pastures dried out between rains and could remain dry for considerable periods, as they did in 1981–82. Heavy rains in the next two years flooded the pastures, creating areas that remained wet for weeks at a time. Most noteworthy of these was a grassy ditch that, when at full flood, cut across the wide bend of a stream, breaking into pools and grassy rapids in several places. Swarms of tiny fish migrated into these temporary pools, growing rapidly in the week or two that followed.

Crows picked up many while walking along ditches, sometimes wading in belly deep and getting heads and bills wet in striking at prey. They preyed on frogs particularly in 1983, the year of an El Niño event. After capturing a frog, a crow usually took it to a dry part of a pasture to tear it apart. On April 1, 1983, a crow flew toward me with a frog about eight centimeters long in its bill. The frog escaped, but the crow recaptured it, then took eight minutes to pound, partly devour, and store what remained. Even small frogs were torn apart before swallowing.

Large fish and salamanders also entered the ditch. Between mid-January and mid-February, 1983, I noted crows working on walking catfish 13 to 20 centimeters long on a number of occasions. The crows sometimes caught catfish on their own. I was watching two crows running back and forth in a shallow rapid in late January when one seized a catfish and flew off with it. On another day a crow caught a fish in a grassy area flooded from a nearby swamp. But most catfish were obtained in other ways. There were three days in late January, 1985, when the temperature fell below freezing. Although the freezing temperature may not have lasted for more than a few hours, it was enough to kill the walking catfish, which are of tropical origin. I found crows as well as Crested Caracaras and Turkey Vultures feeding on ones up to 25 centimeters long for nearly a week afterward.

Crows can be resourceful in finding and capturing fish. Funderburg (1967a) watched American Crows in Florida feeding on dead and dying fish that came to the surface of lakes following cold waves or the use of fish poisons. Dunn (1985) describes a Carrion Crow putting its head under water as it caught fish in a coastal rock pool, and Stahl (1985) observed Hooded Crows hovering over open water like gulls diving for small fish. Hughes (1976) reported an unusually interesting case of fishing for a pair of Carrion Crows. While one of the pair stood on a concrete ledge by a river, its mate plunged into the water and, after being under for a few seconds, reappeared with a fish, which it tossed to the ground. The second crow then killed the fish and flew off with it to feed nestlings.

Robbing Water Birds

Waterbirds came to flooded areas in days after heavy rains. On March 2, 1984, I watched several crows land in shallow water in front of an advancing line of White Ibis. They were apparently using the ibis as beaters, for I saw a crow capture a large salamander in front of the ibis. Several weeks later, following more heavy rains, Great Egrets and White Ibis were catching large eel-like salamanders that were either two-toed amphiumas or greater sirens. Crows were nearly always among them. When an egret captured a salamander, three or four crows would start walking behind it. Egrets usually struck a salamander several times in efforts to subdue it, then dropped it into the water. This gave a waiting crow a chance to dart in and grab it, as I saw on three occasions. Three crows were following an egret on one of these when a Red-shouldered Hawk swooped, causing the egret to drop its prey. While the egret faced the hawk and two crows, a third crow, wading into the water, picked up the salamander, then flew with it to a log below its nest. Here it tore half of its prize to pieces, loaded its antelingual pouch, and flew to the nest to feed the incubating female. It returned to feed her the other half in a few minutes.

On March 26 I noted three crows of a cooperative group chasing White Ibis with salamanders on five occasions. The ibis dropped its prey after three to ten seconds in four of the chases, a single crow dropping to the ground to pick it up. The ibis and crows disappeared over treetops, where I could not follow them in a fifth chase. Relatively few ibis came to the ditch in subsequent weeks until, with another rain, the ditch overflowed again. This time I saw only one chase. A single crow, after causing an ibis to drop a salamander, was working on it when a Red-shouldered Hawk attacked. The hawk hovered within 30 centimeters with talons outstretched, as the crow, still holding the salamander, jumped into the air making a *wraack* note. A second crow, flying in low in what seemed a cooperative effort, drove the hawk away. The first crow then flew to the nest, where it fed the nestlings. The crows seemed to have little fear of the ibis. When six to eight ibis were by the ditch on the following morning, one crow, seeing an ibis occupied with something, supplanted it by jumping onto its back. When the ibis moved over, the crow investigated the spot where the ibis had been.

The drying up of swamps in January and February, 1985, led to a concentration of fish and other prey that attracted hundreds of ibis and smaller numbers of Great Egrets. Although the trees made it difficult to see what the birds were doing, I saw crows chasing and robbing ibis on a few occasions. After the swamps had dried up and the ibis had left, I rarely saw crows with prey of any size. Then suddenly, following a moderate rain on March 23, I began to see crows with salamanders again. On one occasion three crows pursued an ibis for 150 meters along a stream until the ibis dropped its prey into the water. It seemed in this as in other years that crows found robbing White Ibis profitable, more so than any other species, bird or mammal, that they robbed with any regularity. I should emphasize that the crows I watched did all of their foraging in their own group territories.

Robbing Vultures

Crows were occasionally able to get the better of Turkey Vultures if there were not too many of the larger birds. A vulture carried a catfish 30 centimeters long up the bank of a stream to where three others were resting on January 29, 1985. The first vulture was feeding on the fish when two crows landed. One stood a meter in front of the vulture while the other walked behind six times, pulling the vulture's tail at each pass in spite of a second vulture trying to chase it away. The tail projected over a small gully, making it hard for the crow to get a secure hold. The crows left after a few minutes. A vulture was feeding on a catfish at the same place the following morning. This time a crow got a firm grasp on a tail feather and gave a sharp pull. The vulture flew and the crow appropriated the fish.

On February 20 I found two crows walking among two Black Vultures and three Turkey Vultures gathered around the remains of a cottontail rabbit. Every now and then a crow reached in and seized a scrap. Then one crow, seeing an opportunity, grabbed the bulk of the rabbit, consisting mostly of skin and bones, and flew 20 meters across the pasture, with the vultures following. There was a mixed situation for ten minutes, with sometimes a crow, sometimes a vulture, in possession. A crow finally carried the remains to a place to which the vultures did not follow it. In this and other episodes, the crows were generally wary of coming too close to a group of vultures, preferring to wait for chances to seize unguarded scraps.

Attacks on Small Birds

Crows flying over pastures sometimes swooped at robins and Killdeer, and once, when a Lesser Yellowlegs was calling, a crow circled above and swooped at it repeatedly. A crow made a determined effort one morning to catch a small bird struggling against the wind, but without success.

I twice saw crows with freshly killed birds, a robin-sized bird on one occasion and a Blue Jay on the other. In the latter episode the male of one pair flew from a swamp with the Blue Jay in his bill and his mate following right behind. Both birds alighted on the ground facing each other and about two meters apart. The female crouched with tail quivering in a precopulatory pose. When her mate flew to a tree and started to tear the jay apart, she followed and soon had a portion of the bird to herself. Crows appear to become especially excited when they see another crow with a bird in its bill. This may have been why the female went into a precopulatory pose as a way of begging.

I heard an outburst of cawing on February 26, 1984 as seven crows converged on one that had captured a young cotton rat. After being surrounded for a minute, the successful crow flew away with its prey still in its bill. Five crows pursued, but only for a short way. In a similar incident a month later, one crow trying to get into a huddle surrounding a crow with prey jumped onto the back of another. The speed with which a group of crows can converge on one that has caught something unusual was amazing. When a crow captured a robin-sized bird on February 3, seven crows had it surrounded within seconds, even though I had seen no crows in the vicinity beforehand. The crows remained silent, with heads lowered; it looked like a fight. But after a minute the crow with the bird flew to the edge of a wood, where it tore its prey open and ate it undisturbed.

Lack of Fighting over Captured Prey

Crows did not form huddles when any comparatively large supply of food was discovered. When one came upon a mass of what looked like the disgorged stomach contents of a heron, other crows came immediately, and all were soon flying away with portions in their bills. Much the same happened when a crow discovered a cow placenta and three or four crows gathered to carry pieces to the incubating female. Both of these bonanzas lay in the open, and a number of crows could work at the same time. Crows behaved differently when this was not the case. In January, 1984, the crows of one group gathered around a large walking catfish lying dead on the bank of a stream. They fed on it for the next hour and a half, but always one at a time. When one had had all it wanted, another took its place. I think they fed in order of dominance, for several crows that stayed close waiting a turn did not get one until the end.

Discussion

Respect for individual rights. I never saw a cooperative group of crows fight over food that a single crow had caught. What a crow caught it kept, regardless of its social status. The surrounding of one crow by others was, I think, a way incoming crows could form a picture or "search image" (Croze 1970) of what any crow might find by itself.

The absence of intragroup robbery, as noted in other cooperative breeders such as Florida Scrub Jays (Woolfenden and Fitzpatrick 1977), wolves (Mech 1970), and chimpanzees (Lawick-Goodall 1967), may be essential if members of a cooperative group are to stay together. Lawick-Goodall noted that when a male chimpanzee killed a young baboon, three other males sat and watched while the first one, keeping his prize to himself, ate bits at his leisure. There was no sharing until he had eaten all he wanted. The three males that watched were all of higher rank than the one with the meat, of which chimpanzees, according to Lawick-Goodall, are very fond.

Kleptoparasitism. None of the crows' methods of robbing water birds appeared to take much time or energy. To the crows' advantage the water birds had trouble holding large, slippery prey. On several occasions I watched Great Egrets fly to the top of a pine with catfish and toss the fish about to position it for swallowing, only to lose control and have the fish fall to the ground. The crows also benefited by acting together to rob the water birds; their numbers seemed to have a distractive effect. The same has been reported for Skuas robbing Puffins (Grand 1971) and for Laughing Gulls pursuing terns (Hatch 1975).

A difference between the crows and the Skuas and gulls was that the crows were members of a cooperative group. While only one crow was the final recipient of a theft, it was apt to take the prize to the nest and feed the incubating female or nestlings, thus benefiting the group as a whole. Kushlan (1978) observed that Wood Storks, Great Egrets, White Ibis, and other water birds robbed species smaller than themselves. The crows in contrast, in robbing Great Egrets, White Ibis, and in a previous year a river otter, were robbing species heavier than themselves. Their ability to do so, I think, lay in their cooperative efforts. Carrion Crows have been observed robbing a Gray Heron by forcing it to disgorge (Meinertzhagen 1959) and, when five crows were acting together, causing the death of a heron in flight (Walters 1983).

Predation on birds.   Although I did not see crows capturing
birds on the wing, there are accounts of their doing so. Tinbergen
(1953a) watched a Carrion Crow swoop three times on a Lapwing in what he called Peregrine-type hunting. The crow delivered a vicious peck on the first swoop, hung on briefly with
its bill on a second, and then on the third swoop brought the
Lapwing to the ground severely wounded. Walker (1974)
watched an American Crow pursue a Kestrel, catch it in its feet,
then bear it to the ground and kill it. Warren (1969) saw a Carrion Crow and James (1981) a Northwestern Crow catch a Starling, and Erskine (1980) saw crows swooping repeatedly, once
on a Blue Jay and once on a starling, both birds escaping with
difficulty.

One of my hand-raised crows flew after swallows when it
was two or three months of age. This seemed a bit futile, but
Hanford (1969), Radford (1970), and Yapp (1975) all describe
Carrion Crows stooping on swallows or House Martins with
occasional success.

Predation on eggs and chicks.   I was interested in 1984 in the
way a crow circled above a Lesser Yellowlegs that was calling
loudly. Why should the crow have been attracted by the calling? As Sordahl (1979) reports for Willets and Hamas (1984)
for Spotted Sandpipers, the alarm calls of shorebirds also let
crows know where to find chicks. Although the yellowlegs at
the ranch was on migration and not nesting, the crow's interest
was obviously aroused.

Accounts of crows preying on eggs and chicks of other birds
throw light on the birds' resourcefulness. Preston (1953) describes the way American Crows locate Mallard Duck nests
by watching the movements of the females and Erikstad and
associates (1982), a similar strategy used by Hooded Crows in
locating the nests of Willow Ptarmigan.

Crows can take advantage of various situations to get large
birds to leave their nests. Ellison and Cleary (1978) observed
American Crows hovering over and frightening Double-crested
Cormorants from their eggs on windy days. Verbeek (1982),
saw Northwestern Crows stealing eggs of Pelagic Cormorants
when the cormorants happened to be disturbed by Bald Eagles.
In a case, described by Montevecchi (1978), of what appears
to be tool using, Fish Crows dropped Spartina stalks on incubating Laughing Gulls. Fish Crows seem to be fond of eggs
whether they are birds' eggs or not; Carr (1983) observed them
digging through seven centimeters of earth to uncover eggs of
a large turtle, the peninsula cooter.

Versatility and seeming intelligence.   Zach (1979) noted that Northwestern Crows, in contrast to gulls, dropped whelks on rocks to break the shells. The crows selected whelks of a certain size and dropped them from a fixed height, an example, he believed, of learned behavior. Having engineered so productive a form of foraging, the crows had time and energy for other activities. Morse (1980), however, points out that crows feed on a variety of other things, including invertebrates, berries, eggs, and young birds, making it difficult to prove what is most profitable in terms of saving energy. Along the same lines, I would find it difficult to speculate on the time and energy budgets of American Crows. My impression of crows is that they have ample time to rest and look about the year round.

Croze (1970), in experiments with mussel shells, found that Carrion Crows were quick to form search images of where food could be found. Formation of images is doubtless equally important to American Crows. An advantage to their being members of cooperative groups may be that they are able, by means of huddles over unusual food, to share search images more readily.

Many factors go into an animal's ability to exploit a wide range of food, including body size. According to Schoener (1971), "larger animals . . . usually eat a greater range of food size than smaller ones," a concept confirmed by Wilson (1975) from studies of several groups of birds. American Crows would appear to be of a size favorable to exploiting a wide range of resources, from wax myrtle berries and acorns, to dung beetles, frogs, and walking catfish, taken directly, and to large salamanders or other prey, dead or alive, stolen from White Ibis, Great Egrets, and Turkey Vultures. They can also steal from smaller birds. Bird and associates (1973) watched a crow fly to a lawn three times to steal earthworms from a robin. This versatility may help to explain why American Crows are among the few avian species that occur over a large part of North America, and their versatility is more effective, at least in some sections, because they live in cooperative groups.

Foraging in woods.   Lockie (1955) observed that Carrion Crows "feed in woods as well as in pastures and thought they were originally a woodland species. The same may be true of American Crows. Pre-Columbian forests of mature trees with large canopies and no undergrowth could have been more favorable to foraging than the more thickly growing and younger trees of the present day. Crows, however, probably forage more in woods than is realized, since it is difficult to spot them there.

One of the more complete descriptions of a *Corvus* species foraging in forests is that of Sakai and associates (1986) of the Hawaiian Crow. The bird is a generalist, foraging on trunks, branches, and foliage of mature trees in search of invertebrates and other prey, uncovering some of it by flaking off moss and bark in woodpecker fashion. It is also adept at finding birds' nests and feeding on fruits. Tomback (1986) describes similar foraging for the Mariana Crow.

3. Foraging in Relation to Mammals

Feeding on Lice

CATTLE

There are some species of lice in cattle, and particularly the red louse in Florida, that concentrate at the base of the tail. In 1981 I watched one or two crows at a time fly to cows (n = 31) and walk around, pecking at the underside of the tail and adjacent regions with 50 to 150 or more pecks. Crows fed on cattle more extensively in the following year. I had a special opportunity to observe them on March 9 when a herd of fifty cattle spent most of a morning near a nest I was watching. In the course of seventy minutes one to three crows, from a total of five that were attending the nest, fed on the cattle on eight occasions. On the seventh, when a crow perched on a cow's rump, she made things more convenient by elevating her tail. On other occasions a crow might lower itself down a cow's tail like a sailor on a rope to reach inguinal regions more effectively. When cows were especially close I could see that the crows made feeding motions with the tips of their bills. Crows occasionally leaned from cows' backs to pick prey from haunches and shoulders, but were usually tossed off when they perched on a cow's head. Feeding times on a succession of cows ranged from one to twenty minutes. One crow flew directly from feeding on cattle to feeding the female on the nest.

In a different kind of foraging, three crows coming up behind a reclining cow picked up what appeared to be intestinal worms, or segments of them, 20 to 23 centimeters in length. This was on January 29, not long after the cattle had received a dose of medicine against parasites. The worms eaten by the crows, I learned from the College of Veterinary Medicine of the University of Florida, could have been ascarids or tapeworms. Since the ascarid is rare and the tapeworms, or segments of them, more prevalent, the crows had probably partaken of tapeworms.

FERAL HOGS

Sows with litters were prevalent at the ranch in 1981 and 1982, running to feed on corn wherever a ranch hand, who fed wild-life every day, might scatter it. Litters of four to six piglets, after feeding, often fell on their sides to rest. As many as three crows might then search for lice on one suckling pig after another by walking around and reaching in or perching on an exposed flank. The crows worked on all exposed surfaces from head and ears to the back, belly and inguinal regions, pecking at rates of up to sixty times a minute with bills slightly open. The longest I saw crows working was fifteen minutes.

The little pigs never appeared to be disturbed, not even when a crow would stand on a head or try to pull a leg aside. Suckling pigs sometimes solicited the crows by rolling over. On seven mornings I watched crows feeding on sows, and on a few occasions they fed on boars, which were comparatively scarce. One sow solicited on two mornings by walking toward a crow, then rolling on her side. A crow that alighted on her back on one of the mornings did no more than pull her tail and leave.

In an unpublished survey of feral hogs made in January, 1981, just south of where I made my observations, hog lice, Pat Humphrey of the Veterinary School informed me, were found on all hogs, in numbers too great for accurate counting. The only tick found with any regularity was the black-legged tick, an average of 3.2 per hog. Lice being so comparatively minute, it is conceivable that crows pick them up on their tongues, but this was difficult to determine at a distance.

FERAL HOGS

Attacks on Young or Weakened Mammals

The crows at the ranch were quick to notice any animal that looked young or weak. On one occasion they attacked a young raccoon and on another a suckling pig, both animals being the smallest of their litters. On February 11, 1983, in a more intense attack, a crow rode for 20 meters on the back of a suckling pig, flapping its wings and pounding the pig's head as it did so while a second crow hovered overhead.

Two other attacks were on pigs that were moribund but still moving. On March 20 I discovered four Black Vultures standing around a dying pig. They kept the crows away, but otherwise did nothing, as though waiting for the pig to die. The vultures left when I walked over and sat down within 15 meters. The five crows of the local group, being tamer than the vultures, flew in immediately to feed on the pig's still living tissues. The hesitancy of the Black Vultures to attack an animal that was still alive was revealed again on March 6, when a train of eight vultures followed a dying pig without disturbing it. The vultures left when the pig came near where I was sitting. A crow then alighted on the pig's flank as it lay down. Without a pause it tore a hole in front of the pig's ear and, indifferent to the animal's movements, fed on its blood and underlying tissues. A second crow later fed in the same manner. The pig was still living the next morning but died soon afterward.

Attacks on live mammals have been described for other *Corvus* species. Hewson (1981) noted Hooded Crows feeding on eyes and tongues of ewes that had rolled over and were unable to rise, and Rowley saw (1970) crows and ravens similarly attack weakened lambs in Australia. Rowley did not believe that the Australian Ravens caused any significant number of deaths. "When they anticipate a lamb's death by a few hours," he wrote, "it may seem cruel and tragic, but it is neither biologically nor economically wasteful."

Spotted Fawns of Virginia Deer

Jane and I watched attacks on fawns of Virginia deer on two mornings in April, 1982. The fawns were crossing a pasture 200 meters wide that lay between swamps and contained the nest tree of a group of crows. On April 18 I watched a fawn coming toward me. It was about 35 centimeters high and weak on its legs. Although accompanied by its mother at varying distances, it was under constant attack by two breeding adults and three yearlings of the nesting group (Fig. 2). One crow clung to the fawn's back as it ran, while others kept swooping and striking. After running eight to ten meters the fawn collapsed, as if its legs could hold it up no longer. The crows then crowded around, striking about the head, eyes, and other parts. I could not tell whether their bills were closed or slightly open. The doe appeared to be surprisingly unconcerned. She approached the fawn repeatedly with head and neck outstretched to lick

Figure 2. Five crows of a cooperative group attacking a spotted fawn.

it at one end while the crows attacked it at the other. The fawn's only moments of protection were when it nursed under its mother. After fifteen bouts of running, collapsing, and being attacked, the fawn reached the edge of the swamp.

I was then able to walk within three meters of it. Using 8 × 40 binoculars, I was unable to see any injuries done to the fawn's eyes or other parts, in spite of what must have been hundreds of blows. Jane had witnessed similar attacks on a slightly larger fawn nine days previously. A feature of these attacks was that the larger fawn, in one of its periodic collapses, sat back on its haunches and struck at its assailants with its forefeet.

Readers may be surprised that the crows could have struck, or appeared to have struck the first fawn's eyes so many times without causing any apparent injury. I once made the stupid mistake, when clearing woods in New Hampshire, of pushing on a dead balsam to topple it, but without success. Pushing again, I looked up. The top broke off and crashed a painful blow on my upward-looking eye. My wife hurried me to a hospital, but an ophthalmologist examined my eye under a slit lamp and could find nothing wrong. The human cornea and sclerae, like those of most vertebrates, have been selected for toughness over millions of years. So I was not surprised that the crows had not damaged the fawn's eyes, severe as the attacks appeared. It is also possible that the fawn protected itself by closing its eyes.

River Otter:
Scats and Catfish Heads

Tail Pulling and Catfish Heads

One of the more exciting events watched at the ranch was in a drought year when walking catfish moved into a water hole from a neighboring swamp. The hole, which measured 7 by 20 meters, was free of vegetation, and when an otter came running across the pasture to catch fish there, Jane and I had an unobstructed view of its activities. There were actually two otters, a large and a small one, but only one ever came at a time. In the first week it took an otter only a few seconds to catch a fish. On January 4, 1981, one of them caught and ate eight catfish 15 to 30 centimeters long in an hour and, on January 15, nine in two hours. After this the number of catfish declined until, by February, there appeared to be none of any size remaining.

Although the otters were tame and easy to watch, it was their interactions with crows that interested us particularly. Three to four crows generally flew to the pool to stand nearby when an otter came out of the water to rest, roll in the sand, or eat a catfish. A favorite ploy, seen twenty-seven times, was to pull the otter's tail. Although the attacks looked like simple pecking, we noted on several occasions that the blows were delivered with the bill slightly open. It seemed likely, therefore, that the crows were really pinching and pulling. Although the otters might whirl around on a crow, they generally paid little attention. They ate catfish tail first, holding the body vertical in their forepaws until they reached the head, which they discarded. Crows then scavenged the heads. On one occasion the crows robbed an otter while it was still eating. On January 15 the otter was lying partly out of the water when four crows gathered in front of it. A fifth crow, alighting by the otter's tail, gave it a tweak. The otter dropped its fish, and, while swinging around to attack its assailant, a crow in front seized the fish and flew off with it.

Another episode was curious. An otter was resting on the

shore one morning when a crow carrying a catfish head walked around and pulled its tail. The otter got up and left. The crow then buried the fish head where the otter had been lying.

Eating and Storing Scats

In January and February of 1984 I watched crows eating and storing the dung of river otters. The three juvenile and two adult otters that came to the ranch deposited their dung at three marking sites along a stream. The A1 crows were quick to recognize the sites, and often (n = 29) one or two of them flew to a site as soon as an otter started to leave. They also visited (n = 9) sites when there were no otters to be seen at all. Once there, the crows either ate scats or loaded them into their bills and walked or flew to store them elsewhere. They poked scats into clumps of grass (n = 9), covering them with wads of turf or other debris. In one instance a crow pushed a scat under a cow pie and in another, into a bromeliad growing on a bay tree.

Robbing Squirrels

I twice saw crows attack squirrels that had uncovered what looked like the yellow meat of acorns. A fox squirrel was eating by a cache one morning when two crows walked close to it. One walked behind and gave the squirrel a hard peck. The squirrel left without any attempt to defend its stores. A gray squirrel feeding by its cache, in contrast, rushed at one then the other of two crows that approached. Although crows are able to rob squirrels, it seems probable that squirrels, with their sharp sense of smell, are better equipped to rob crows of corn, acorns, and other food stored in the ground. I noticed the strength of a fox squirrel's sense of smell in one that would follow me, sometimes for several hundred meters, if I carried corn in my pockets but not if my pockets were empty.

Scab Wounds

Wounds and Carrion

I watched a crow peck at a branding scab on the haunch of a Hereford bull on three occasions. Linsdale (1937) collected many accounts of Black-billed Magpies attacking open sores on cattle and horses. My hand-raised crows pecked at any scabs, no matter how small, that I had on my hands.

CATTLE CARCASSES

Crows were often prevented from feeding on carrion by competition from large numbers, up to hundreds, of Black and Turkey Vultures. But even with vultures, I was surprised at how little of a carcass they might consume before blowfly and other larvae took over. Each large carcass had a history. When a Hereford bull died on February 6, 1984, a hundred Black Vultures stood around for several days, making little progress. They pulled tissues from the bull's mouth and anus but could not penetrate the hide. When they left on February 8, four crows took turns pulling bits of intestines through a small hole in the abdomen. After this neither the vultures nor the crows were able to get anything from the now greatly distended carcass. The crows, however, continued to walk around the bull for several weeks, picking off flies, especially by the neck, where there were numbers of them. When the bull had been dead for several weeks I noticed the resident pair of crows moving at distances of five to ten meters, behaving like robins in the way they hopped a few meters, then stopped with heads up to look about before hopping now here, now there, to pick up prey. They continued in this way for four days. On searching the grass, I found larvae of carrion beetles about two centimeters long. The larvae were highly mobile and seemed to be migrating out from the dead bull. On March 3, about a month after the bull died, some animal tore the abdomen open, scattering the viscera on the ground. When I arrived, two crows were seizing portions of the well-decayed viscera and storing them in oaks at distances of 30 to 60 meters.

Another carcass lay not far from the nest of the B crows. The crows entered the pelvis, torn open by a broken femur, to tear off pieces of meat, which they carried directly to their nestlings. Because the hide was so tough, they were unable to reach any more flesh after two days, but they continued making visits to pick off blowflies and other insects for some weeks.

HOGS

Vultures dealt more effectively with dead hogs, giving the crows little chance of getting close unless on special occasions. Twenty to thirty Black Vultures were feeding on a hog carcass when a Bald Eagle frightened them away. When the eagle left, four crows immediately came to feed. Two were by the carcass a few days later when a Black Vulture arrived. While one crow fed, the other chivied the vulture to get it moving. Once the vulture started to move, the crow jumped over its back twice, as if to hurry it along. When the vulture stopped, the crow crouched, first on one side, then on the other, giving *g-wal-ops*, one of the loudest vocalizations a crow can make. The vulture finally flew, with the crow swooping on it for a short way. Erskine (1968) describes a somewhat similar case of cooperation in New Brunswick province. A Bald Eagle had left the carcass of a fish in order to get a drink, when two crows flew to it. While one fed, the other "chivvied the eagle by hopping around it, flying low over it, once landing momentarily on its back, and constantly calling."

I have watched both Crested Caracaras and crows come to the final remains of carcasses, ones that were nothing but skin, tendons, and bones, to pull off and eat tendons. Crows did the same to skeletal remains as small as those of frogs and snakes.

EXPERIMENT WITH ROADKILLS

I scattered corn from 10 to about 12 meters from the base of the nest tree (used by crows from what I called group A2) in March and April, 1985, then sat four meters farther away to watch the crows when they came either to the corn or to the nest above. This gave me a front-row seat when, on March 25, I placed a freshly killed cottontail rabbit with the corn and on April 14, an armadillo. The response of the crows was immediate in both cases. Gathering around, two to three stood a little back while four or five tore, bit, and tugged with their bills on the roadkills. It took a minute or less for a crow to fill its pouch, then fly away as another crow took its place. The crows worked silently and without signs of conflict or dominance. Those leaving flew 100 to 150 meters away to store their loads in grass or in trees. The remaining flights on March 25 (n = 23) and April 14 (n = 26) were to the nest to feed the young. Within 30 to 40 minutes on both days, all of the readily accessible muscle and viscera of the roadkills, which were of approximately the same size, had been removed. After that only a few crows continued working on what was left.

The crows were so efficient in tearing up the roadkills and storing the pieces that they may have been aware that they had best make the most of what they had while they had it. When I was sitting close there was no danger of vultures coming to the kills. Under usual circumstances, however, vultures, which are always present at the ranch, would have arrived and the crows would have gotten relatively little.

The way that the seven of the group designated A2 worked without conflict was similar to Hope Ryden's (1979) description of coyotes, which are also cooperative breeders, working on a carcass in Wyoming. "Usually," wrote Ryden, "no more than four coyotes tried to feed together on an ample carcass at one time. They seemed to understand that crowding could lead to trouble."

Discussion

Eating otter scats.   Why should the crows have eaten and stored scats of otters? Scats collected in early February and examined by James N. Layne of the Archbold Biological Station gave little clue. The scats consisted almost entirely of fragments of crayfish exoskeletons held together with mucus. Other than the mucus, it was difficult to see what the nutritive value of them could have been. Crows eat sand, as do Blue Jays (Kilham 1960), and it is conceivable that the sharp-edged pieces of exoskeletons could have served the same purpose. But sand is everywhere in Florida, and I have been unable to find any good explanation for crows eating otter scats, unless for bulk or roughage in their digestive tracts.

Other birds eating dung include Common Ravens (Bent 1946), Black-billed Magpies (Summers-Smith 1983), starlings (Simmons 1983), and Black Vultures (Welty 1982), all of which eat dog feces, and Ivory Gulls (Welty 1982), which eat the dung of polar bears, walrus, and seals. It is conceivable in all of these examples that birds are able to extract nutrients from items that remain undigested in passage through mammals.

Tail pulling.   Tail pulling is a habit common to a number of corvids (Goodwin 1976). The crow that robbed the otter by pulling its tail could have done so by happenstance or as a deliberate piece of strategy. It is hard to know. The crows had pulled the otters' tails many times before, to no seeming purpose except an urge, shared by Black-billed Magpies (Lorenz 1970) and Common Ravens, to provoke animals larger than themselves, whether there is any immediate advantage to doing so or not. Bent (1946) reported three Common Ravens robbing a dog of a bone, one bird pulling the dog's tail while others stood by its head. It is conceivable that crows, like ravens, are capable after trial and error of seizing upon the right moment for pulling a tail to advantage. Another use of tail pull-

ing can be to get a larger bird or mammal to move from a carcass, as I describe later for Common Ravens contending with
Turkey Vultures and as Hewson (1981) did for Hooded Crows
contending with a Buzzard. Goodwin (1976) described crows
and magpies pulling the tails of mobbing predators.

The behavior appears to be innate, for one of my hand-raised
crows pulled a sheep's tail and a hand-raised raven a cat's tail
when they were less than three months of age.

Cleaning/feeding symbioses.   I have been unable to find previous reports of American Crows feeding on ectoparasites of
other animals. Bent (1946) mentions Fish Crows picking ticks
from the backs of cows. Hundreds of Fish Crows passed over
the crow territories at the Hendrie ranch in late winters and
springs, but I saw only a few alight. Each of these few times
was a visit to a markedly pregnant cow, with special attention
to the root of her tail. If bovine ectoparasites, or some of them,
are controlled by the reproductive hormones of the host, as
has been shown for rabbit fleas by Rothschild and Ford (1964),
then cows in advanced pregnancy might be a rewarding place
for crows to look for them.

Other corvids reported as engaging in cleaning/feeding symbioses include the Pied Crow on white rhinos (Stutterheim
1980), Black-billed Magpies on elk and mule deer (Linsdale
1946), Florida Scrub Jays on feral hogs (Baker and Morris
1980), and Scrub Jays on black-tailed deer (Isenhart and De-
Sante 1985).

Christian (1980) raises the question as to whether cleaning/
feeding symbioses between birds and reptiles in the Galapagos
Islands arose through a genetically determined mechanism or
the discovery of some avian genius. I do not think that any
special mechanisms need to be invoked for crows. Crows are
curious about a wide variety of things that may yield something to eat, from cow pies to cabbage palms, and from this
point of view there is nothing unusual about their looking over
cattle and hogs, if such are part of their environment. A wide-
ranging curiosity is, indeed, characteristic of many corvids, a
fact brought out by Dean and MacDonald (1981) in their list
of corvids associated with mammals in Africa.

Attacks on young or weakened mammals.   Crow behavior can
be difficult to interpret. One could say that the crows were defending their nest in attacking the fawns. But this seems im-
probable. The fawns were well away from the nest tree most
of the time, and I have frequently watched sows with litters

passing under nests without creating any disturbance. An alternative explanation is that crows are not limited to being scavengers but become predators when they find higher vertebrate young weak or small enough to be attacked.

Attacks can be a way of testing whether the prey is feeble or incapacitated enough to subdue. In this the crows resemble wolves, which, according to Mech (1970), regularly search for large prey that have a weakness they can exploit. Lorenz (1970) called this type of predation a "sensitive response to symptoms of illness in animals, which would never serve as prey when healthy." Crows, like wolves and ravens, can be likened to sensitive clinicians, and their ability to spot weakness enhances their ability to survive. Rowley (1970) remarks that an Australian Raven is no match for a healthy lamb, and I would think, from my observations, that American Crows are no match for a healthy fawn. Chadwick (1983) gives an account, illustrated with photographs, of a Pied Crow in Africa seizing a young and apparently healthy bat-eared fox by the tail and trying, without success, to fly off with it.

Cooperation in foraging.   American Crows that belong to groups cooperate in defending territories as well as in nesting. How much of this ability to cooperate is carried over into foraging? While the question is not easy to answer in depth, I think that crows of a group benefit from foraging together. This was seen when several were in the cabbage palms dislodging prey while others waited below. Crows gathered in much the same way when feeding on wax myrtle berries. Another occasion when crows acted together was when they pursued White Ibis and Great Egrets carrying salamanders. While only one crow benefited from a theft, pursuit by two to four crows served as a distraction. Crows also acted together when one or more stood in front of an otter or vulture with prey while another walked behind to pull the animal's tail. And effective at times was the way one crow might chivy a Black or Turkey Vulture away from a carcass, enabling a second one to feed.

The benefits of group membership were less evident when crows were scattered over pastures, but observation indicated that they could still be benefiting from each other's presence. If one found something, the nearest crow or two flew over to have a look. If the item was sizable or unusual, crows gathered from a distance to huddle about the captor. Interest of each crow in what others find doubtless leads to formation of search images of what prey is available at any particular locality or time of day. The five to seven crows of a group may thus constitute, at times, an intelligence network that enables them to make the most of food resources.

The almost complete lack of fighting in cooperative groups as compared to wandering flocks (see chap. 10) is another asset to foraging within a territory. Sentinel behavior, in which one or two crows remain on guard while others of a group forage, can also be a part of cooperative foraging, as noted by Montevecchi (1976) for crows in a salt marsh. It was a behavior seldom seen on the Hendrie ranch, however, where the crows were not persecuted by humans.

4. Territory and Food Storing

Territorial Behavior

Along the boundary between the A and B groups of crows I witnessed forty-seven territorial encounters between 1981 and 1983, nearly all of which (n = 44) were aerial. A feature common to most was that one crow usually swooped on and attacked a fleeing intruder while two to five crows followed. When close, I could hear *kr-aack, kr-aack* vocalizations as the attacker swooped on the intruder, or even a whack when it struck. I saw general melees on three occasions, with eight to ten crows whirling up into the air (Fig. 3, bottom). In severe encounters (n = 3) two crows hovered beak to beak or grappled and fell toward the ground. A feature of all encounters was that once they were over, the A crows flew to their territory and the B crows in the opposite direction to theirs.

Encounters were most frequent at the start of the breeding season. I found that, although encounters were infrequent during nesting, I could induce them according to where I scattered corn. When I scattered corn 12 to 15 meters on the B side of the boundary on April 13, the A crows cawed from the edge of their oak grove and the B crows from a leafless tree on their side. After five minutes of cawing the eight B crows flew not toward the A crows but back into their territory to bunch together on the ground (Fig. 3, top). They then flew at their opponents. After mixing at the edge of the grove with one jump-up fight, the A crows left and the B crows flew to feed on their corn for the first time. The encounter was the first in which I observed crows bunching before an attack.

The A crows' behavior in 1984 differed from the three previous years in that the A crows, possibly from an accumulation of auxiliaries that had become sexually mature, divided into three groups—A1, A2, and A3—each nesting in a division of the original A territory. The relative crowding increased

Figure 3.   Behavior in territorial conflicts: (*bottom*) aerial melee; (*top*) cooperative group bunching prior to an attack.

the number of conflicts. From where I sat watching the nest of the A2 crows, I was able to follow conflicts along three boundaries. With these three borders to protect, the A2's flew to one boundary or another almost daily to enter into cawing contests with neighbors. Female A2, whether incubating, brooding, or feeding nestlings, took an active or leading part in driving intruders away. The most frequent encounters were with the A1 crows whose nest had failed in March. The A1's did not renest, and, with no nest to attend to and time to spare, they took a renewed interest in territory, a phenomenon that I once noted for a pair of Yellow-bellied Sapsuckers (Kilham 1962).

Another situation leading to conflicts was flooding of ditches and low places following heavy rains. The floodings led to an influx of fish and salamanders pursued by White Ibis and Great Egrets. Two shallows where foraging or robbing the water birds was particularly good were along boundaries. This led to clashes between the A2 and the A3 crows in one direction and the A2 and the B crows in another.

The A and the B crows had territories of about 90 hectares each until the A territory division, after which two groups had territories of about 40 hectares and the A1's expanded theirs into swampy areas where I could not follow them. These areas were still large compared to the 0.49 hectares described for Northwestern Crows by Butler and associates (1984) and the 26.7 for Carrion Crows observed by Wittenberg (1968).

Territorial Groups

SIZES OF GROUPS

Table 1 shows the sizes of thirteen territorial groups I observed over a period of five years. All remained the same in size from January through April, in spite of attacks by breeding males on some of the older auxiliaries. It seemed probable, therefore, that changes in groups other than recruitment from fledglings took place at other times of the year. The average size of groups in the five years I watched was 7.2. Seven to eight may be an optimal size for territorial groups of crows in some localities, for these have been recurring numbers in New Hampshire as well as in Florida. Rowley (1978), who believed that the commonest sizes found in nature are probably optimal, found 6.7 to be the optimal size for groups of cooperatively breeding White-winged Choughs.

The size of groups in Florida remained about the same whether nestings in a previous year were successful or not. When a nesting was successful, there might be one to three yearlings in a group the following January (see Table 1). But when a nest failed the year before and there were no yearlings, the numbers in groups, as illustrated by the B group in 1984 and 1985, remained equally high, with adult auxiliaries seemingly filling the places of yearlings, had they been present.

Table 1. Numbers of American Crows in each of thirteen territorial groups observed during breeding seasons, and age categories of helpers

		TERRITORIAL GROUPS										
	A1			A2			A3			A4		
		Helpers			Helpers			Helpers			Helpers	
Year	Total	Ad.	Yr.	Total	Ad.	Yr.	Total	Ad.	Yr.	Total	Ad.	Yr.
1981	9	3	4	—			—					
1982	9	4	3	—			—			9	4	3
1983	7	5	0	—			—			9	6	1
1984	8	4	2	5	3	0	4	2	0	8	6	0
1985	5	3	0	7	3	2	7	2	3	7	5	0

NOTE: Ad. = helpers in adult plumage; Yr. = yearlings. Breeding seasons observed were January–April, 1981–85.

In 1985, following successful nestings in 1984, the A2 and A3 groups contained approximately equal numbers of yearling and adult auxiliaries.

IRREGULAR CROWS

In 1984 and 1985 I noticed an A2 crow that kept trying to join the B crows. The scenario was almost always the same. When I put out corn for the B crows, the A2 crow flew about 100 meters to try to join them. But as soon as male B arrived, he chased the intruder back the way it had come. Once back in its own territory, the trespasser rested on a fence post at the boundary, a habit repeated almost daily. Its motivation was not food, seemingly, for on some mornings it ceased feeding on corn with its own group to try joining the B group at theirs.

There was another irregular crow from the A2 group. He had a small broken feather that projected at a right angle from his folded right wing, a seemingly permanent defect, for it was there in two successive years. In each of two early breeding seasons, X, as I called him, tried to join the A1 crows, but, as described in the next chapter, he was persistently driven away by the breeding male.

A Lone Crow

Yearlings have a strong urge to belong. If something happens and a yearling finds itself alone, it will persist in efforts to join a group, even though driven away over and over again. I en-

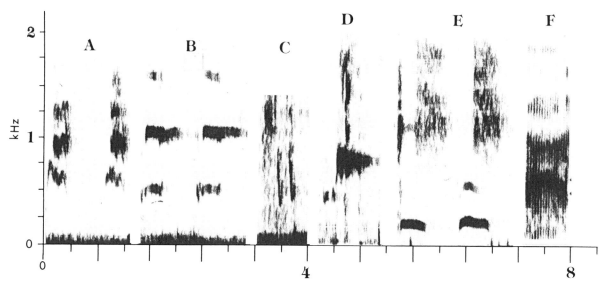

Figure 4.　Special vocalizations of American Crows in Florida: (A) *G-wal-op, g-wal-op;* (B) *G-wong, g-wong;* (C) *Cu-koo;* (D) *Kuck-woo;* (E) play vocalizations of yearling; (F) rattling cry.

countered a lone crow in Florida in 1984, marked by a forked tail that enabled me to follow it for four months as it tried to join one group then another.

When I scattered corn for the A1 crows early in January, eight came to feed almost immediately. The lone crow, LC, perched 100 meters away and, afraid to come down, gave monotonous caws in series of three. On January 11 it kept these up for forty-five minutes. LC made a number of attempts to land among the crows feeding on corn, but the breeding male always drove it away. By January 27 LC had ceased trying to join the A1 crows and was trying to attach itself to the A3's. It was driven away, however, by male A3 as vigorously as it had been by male A1. The others of the A3 group, the breeding female and two auxiliaries, were more tolerant. LC had now adopted a rattling vocalization [Fig. 4(F)], which it repeated almost incessantly. As other crows rarely gave rattles and the vocalization was striking, I called LC "Rattles."

By late February Rattles was coming to perch by the A2 nest, but only until male A2 returned and drove it back to A3 territory. By the first of April Rattles was attaching itself to the B crows with some success. Although driven away from the vicinity of the nest when male B was near, Rattles fed nestlings when he was away and was tolerated by others of the group.

Rattles was back with the A3 crows in 1985. When the seven

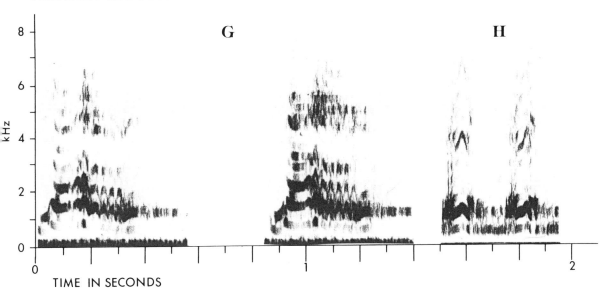

(G) *Kwarr-uck, kwarr-uck;* (H) *Kuk, kuk.* Note different frequency and temporal scales above and below.

crows of the A3 group came for corn, Rattles perched not far away, making *g-wong*s and *kwar-uck*s and other odd vocalizations in addition to rattling. The male and female of pair A3 were quick to chase it, and the chases were nearly always spectacular. With the two of the pair flying hard after it, Rattles flew up into the sky, the three crows turning and twisting until they had moved well toward the horizon. But the efforts of the pair were to little avail. Soon after the two returned, Rattles was back also. Sometimes, at the start of the nesting season, the pair pursued the unwanted crow as often as three times in fifteen minutes. Judged by the intensity with which Rattles was attacked not only by pair A3, but also by the A1, A2, and B pairs when it wandered into their territories, it seemed to be a bird that aroused a special animosity.

The pairs that chased Rattles expended considerable time and energy in doing so. When Rattles came to the A2 territory on March 6, 1985, female A2 started giving *caw-caw-caw*s from her nest, then flew to join her mate in driving Rattles away. She returned in two minutes, but continued cawing as she resumed incubating. Her cawing, with caws of the same length, type, and given at constant intervals, fits Bossema and Benus's description (1985) of the cawing of Carrion Crows defending their territories in the nesting season.

Florida Scrub Jays also have a strong drive to be members

of a group (Woolfenden and Fitzpatrick 1977). But unlike the lone crow I watched at the ranch, persistent lone jays that Woolfenden and Fitzpatrick watched in some cases finally succeeded in joining an established group.

Wandering Flocks

On six occasions between 1981 and 1985, all in January, flocks of thirty to forty outside crows alighted in one territory or another to remain for twenty to thirty minutes, in spite of a few jump-up fights and much cawing. It seemed likely that these flocks consisted of nonbreeders, comparable to those described by Wittenberg (1968), Charles (1972), and Loman (1985), among others, for Carrion Crows.

A phenomenon occurring in late winter and early spring of all years was when groups of five to eight American Crows would fly over the ranch at a little above treetop height and always in a northeasterly direction. Neither the A nor the B crows paid much attention to these outsiders, even though on several days they circled upon seeing the resident crows feeding on corn. Skead (1952) described Black Crows as having year-round territories with rigid boundaries. He noted, however, that intruders were not attacked if they flew high enough. In Florida it seemed that height was not always as important as the fact that the aliens flew on a set course, as if flying to a distant objective with no intention of landing.

Food Storing
in the Breeding Season

CORN

One of the benefits of maintaining territories was that the crows of a group could store food without danger of its being stolen by outsiders. When I scattered corn, five to eight crows of the local territorial group came to fill throat pouches and bills before flying 7 to 100 meters to store it in various parts of the pasture. A crow, once alone, might push its bill into a depression and then, widening the hole by opening its mandibles, disgorge the corn into it. Concealing was done with a few quick snatches of dry grass or other debris. Crows sometimes stored a single load of corn in two or three places by disgorging and then carrying portions in several directions. The crows were not adverse to storing in wet places, for on two occasions I watched one storing under water. Storing the corn I provided was a daily activity; I saw it done hundreds of times.

I seldom saw corn fed to incubating females, but if a female on the nest saw a crow storing in a pasture, she might fly over (n = 5) and eat some. I noticed breeding males on a number of occasions (n = 4) share stored or about-to-be-stored corn with an auxiliary. But in most instances crows stored individually.

PREY

Crows stored frogs, catfish, and other prey larger than what they could eat at any one time, especially in wet years when prey was more abundant. A crow on March 3, 1984, tore up the body of a frog held down with its toes, then walked in four directions to store portions of it before flying off with the carcass. Another crow, after working on a catfish, poked 15 centimeters of body and tail into a tuft of grass, hiding it with four or five pieces of turf and cow dung. The crow then concealed the head elsewhere. Crows were able to hide fairly large items. One used pieces of cow dung and turf 10 to 12 centimeters across in concealing the body of an amphiuma.

The crows did not appear to have difficulty recovering what they cached. One crow, landing five meters from where I had seen a fish cached a few hours previously, walked a few steps, then ran and hopped directly to the place where the food was hidden.

Food was stored in trees as well as in the ground. Female A gave begging calls while incubating on March 14, 1984. When no crow came to feed her, she flew to an air plant at the same height as her nest and 12 meters away, took out the remains of a frog, which she ate for two minutes, and then returned to her nest.

A male by another nest dropped to the ground to catch a snake about 25 centimeters long, then carried it into an oak. The same crow, identified by a broken tail feather, was back on the oak the following morning. This time he perched above what I supposed was 15 centimeters of the same snake. After flying to feed the female on the nest, the male returned to store the remainder of the snake in an air plant, covering it with bits of Spanish moss and other debris.

I seldom saw crows store food on the ground by a nest tree. When male A approached his mate on February 23, 1983, however, he paused, then dropped to the ground to disgorge the contents of his antelingual pouch. After storing half of the contents, he took the remainder to the female.

A nest watched in 1983 was among oaks where storage was

largely (n = 16) in the long needle tufts of the air plant *Til-landsia setacea*. Nests watched in 1984 were more in the open, and caches (n = 21) were in ball moss that grew in oaks that, in late winter, were bare of foliage. Male A took food from ball moss to feed his incubating mate on a number (n = 5) of cold early mornings when foraging appeared to be poor.

CARRION

Crows cached carrion as well as prey. When we arrived at the ranch in early January, 1984, I found crows storing and re-storing walking catfish killed by a cold wave in late December, or feeding on ones that had been stored previously.

When a bull died in the warmer weather of late winter, crows, unable to penetrate the hide, did little more than walk around it for three weeks. When unidentified scavengers tore the ab-domen open, I found a pair of crows storing pieces of viscera and fat in trees and on the ground on the following morning. It seemed from this and other observations that neither ad-vanced decomposition nor warm weather had much effect on storing.

Discussion

Territory. Good (1952) wrote that "Crows do not exhibit the strong territorial behavior common to so many other birds." I, on the other hand, found the behavior well developed in Florida and New Hampshire. A possible reason for the differ-ence is that territorial behavior can be missed, especially in localities where woods obscure the boundaries. I was fortu-nate in both Florida and New Hampshire in finding sections of boundaries where encounters took place repeatedly in the same as well as in succeeding years.

As summarized by Morse (1980), the functions of territories are much the same for various birds. Territories provide im-proved protection through greater familiarity with safe areas; reduced interference with nest building and copulations; greater protection of stored food; and increased assurance of a good food supply. Songbirds of some species and woodpeckers de-fend considerably larger areas at the time a territory is estab-lished in late winter and early spring than during the nesting period. The territories of crows in Florida, in contrast, remained the same in size in the months Jane and I were there.

Corvus species defending territories include Carrion Crows

(Wittenberg 1968; Charles 1972; Coombs 1978); Northwestern Crows (Butler et al. 1984), Black Crows (Skead 1952), and Jungle Crows (Kuroda 1975); and Australian and Little Ravens (Rowley 1967). The sizes of territories vary widely among species. Northwestern Crows that have at most a single helper and usually none (Verbeek and Butler 1981) defend areas of 0.49 hectares and do much of their foraging outside of them. This contrasts with the 90 hectares defended by crows in Florida that had up to five or six helpers and did nearly all of their foraging within their territories. Factors regulating territory size doubtless involve a complex of ecological and other factors. Among species nesting as pairs Wittenberg (1968) gives 14 to 41 hectares for Carrion Crows; Kuroda (1975), 45 hectares for Jungle Crows breeding in Tokyo; and Rowley (1975), 110 hectares for Australian Ravens.

Colonial nesters, including the Rook (Coombs 1978), the Fish Crow (Kilham, unpublished data), and the Little Raven (Rowley 1974), do the main part of their foraging outside of their territories, which do not extend far from the nests. Rowley (1967) discovered that up to twelve pairs of Little Ravens could nest in the year-round territory of one pair of Australian Ravens without conflict. Among reasons for the peaceful coexistence, Rowley found, were that the Little Ravens did their foraging elsewhere and migrated soon after young were fledged. These types of behavior are worth considering because so little is known about American Crows and still less is known about Fish Crows. Emlen (1942) observed a colony of sixty pairs of American Crows in California that nested in a walnut grove of 40 hectares, a density of one pair to less than a hectare. It is conceivable that much diversity might be discovered in relation to territories and breeding if American Crows were studied throughout their range, which covers a large part of North America. Diversity in territorial behavior and nesting have also been described for Carrion Crows. Although they normally nest in comparatively large individual territories of up to 41 hectares (Wittenberg 1968), Rebecca (1985) found a colony of six nests with eggs and young in an area of 25 hectares.

Sex and territorial defense. Territorial behavior in Florida reached a peak from prior to nest building until copulatory behavior ceased in the early part of incubation, a period in which the breeding male took the lead. After this the aggressiveness of males declined, a phenomenon that I have also noted in woodpeckers (Kilham 1983). Females became increasingly territorial as incubation progressed, flying from their nests to attack intruders as much as several hundred meters away. Similar aggressiveness in females while incubating and brooding has been noted by Kuroda (1975) for Jungle Crows, Stiehl (1985) for Common Ravens, and Woolfenden and Fitzpatrick (1977) for Florida Scrub Jays.

Storing food.   Storing food is an important habit of American Crows but has been little studied except as noted by Montevecchi (1976), George and Kimmel (1977), and Hess (1978). There could be several reasons for this. Crows may do little storing when they are in their winter flocks, on migration, or otherwise away from breeding or year-round territories. Even when on their territories, they are unlikely to store in the course of ordinary foraging, such as walking about fields picking up miscellaneous prey. Storing is nearly always associated with a surplus of food of one kind or another, as described by Montevecchi (1976) for gull eggs and by George and Kimmel (1977) for laboratory mice dumped on a field in winter.

If one sees a crow flying away with food, marks carefully where the crow stores it, then walks over to inspect, it is frustratingly difficult to locate the spot that seemed obvious at a distance. I say to myself that the storage place is "right between those two clumps of grass." But when I get there I find one clump is much nearer to my original position than I had thought, the other farther away. Without precise markers, all becomes confusing. In spite of such difficulties, I have been successful when a crow stored on an upslope (where I could get perspective), was at close range (as in Florida), or I was aided by fresh snow (as in New Hampshire).

An advantage of storing, in terms of natural selection, is to secure as much of a local surplus as possible before larger and more powerful competitors arrive. In Florida competitors for corn included Wild Turkeys, Sandhill Cranes, feral hogs, and squirrels. The crows cached a small amount of corn nearby, but most of their flights were to parts of open pasture 50 to 150 meters away, seemingly to lessen the chances of their competitors' finding it. Some turkeys, with a sense of what crows were doing, ran as much as 100 meters to a crow that was storing or about to store. Fox squirrels can smell corn, and along with gray squirrels, are probably well equipped for locating food concealed in the ground.

Crows that I observed sometimes stored within four to seven meters of where I scattered corn, making little effort to conceal what they were doing from other crows. But even if crows found and ate each others' stores in the course of random foraging,

I do not think that it would make much difference. James and Verbeek (1983) found that only a small part of stores of Northwestern Crows were stolen by others of the same species. As Wall (1982) states for Clark's Nutcrackers, only the bird that prepares a cache has the information to find it directly.

Crows in Florida faced much competition in feeding on carrion. Black and Turkey Vultures, Crested Caracaras, and occasionally Bald Eagles competed for remains of catfish, hogs, and cattle. There was a premium, therefore, in carrying away as much as possible before competitors took over. I saw this when I placed fresh roadkills on the ground near the nest of the group A crows. All seven A crows worked intensively at tearing the meat, then carrying it 20 to 100 meters for caching in trees or clumps of grass. Turkey Vultures soared overhead and would have come down had I not been sitting nearby. Hewson (1981, 1982) described storing by Hooded Crows in Scotland, where the crows are dominated at carrion by the larger Buzzards, Great Black-backed Gulls, and Common Ravens.

Turcek and Kelso (1968) emphasized that foods such as corn and acorns are ideal for storage because of their hardness and durability. This would seem to hold more for long-term than for short-term storage, where spoilage might be less likely to have occurred. Crows stored animal matter in Florida — fish, frogs, roadkills — that was neither hard nor easily preserved. Varying degrees of spoilage in hot weather would not make much difference to crows that readily eat meat that is rotten, desiccated, or both. Waite (1985) found that both Rooks and Carrion Crows stored invertebrates on warm days, when prey intake was above average.

Storing observed in Florida and New Hampshire was all within group territories. Most birds or mammals that store are territorial, as I have noted for red squirrels, pikas, and Red-headed Woodpeckers (Kilham 1954, 1958, 1959) and Swanberg (1951) for Thick-billed Nutcrackers. Rooks, which are not territorial in foraging, store food on common ground (Purchas 1980). They also appear to be unusual among *Corvus* species in digging holes to bury their stores (Simmons 1970; Andrew 1969).

A feature of crows at the ranch was the way they stored prey used later in feeding the incubating female. Morse (1980) states that few birds cache food for use during the breeding season. A number of *Corvus* species do so, however, as Kuroda (1975) noted for Jungle Crows; Giffin (1983) and Sakai and associates (1986) for Hawaiian Crows; and Verbeek and Butler (1981) for Northwestern Crows. James and Verbeek (1984) found that

Northwestern Crows did most of their storing when females were forming and laying eggs.

Foraging opportunities for *Corvus* species may vary with the time of day, the weather, and, for the Northwestern Crow (James and Verbeek 1983), the rise and fall of the tides. Temporary storage may counterbalance such vicissitudes, enabling crows to feed either incubating females or nestlings on a steadier basis than would be possible otherwise. Storage in trees during the nesting season has been noted by McNair (1985) for Fish Crows, Sakai and associates (1986) for Hawaiian Crows, and Kuroda (1975) for a male Jungle Crow that also stored on house tops and under eaves.

5. Behavior in the Early Part of the Breeding Cycle

The dominance of breeding males was a leading feature of early breeding-season behavior. When I scattered corn in territory A1 in early January, 1984, eight crows came to feed. I identified the breeding male, MA, by both physical and behavioral characteristics. He did the most cawing and wing-tail flicking and waited several minutes before flying down. He stood out in being heavier and broader than the others, a size difference enhanced by his standing with head up and holding his "shoulders" out. While picking up corn he tried continually to edge another crow away. This crow, X, had a deformed feather projecting from the middle portion of his right wing. Since X was aggressive and in the absence of MA, drove away another crow, he also appeared to be a male. MA became increasingly intolerant of X. From walking behind to drive him away, MA changed to attacking and pursuing by early February. On February 14 he supplanted X on nine fence posts in succession. By the end of the month X ceased to appear and MA was driving away another adult. Almost exactly the same events happened in 1985, with X being driven away again. In both years X returned to the A2 group, where he was accepted.

In 1984 I found that the size of the A1 group varied according to where I scattered corn. If I placed corn within 90 meters of the nest that was being built, four crows of what I called the inner group (the breeding pair plus two yearlings) came down, but if at 200 meters, seven crows gathered, the extras being adult auxiliaries tolerated at the greater distance.

All groups followed much the same behavior pattern in the five years of my watching, with an original group of seven to nine crows being reduced to an inner one of four to six as nesting approached. Here it seemed that if the pair had nested successfully the year before and had two to four yearlings as helpers the next breeding season, the nuclear male drove away adult auxiliaries and formed the inner group. But if there were no yearlings or only one, adult auxiliaries were tolerated.

Adult auxiliaries that were driven away remained on their group territories, coming to nests later to feed nestlings. By this time the aggressiveness of breeding males was greatly diminished. Raitt and Hardy (1979) describe breeding male Beechey Jays as restricting groups to yearling helpers by driving away adults at the start of the nesting period.

The dominance of breeding males served, it seemed, to suppress sexual maturation in adult auxiliaries and, by special attacks on males in adult plumage, to ensure that only the genes of the breeding male were passed to the next generation. These functions of male dominance parallel those described by Woolfenden and Fitzpatrick (1977) for Florida Scrub Jays. An additional effect of male dominance was to reduce groups to a size and composition compatible with cooperative nesting in its early stages.

Male American Crows are larger and weigh more than females (Hicks and Dambach 1935; Imler and McMurray 1939; Hartman 1955), and their size aids them in being dominant within a group and taking the lead in territorial encounters. Sexual dimorphism appears to be general in *Corvus* species, as Holyoak (1970), Picozzi (1975), and Slagsvold (1982) describe for Carrion Crows; Dhindsa and Sandhu (1984) for House Crows; and Rowley (1975) for Australian Ravens.

Allopreening

Female A was recognizable by being about five centimeters shorter than her mate, a difference seen when the two perched together. She was also the only one of her group to give *g-wong, g-wong* vocalizations [see Fig. 4(B)]. MA and his mate were perched on a limb five meters above my head on February 10, 1984. This was in an interim of several weeks between completion of nest building and egg laying. When MA held his head low, she allopreened the feathers on the top of his head. In the midst of this she put her bill under his to tip his head up so that she could reach the feathers of his throat. MA closed his nictitans when she nibbled around his eye. FA paused at times to preen herself. She was on a canal bank giving *g-wong*s on February 9 when MA alighted near her. He picked up a rootlet and, moving close, bent his head as she allopreened him. After a few minutes he dropped the rootlet, picked up some fibrous material, then returned for more allopreening. She mounted a cow pie three times to preen the top of his head.

Allopreening largely ceased during incubation. FA tried to alloppreen a yearling when it came to feed her on incubation day three, and when MA came, she succeeded in allopreening him for three seconds. The nest failed late in incubation and pair A did not renest. With seemingly little to occupy their time, pair A reverted to allopreening in late March. Although nearly all allopreenings that I have watched have been by one of the pair (n = 100+), they are occasionally reciprocal. When MA came to feed his mate early in incubation, she allopreened him for a minute, standing on the nest rim to do so. She then settled on the nest and he allopreened her for several minutes.

Allopreening—the preening of one bird by another—is a kind of social cement for the pair and the cooperative group as a whole. The habit is widespread in *Corvus* species, with females taking the lead. Lorenz (1970) describes it for Jackdaws and Common Ravens, Schaller (1964) for White-necked Ravens, Richards (1976) for Rooks, Wittenberg (1968) for Carrion Crows, Bijlsma and Meininger (1984) for House Crows, and McNair (1985) for Fish Crows. Harrison (1965) considers the birds doing the allopreening to be dominant. In birds that I have studied, however, which have included Casqued Hornbills (Kilham 1956a), Crested Caracaras (Kilham 1979), and Common Ravens, (see chap. 15), allopreening has been pair bonding, with females taking the lead and with no indication that one sex or the other was dominant. Shepherd and Mathews (1983), who rescued a Fish Crow from a Red-tailed Hawk, report that "the rescued crow behaved calmly when handled and appeared to enjoy being scratched behind the head, even pushing its head back to maintain the pressure." My hand-raised raven liked to be scratched around the head and, in an interchange of affection, to allopreen my eyebrows.

Trios

A feature of most breeding pairs of crows studied in Florida (n = 13) in the early breeding season was the persistence with which they were attended by third crows. A third crow might be a yearling or, if there were no yearlings, a nonbreeding adult. The third crow with pair A in 1984 was a yearling. When MA flew away after being allopreened by his mate on February 12, the yearling took his place, and female A allopreened it for three minutes (Fig. 5). A few days later the yearling crowded close along a wire when FA was on a fence post. MA, returning, hovered and then settled between the two, forcing the

Figure 5.   A "third crow" of a trio solicits (*upper left*) from the breeding female and is allopreened (*lower right*).

yearling away. Although males drove older third crows away by rougher methods, such as pecking at their feet, MA never more than nudged the yearling. The yearling responded at times by holding its wings out in appeasement begging or, rarely, by holding a foot out sideways to keep the male at a distance.

Third crows in 1982 were yearlings. Of twenty-nine episodes particularly noted, a third crow tried to crowd in on a pair when they were allopreening on five occasions and when they were engaged in copulatory behavior on three. On February 10 a yearling flew to the nest immediately after pair B had copulated and tried to push its head under them. On another occasion, when a pair was flying, the male tried to drive the third crow away, without success. When the three landed on a branch with little room, the third crow hung upside down below the pair.

Forbush (1927) devotes nearly a page in his account of American Crows to reports by various observers of third crows. When a pair of crows were building a nest in Boston, a "third crow was a very interested spectator and close companion of the other two." Trios can often be noticed when one is traveling along highways. Amusingly, when delegates from the Hartford Convention were en route to Washington in 1814, Harri-

son Grey Otis wrote home that they were constantly pre-
ceded by three black crows (Greenslet 1946). Third birds particularly associated with breeding pairs have been noted for
other *Corvus* species. Charles (1972) noted the persistence
with which "third birds" attended pairs of Carrion Crows in
spite of efforts of breeding males to drive them away. Bijlsma
and Meininger (1984) observed trios regularly in flocks of
House Crows at Suez and Verbeek and Butler (1981) a trio of
Northwestern Crows in which the third bird was an unmated
female with a deformed bill. She begged and was fed by the
male.

Forms of courtship other than allopreening and perching together included bowing, billing, and exchange of low notes.
The members of breeding pairs frequently rested within five
or six centimeters of each other. While MA and FA might allopreen at these times, the two occasionally (n = 3) bowed together, both facing out in the same direction. On January 8,
1984, MA, with head feathers raised and wings a little out,
made a moaning sound, then a *cu-koo* in bowing deeply. FA
also bowed, but more mildly. These performances were repeated
six times. I saw similar bowings on January 9 and 10. In 1982
the same pair bowed together on the back of a cow. One then
tried to mount the other.

Other Forms of Courtship

Bowing was not all done in courtship. When MA alighted
at corn on one occasion, in the presence of rival male X, he
assumed an upright posture with tail spread and wings a little
out, then bowed deeply in giving a *cu-koo*.

Billing was a less frequent form of courtship. When MA and
FA came close to each other on February 13, 1984, they fenced
gently with their bills, with one grasping the terminal half of
the bill of the other. I heard low notes, particularly at times
when the two of a pair settled together on nests prior to egg
laying.

Good (1952), who studied crows that were wary and could
be viewed only from a distance, believed that they had little
courtship, which he thought to be a characteristic of birds that
mate for life. Birds mated for life, however, still need pair-
bonding activities to synchronize sexual development as well
as to ensure cooperation in reproduction. The activities that
I have noted in American Crows in the early breeding season,
such as bowing, are common in varying degrees to other *Corvus* species (Goodwin 1976; Coombs 1978).

Special Vocalizations

The vocalizations of American Crows fall into two categories. One is the familiar cawing and the other, a variety of "uncrow-like" vocalizations that are for the most part either inaudible at close range (i.e., within 20 meters) or not recognizable as coming from a crow unless one has a good look at the performer. A difficulty in studying these vocalizations is the extent to which their use can vary. Vocalizations may reflect individual peculiarities as well as the varying composition of cooperatively breeding groups, particularly the ages and sexes of the auxiliaries and how many of those in adult plumage are close to sexual maturity. Some vocalizations have sounded as if the performers were practicing or playing with their voices. Regardless of these difficulties, certain vocalizations were given repeatedly and appeared on some occasions to convey definite meanings.

G-WAL-OP, G-WAL-OPS

These calls [see Fig. 4(A)] were usually given as doublets and were loud enough to carry throughout a territory. The adults giving these calls were primarily breeding males. One such male came to a tall stub, where we sometimes got out of our car in the morning, and repeated *g-wal-op, g-wal-op*s, accompanied by bows, the back of his neck appearing humped because of his raised feathers. This was for about ten days at the start of nesting.

Territory was the most recognizable of contexts. On January 16, 1983, when *g-wal-op*s from A crows were answered with *g-wal-op*s from a neighboring group, the A crows flew to their territorial boundary. *G-wal-op*s were seldom given near nests unless singly at times of copulation and once, repeatedly, when a nest was visited by a Red-tailed Hawk.

A confusing situation was that *g-wal-op*s were one of a series of vocalizations related in that they were loud and delivered as doublets. Among commoner variants were *g-wong, g-wong*s [Fig. 4(B)]; *kwar-uck, kwar-uck*s [Fig. 4(G)] and *kuk, kuk*s [Fig. 4(H)]. Some yearlings gave *g-wal-op*s and one or more of the variants so often that I could recognize them individually. Adult auxiliaries giving odd vocalizations were nearly always ones driven away by the breeding male and apt to stay by themselves. Some of the vocalizations that I have described might sound different to others. Chamberlain and Cornwell (1971), who made a recording of *g-wal-op*s, refer to them as

"*C. b. pascuus* screams." Stoddard (1978) describes a crow in Georgia that, bowing repeatedly below the horizontal, gave a strange *too-o-t-o-o-w-ah* that carried a quarter of a mile away. It may be that these loud vocalizations are restricted to the Florida race of the American Crow, *C. b. pascuus;* were they given in Maryland or New Hampshire, I am sure that I would have heard them.

Cu-koos

Cu-koos [Fig. 4(C)] are one of the more distinctive of crow vocalizations and possibly one of the more important in terms of social bonds. Unlike the *g-wal-op* group of vocalizations, they were given singly, without variants and softly, at the end of a deep bow, or by themselves. While the contexts in which they were given were often undecipherable, circumstances related to others, along with the number of times that I recorded them, were as follows.

Cu-koos counted in 1983 were given when the two of a pair were together (n = 45), or nearly as frequently (n = 43) when a crow was alone. Crows appeared at times to use *cu-koos* as a greeting. A yearling walking below a nest early in March gave a *cu-koo* when the female above flew off. In another episode a female incubating on her nest uttered a *cu-koo* when her mate came to a perch seven meters away. *Cu-koos* were sometimes given to a crow flying by. In one incident a crow was resting on a low branch. When a second crow passed near on a long, low flight, the first one bowed and gave a *cu-koo*. A similar incident occurred on another day when a crow, walking on a pasture, bowed and gave a *cu-koo* when another one flew overhead.

I heard *cu-koos* occasionally (n = 26) when the two of a pair were together on or by a nest prior to egg laying. On three occasions a female incubating on a nest gave a low *cu-koo* on hearing *g-wal-ops* in the distance. Some females (n = 3) gave a *cu-koo* when returning to their nest during incubation, either on landing or on the wing. In 1985 two breeding males were alike in giving a *cu-koo* with bowing displays when landing among others of their group to feed on corn, possibly as an expression of dominance. Single *cu-koos* were the most frequent of vocalizations given before copulations.

A feature noted in all years was the way a crow might seemingly address *cu-koos* to my wife or me directly, often flying to a perch four to five meters overhead to do so. When male

B, one of the tamest of the crows, did this on February 20, he bowed and gave bill clacks along with a *cu-koo*. In 1981, unfamiliar with the crows and afraid of frightening them, I hesitated to come below the nest tree of pair A. Finally, seeing no crows, I walked as close as I could to the nest. Then I found that a crow had come up silently to within six meters of where I stood. Looking at me it gave a single soft *cu-koo* and left. Not all incidents were near nests. A crow was perched silently on a fence post on February 7. When I walked passed, it bowed and gave a *cu-koo* in the same way that I had seen crows greet other crows.

I heard a *cu-koo* on January 15, 1985, when walking across a pasture and thinking that no crows were around. On turning I found that a crow had alighted behind me. It gave five more *cu-koo*s and left. Somewhat the same events happened on a another morning when I turned to find five crows that had apparently followed me. They were thickly bunched and making motions as if feeding on corn, although none was there. It was striking on these occasions when crows seemed to be asking for corn that *cu-koo*s were the only vocalization given.

*Cu-koo*s have been described by others. Mortimer (in Bent 1946) heard a note like the "cry of a cuckoo" in 1890 and Chamberlain and Cornwell (1971) a "*coo-coo*" from a family of crows, also in Florida. The vocalization is not limited to the south, for Townsend (1927), on getting close to a crow's nest in Massachusetts, heard "a pleasing sound . . . like the note of a cuckoo clock." I have not read of other corvids having any special way of greeting each other except for the remarkable "up-fluffing" that Hardy (1974) describes for neotropical jays (*Cissilopha*). It is due to this development, Hardy believes, that aggression and threat are so rare among them.

*KUCK-WOO-OO*s

These vocalizations [Fig. 4(D)] were like *cu-koo*s in being associated with bowing and in having an exotic quality, like the cooing of some tropical dove. The two calls, however, were distinct. *Kuck-woo*s differed from other vocalizations in having a faraway quality. When sitting by a nest being built on February 2, I heard what I thought a distant *kuck-woo*. I wondered if it came from the top of an oak, and it took a minute to discover that the performer was on a branch only five

meters away. The bird bowed twelve times, giving *kuck-woo*s
on the way down. A suggestion that *kuck-woo*s may serve as
a low warning at times was suggested on three mornings when
a breeding male made them in driving away a gray squirrel.
A yearling that aided him on two mornings remained silent.
The most continuous performances I heard were when a crow,
perched on a cabbage palm, gave *kuck-woo*s at a rate of twelve
a minute for five minutes. A single interruption was to make
a *hoo-hoo-hoo-ah* like the hooting of a Barred Owl.

Song

It is impossible to describe the mixtures of *coh*s, *caa*s, moans
and growls, mingled with caws, low *cu-koo*s, *g-wal-op*s, and
*kuck-woo*s, given at rates of up to sixty a minute, that make
up the "songs" of crows. The effect is that one of the breeding
pair or an auxiliary is going over the gamut of sounds that it
can make. A curious use of singing, noted on one occasion,
was when a Red-shouldered Hawk, after robbing a crow of a
walking catfish, took the fish into the depths of a live oak. A
crow followed and, perching within 30 centimeters, sang a conglomeration of sounds for nearly forty minutes, as if to dis-
tract the hawk.

   Among other corvids having songs are Carrion Crows (Bacchus 1943), Rooks (Coombs 1978; Richards 1976), Common
Ravens (chap. 15; Bent 1946), Jackdaws (Lorenz 1970), and
Black-billed Magpies (Baeyens 1979), Baeyens noting that the
observer must be close to hear them. Brown (1985) has reported on song and its use by captive American Crows.

Rattling Calls

I heard rattles [see Fig. 4(F)] only a few times, and these were
in conflicts between crows and Red-shouldered and Red-tailed
Hawks. The repeated rattles given by a lone crow when trying
to join one group of crows and then another in 1984 and 1985
were an exception. Others give a variety of contexts for rattling calls. Chamberlain and Cornwell (1971) heard them when
American Crows were in roosts or in flocks, Goodwin (1976)
in Carrion Crows when they were attacking birds of prey, and
Roskaft and Espmark (1982) in Rooks when a pair was in close
contact.

Low Notes

I heard varieties of soft sounds that might include moans, caws, and growly notes when the members of pairs were on a nest prior to egg laying, or again at the end of nesting in what appeared to be a renewal of courtship. Lamm (1958), in observations of Pied Crows, describes low notes as close vocal contact or "talking."

Bowing, Vocalizations, and Bill Clacks

When bowing at full intensity, a crow might give a few shakes of its head accompanied by mammalianlike moans, then pull its bill in against its breast and lower its head to its toes while opening and clacking its bill. A *cu-koo*, a *kuck-woo*, or no audible vocalization at all might end the performance as the crow pulled its head up sharply. I observed crows performing, but without being able to hear any sounds. Performers that I have been able to identify have been breeding males.

Calls associated with contortions of the head and neck are characteristic of a number of corvids. Among descriptions are Amadon's (1944), of the pistonlike thrusts accompanying the "hiccups" of the Florida Scrub Jays, and Goodwin's (1976), of the odd postures assumed by European Jays. In the latter, the back of the neck is humped as the head is bent downward. American and Carrion Crows (Wittenberg 1968) have a similar silhouette when producing their calls, which, like those of the European Jays, terminate with an upward jerk of the head.

Bill clacking is reported by Bacchus (1943) for Carrion Crows, by Gwinner (1964) and Brown (1974) for Common Ravens, and by Lawrence (in Bent 1946), who speaks of Northwestern Crows as "making a curious clattering of the bill which resembled horny plates struck together."

Vocal Mimicry: Barred Owl Call

I first heard crows making Barred Owl calls when close to a pair in Seneca, Maryland, in March, 1953. One crow was making a conglomeration of guttural sounds when it interrupted them to give a *hoo-hoo-hoo-ah*. I did not hear the call again until 1983, in Florida. The owl call was again mixed with a variety of vocalizations. The *hoo-hoo-hoo-ah*s are the only sounds I have heard (n = 4) from wild crows that sounded imitative. When near two crows mobbing a Barred Owl in Maryland, I heard the owl give *hoo-hoo-hoo-ah*s that sounded much the same as the crow imitations. It is well known that birds and animals as well as men may learn sights and sounds in moments of stress. Lorenz (1970) gives several examples of this, one of a pet Hooded Crow that had been caught in a trap. Crows become excited by Barred Owls, especially if one comes near a nest, and might pick up *hoo-ah*s under the stress of trying to drive it away.

Vocalizations and Individual Recognition

In seeking meanings of some of the "uncrowlike" vocalizations of American Crows, I have never been able to note any response of one crow to another giving a *cu-koo*, a *kuck-woo-oo*, or *g-wal-op*s. An impression is that American Crows express individuality in a range of vocal peculiarities. One yearling gave repeated *cu-koo*s whenever I passed in its vicinity, which was daily during the nesting period. Its two siblings made repetitions of other vocalizations, one of *g-wal-op*s and the other of choking sounds as if it were about to produce some vocalization but was not succeeding. A female gave *g-wong*, *g-wong*s when with her mate and another crow, *kuk-kuk*s for several years when no other member of its group was giving them. A lone crow that belonged to no group gave seemingly endless rattles. Although vocal peculiarities were most marked in yearlings, they persisted in some individuals from year to year.

Discussion

Selective values of individual recognition. Crows recognize each other individually; otherwise breeding males would not try to drive certain adult auxiliaries away in the early breeding season or members of a group be so quick to recognize a territorial intruder. But crows are sexually monomorphic. Their uniformly black plumages may make it difficult to recognize close kin at a distance; hence the value of recognition by vocalizations. Roskaft and Espmark (1982) report that the *caws* made by adult Rooks are structurally characteristic for each individual, and Thompson (1969) and Richards and Thompson (1978) have suggested the same for the cawing of American Crows. Individual and sexual recognition by the *caw* sound in Rooks is, according to Roskaft and Espmark (1982), a mechanism by which the two members of a pair can maintain contact under various seasonal conditions.

The selective advantage of the individuality of yearling vocalizations that I noted in American Crows may lie in Goodwin's (1976) observation that "captive corvids of some species . . . appear to pair more readily with strangers introduced to them at an appropriate time than they do with conspecifics which they have been reared and constantly kept with." Prevention of inbreeding could be a selective advantage of individual recognition among siblings. As Bateson (1978) has demonstrated for Japanese Quail and Miller (1979) for Zebra Finches, some birds, having learned the auditory characteristics of their immediate kin in early life, may later choose mates from among individuals that differ vocally from those with whom they were raised. Mechanisms leading to avoidance of inbreeding may be particularly important among cooperative breeders such as American Crows, where young can remain on natal territories long enough to become sexually mature.

Vocal mimicry.   A question is why crows should mimic Barred Owl calls and not those of Red-tailed Hawks and other raptors with which they are sympatric, as do Blue Jays (Bent 1946). This could be a matter of vocal capabilities. A crow's vocal apparatus is pre-adapted to making *oo-oo* sounds, and the *hoo-hoo*s of the Barred Owl come easily. The *scree* of a Red-tailed Hawk, on the other hand, may be beyond a crow's potential. The reverse may be true of Blue Jays. Although they mimic the calls of a number of Buteos, as well as of Screech Owls (Bent 1946), I have never heard, nor read of anyone as having heard, Blue Jays mimic Barred Owls. The *hoo*s of these owls are, conceivably, beyond a Blue Jay's potential.

Vocal mimicry can be of conspecifics or of other birds and animals. Goodwin (1976) notes two classes of the second type in corvids: (a) ravens and magpies, which mimic if they are hand-raised but not if they are wild, and (b), jays such as Common and Blue Jays that habitually practice mimicry in the wild state. American Crows are well known to mimic "hello" and other words in captivity (Chamberlain and Cornwell 1971). As far as I am aware no one has ever described them as mimicking the vocalizations of any animal or bird in the wild. One might be led, therefore, to include them in Goodwin's (1976) category of corvids that mimic only in captivity. But one can question whether Goodwin's categories are valid. Mimicking of other birds and animals by ravens, magpies, and American

Crows could occur in the wild but be difficult to detect. If, without having studied crows, I heard a *hoo-hoo-hoo-ah* in the wild, I would assume that it came from a Barred Owl, even though I might hear crow vocalizations intermixed. It was only by being close to crows on four occasions that I found that they can make remarkably close imitations.

6. Onset of Nesting

Nest Building

The first evidence I had that pair A was getting ready to nest was when the female tried to lay sticks in a bay tree in January. I watched crows carrying sticks to various places in the next week and even dropping them when flying across a pasture. By the first of February the two of the pair were carrying sticks from the ground into an oak growing more or less in the open. When I went to look, the sticks laid were so few that I could see nothing definite. I assumed, therefore, that this was day one of nest building. The adults appeared to do all of the building at first, and it was not until February 6 that Jane and I noted three crows at the nest, which was located 30 centimeters within the canopy and eight meters above the ground. The inner group of these crows consisted of the breeding pair plus three yearlings. That the yearlings helped with nest building was indicated on the same morning when three crows flew to the nest, each carrying a lump of black mud and turf. On February 8 we noted four crows on the nest on two occasions. The nest was completed in nine days.

Pair B tried several sites before deciding on a final one on February 5. The site was on the trunk of a slanting oak, seven meters above the ground and 15 meters within a grove. On February 6 there was almost constant activity as the crows brought in crooked sticks, which took time to work into a structure. This meant that crows coming with sticks had to wait for a chance to get to the nest. It was apparent that the three yearlings were taking part, for I noted three crows by the nest on three occasions, four on two, and all five members of the group on one (Fig. 6). The yearlings usually left their sticks for the female to work in. The situation changed in the next

Figure 6. Five members of a cooperatively breeding group of American Crows at a nest. Yearlings bring in sticks and the breeding female arranges them while the male (foreground) is on guard.

few days, when, with the stick phase completed, the crows started bringing in mud and finer lining materials. These could be placed more quickly, and the wait to get at the nest disappeared. Rowley (1978) describes crowding by nests of White-winged Choughs where members of a group formed queues in awaiting turns.

I watched pair B and their yearlings walking on the floor of the grove one morning, searching the fallen leaves of cabbage palms for fibers. The yearlings worked in the same manner as the adults in flying them to the nest. On February 9, the last day of nest building, I noted three crows at the nest on five occasions and four on one occasion in a period of ninety minutes. Pair B, with the help of their yearlings, completed their nest in five days. The times for groups A and B in 1982, nine and five days, respectively, were shorter than those noted by Emlen (1942), who, in a much larger series, noted that crows in California took thirteen days to complete their nests.

SHUDDER CALLS OF FEMALES

The males and females of breeding pairs often flew to and from the nest construction site together, the female or, less often, both sexes carrying sticks. In either case the male left after a few moments to guard from a distance. His mate then began giving growly notes as she worked sticks into place. Many of the sticks were long (about 30 centimeters) and crooked. When a female seized one in her bill and tried to force it in place by shaking her head, while still making growly notes, the result was a shudder call [Fig. 7(A)] audible at a considerable distance. The vocalizations were loud enough on three occasions to lead us to nests that we had been unable to find.

Wittenberg (1968) reports shudder calls, as I have termed them, in Carrion Crows and Goodwin (1976) in Rooks. "When building, particularly and perhaps only if the stick or other material gets temporarily jammed in an unsuitable position," wrote Goodwin, "the Rook utters a long drawn out hoarse call with an almost human tone of exasperation and complaint."

START NESTS

The helpers of pair A, those that the breeding male allowed to come near at the start of nesting, were all yearlings. On February 20, 1982, ten days after completion of the nest and

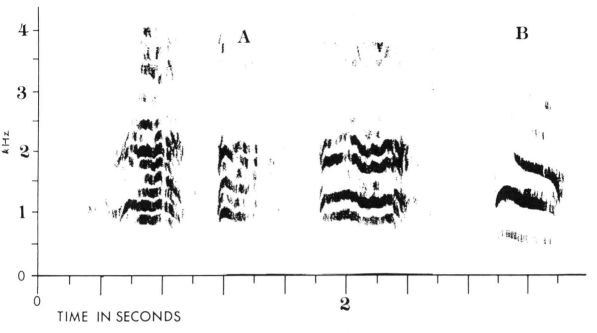

Figure 7.   (A) Shudder call; (B) nest call.

prior to egg laying, I found a yearling building a nest by itself, doing much cawing as it broke sticks from neighboring bay trees. The adults of the pair and the other two yearlings came to look several times, but none gave any help in the hour that I watched. The yearling worked ten minutes on the following day and then lost interest.

The six auxiliaries of pair B in 1983 were in adult plumage with the exception of a single yearling (see Table 4). When the breeding pair were building their first and later a second or replacement nest, the auxiliaries built nest foundations of their own 40 to 50 meters away. This, I believe, was due to the aggressiveness of male B. Thwarted at the main nest and having an urge to build, the auxiliaries brought their sticks to a second nest. Things changed when the main nest was ready to be chinked with mud and lined. Since these materials were easier to bring in than crooked sticks, an auxiliary had time to come and go before the male arrived. Lawton and Lawton (1985) describe Brown Jays building two nests at a time, then abandoning one, as the crows did.

A Faulty Nest Corrected

When five adult auxiliaries brought sticks to nest B in 1984, the nest fell into disarray. Some sticks rested above a supporting fork but many were to one side with little to hold them. Work ceased for several days, and I thought the nest abandoned. But female B, recognizable by small holes in the vanes of her rectrices, now began pulling sticks from the unbalanced side, often hanging upside down to do so, then flying them around to the top. The other crows, meanwhile, ceased coming. After female B had spent two weeks reconstructing the nest, the others of her group returned to help finish it. It seemed in this case that, with five adult auxiliaries bringing in sticks faster than the female could handle them, the nest became disorganized. There is a limit, conceivably, to the number of adult auxiliaries that can be of help rather than a hindrance. Dow (1984) found that building rates in Gray-crowned Babblers, which are also cooperative breeders, were lower in groups with seven auxiliaries than in ones with fewer.

Interim Period

There was usually little or no activity around nests for six to sixteen days following their completion. Females accompanied by their mates occasionally flew to a nest to add a few bits of nest lining, but otherwise stayed away, as if no longer interested. Verbeek (1972b) noted that Yellow-billed Magpies fed and loafed for about ten days following completion of nests, and Erpino (1968) describes the same for Black-billed Magpies. Woolfenden (1973) found intervals between nest building and egg laying were longer in Florida Scrub Jays for the first nesting of a year than for renestings. Nest building is a strenuous activity, and it may be that females need an inactive or interim period in which to develop nutritional reserves for egg laying.

Precopulatory Displays

The female, the male, or both crouched, with body horizontal, wings out and drooping, and tail vibrating up and down prior to some of the copulations described below. Coombs (1978) describes precopulatory displays with tail quivers in both sexes of Rooks, James (1984) the same for Northwestern Crows, and I for Common Ravens. Tail quivers can also be used in appeasement.

HOLDING OBJECTS IN BILL

Breeding males sometimes picked up objects as part of copulatory behavior. When the two of pair A performed precopulatory displays on the ground below their nest on March 6, the male picked up a raccoon vertebral column, with pelvis and a femur attached, and leaned it against his mate. When the female flew from the nest four days later, on day two of incubation, the male performed a vigorous precopulatory display by himself, then picked up the raccoon skeleton again.

Some precopulatory displays were playlike. When the two of pair A were on a canal bank near their nest four days before incubation began, MA picked up a wad of debris and walked to his mate. She immediately crouched in a precopulatory display. But MA, instead of mounting, lay on his side holding the debris toward her. Then he assumed a precopulatory pose and she attempted to mount him in a reverse mounting. This play of the adults was later mimicked, to some extent, by the two yearlings of the group. I once saw a male holding debris in his bill while copulating. James (1984) noted a male Northwestern Crow holding a feather in his bill prior to one complete and one incomplete copulation and Verbeek (1972b), female Yellow-billed Magpies holding objects in their bills in two of six copulations.

INTRAPAIR

Intra- and Extrapair Copulatory Behavior

I observed twenty-eight copulations of American Crows in Florida, of which seventeen were on nests, nine on the ground, and two on branches. Details of some of them are as follows: A female was giving slow *caw-caw-caw*s on her nest on January 13 when her mate came to the nest rim and mounted. I heard a single *cu-koo*. The male settled on his mate, waving his outspread wings, which came to hang over the edge of the nest. The female stood up beneath him, her tail vibrating up and down as he worked his tail under hers. On the next day, the second of egg laying, he again came to the rim, placing a foot on her neck before mounting. This time her body sank low as her head tilted way back. The crows vocalized so loudly that Jane heard them from a distance of 250 meters. Loud cries accompanied nearly half (n = 11) the other copulations. Wittenberg (1968) describes similar vocalizations for Carrion Crows.

I was watching a crow flying over a pasture on February 2, when it stopped abruptly to drop down on a female that was crouching in the grass. She put her head way back in the copulation that followed. This was 70 meters from the nest. I watched the same female on the ground later when her mate, alighting five meters away, went into a precopulatory display. She flew to him immediately to do the same. He then took a piece of debris about seven centimeters long and, holding it in his bill, mounted and copulated.

Female A gave a prolonged series of nest calls on March 6, then flew to the ground below her nest. Here she performed a precopulatory display as her mate arrived and did the same. As described above, he picked up a raccoon skeleton and leaned it against her. She then mounted his back in reverse mounting, and the male then mounted her.

Copulations lasted from four to twelve seconds and took place over a period of two to three weeks. Those for one pair started during nest building and, continuing through an interim period of two weeks, ended with one on the third day of incubation.

I have found no descriptions of the copulatory behavior of American Crows by others, but that of the related Northwestern Crow (James 1984) appears to be similar. Seven copulations witnessed by Wittenberg (1968) in Carrion Crows were on nests and one by Gent (1949) on the ground.

Reverse Mounting

I noted reverse mounting twice, once in a complete and once in an incomplete copulation. It has also been noted by Coombs (1978) in Rooks and by James (1984) in Northwestern Crows. The reverse mounting described by James followed a nest failure, and he thought that mounting by the female may have been an effort to restimulate the male. The reverse mounting I witnessed, on the other hand, was at the start of egg laying and below a nest that was later successful. Having observed reverse mounting in Red-bellied and Red-headed Woodpeckers (Kilham 1961, 1977), I think it is apt to occur in species that exhibit what I call mutualism in courtship. A form of this in *Melanerpes* woodpeckers was the way a male and a female tapped together. While mutualism is less constant between the sexes of American Crows, it is exemplified by both sexes squatting in the same precopulatory crouch with tail quiver, carrying debris in the bill, or bowing together. From this point of view, mounting by females, although infrequent, can be regarded as one of a number of forms of courtship in which both partners behave in the same way.

EXTRAPAIR COPULATIONS WITHIN A GROUP

The Crows in 1983 were in two groups: A with five and B with six adult auxiliaries (see Table 1). About half of these, although attacked repeatedly by the breeding males, still exhibited signs of sexuality in periods when copulations of the pair were taking place. Pair A had nearly finished a copulation on the nest on January 14 when a second male, an auxiliary, flew to land beside the copulating male on the back of the female. Both males flapped their wings with all three crows rising and falling as the female moved underneath. After a few seconds, the males flew, one chasing the other mildly.

Other instances of extrapair activity took place on the ground. Female B was giving nest calls while feeding in a pasture one morning when an auxiliary, first flying to the unattended nest, flew to her and mounted. The breeding male knocked him away almost immediately and then returned to his mate three times in twelve minutes in attempts to copulate.

Two other instances of extrapair copulations were initiated by a female auxiliary. This "thwarted female," on coming below the nest where female B was incubating, crouched in a precopulatory display, and male B mounted. Female B flew down, lowered her head, and nudged the auxiliary away. Male B mounted the auxiliary a second time two days later, again after she had given a precopulatory display. Neither of these attempts was successful. The auxiliary continued trying to seduce the breeding male for a week, accompanying her efforts with bowing and bill clacks ending with *cu-koo*s and picking up debris, which included a white feather.

COPULATORY ATTEMPTS BY OUTSIDE MALES

Territorial intrusions by single crows were commonest when the sexual activity of a breeding pair was at a peak. I witnessed twelve intrusions at nest B between February 6, when it was being built, and February 28, when the first egg was laid. The intruders usually circled a nest, then headed back for the territorial border with male B and often a few auxiliaries in pursuit. One intruder tried to copulate with female B on four occasions when she was laying, but was driven off each time.

Efforts of females to avoid copulations varied. An intruder on March 12 flew directly to the rim of nest B. Female B (FB) kept turning, and the male (I presumed the same one) was back in fifteen minutes. He tried to flutter on the female's back, but she left the nest. When he followed, she returned making *ca-ca-ca* notes. The intruder again fluttered on her back and she again left the nest. Her assailant then flew to perch within five meters of me. This was when male B (MB) returned to feed his mate. MB paused, then bent low as if for a better look at the intruder that he now saw for the first time. The result was another pursuit to the boundary.

In contrast to female B, female A seemed not to resist when an intruder landed on her back. But within seconds male A struck the nest so hard that he knocked both his mate and the intruder out of it.

From watching both the intra- and extrapair copulatory behavior of American Crows, I think that an outside male's chances of forcing a copulation on a breeding female, especially when she is sitting on her nest where most crow copulations take place, are slim. Her attachment to nest and mate would seem enough to make her resistant to a foreign male alighting on her back, especially when he has no time for preliminaries. Turning on the nest, standing up, and leaving were all effective in preventing an intruder from mounting. At a minimum the evasive actions of females gained time for their mates to return and chase an intruder away.

Promiscuity is especially prevalent in colonial nesters (Gladstone 1979). This may explain why extrapair copulations appear to be commoner among Rooks (Roskaft 1983) than other *Corvus* species. Among eleven copulations observed by Wittenberg (1968) for Carrion Crows, four were by intruding males. In one of these, two males mounted one female simultaneously, a situation that I observed, as described above, for a breeding male and an auxiliary American Crow.

Mate Guarding

Breeding males guarded their mates during the time of sexual receptiveness. The onset of mate guarding was difficult to determine, however, because males perched and flew with their mates as part of courtship before protection against stolen matings was especially needed. One of the earliest signs of nest guarding was the way a male flew with his mate to the nest when she carried sticks, waited on a branch nearby while she worked them in, then followed when she left. When nest calls began at the start of egg laying and a female was sexually receptive, a male might perch in her vicinity for thirty minutes while she made her monotonous *caa*s. Once a female began to sit on her nest, her mate generally had two or three special perches from which to watch. Male B in 1983 watched from a fence post 150 meters from the nest; from a spot on the ground in open pasture 60 meters away; on the ground below the nest; and, least often, from the top of a tree. An advantage to the low perches was that intruding males usually flew in low through the grove where the nest was located.

Males occupied with guarding spent little time feeding their mates in the first days of incubation. In several hours of watching on February 27, the second day of incubation, auxiliaries fed female B ten times and the male not at all. He tried to drive the auxiliaries away but without success. In 1984 male B drove three territorial intruders away from the nest on the second day of incubation and two on the third.

Sexually Thwarted Females

Peculiarities of Group Behavior

A phenomenon noted in four of five years was the presence of one or two adult auxiliaries that begged in the manner of juveniles. They started about the time breeding females began giving nest calls, and it seemed probable that they were sexually thwarted females. One of them in 1983 spent much time below the nest where female B was incubating, as if waiting for male B to return. When he did so, he sometimes walked closely behind as though trying to drive her away. She walked just ahead, picking up and dropping pieces of debris and giving an occasional *cu-koo*. At other times he flew to her as if seeking company. She once solicited copulation and he twice mounted her, as detailed previously. As nesting progressed, MB became mildly hostile, driving the auxiliary away when she came close. In 1984, when there were five young in the nest, a maximum number, MB paid little attention to the two begging females of his group. The two seemed to set each other off. When one begged, the other did also. Late in the nestling period when the lone crow LC, an outsider that belonged to no group, was present, it joined in the clamor. In spite of their begging, all three — the two thwarted females and LC — fed nestlings.

Group A2 in 1984 consisted of a breeding pair plus three adult auxiliaries, two of which were females. Female A2 was unusual in joining in the begging of the auxiliaries while sitting on the nest. The begging helpers tried at times to get close to the male when he was resting. This appeared to annoy him, for he nearly always made efforts to drive them away. When one of the females came within ten centimeters on April 10, he drove her along the limb they were on, bending low and pecking at her feet (Fig. 8).

I have heard people remark that they knew when crows had young because they could hear the begging cries, yet this was, in Florida, before any eggs had been laid! As described in chapter 7, the vocalizations of nestlings are low and unlikely to carry any distance. Loud begging that I heard during nesting came either from auxiliaries that were thwarted females or, for a short time at the start of incubation, from the female giving nest calls.

ALLOFEEDINGS

There were occasions when an auxiliary, whether a yearling or an adult, begged from another member of its group and got fed. In 1982, when auxiliaries were all yearlings at the start of nesting, I saw this happen twice before nesting began and twelve times afterward. Begging auxiliaries sometimes flew to the nest at the moment when another crow was arriving with food, then begged, and got fed. But the food might be only sidetracked, for the auxiliary usually passed it on to the incubating female or to nestlings. Male B and a begging female had been perched side by side on March 21 when MB flew off and caught an anole. She begged with wings out and he gave it to her. She then flew to the nest to feed the breeding female.

Crows coming to a nest frequently paused to disgorge the contents of their antelingual pouches on the ground, then tear it into smaller pieces. When male A did this early in incubation, a yearling, as if seeing an opportunity, flew down to beg and was fed by MA. Female A then flew over to beg from the yearling. The yearling, instead of feeding her, flew with her to the nest where, in a roundabout way, she received the food intended for her originally. Thwarted or begging female auxiliaries did not seem to want food per se. What they sought was attention, for I several times saw one beg when her bill was already full.

I have not seen courtship feeding, that is, feeding of the female in weeks prior to egg laying in American Crows. Breeding females that I have watched have been fed regularly only when incubating or about to start doing so. Verbeek and Butler (1981) observed yearling helpers being fed by male North-

Figure 8. Breeding male of a cooperative group of American Crows driving away a "thwarted female" helper by biting at her feet.

western Crows. They refer to this as the cost to the breeding adults of having helpers. Close analysis of costs has seemed impossible with American Crows that I have watched, since helpers, whether yearlings or adult, had a strong desire to feed the incubating female as well as nestlings, and while they might occasionally beg to be fed, they still had an urge to carry the food to the nest. Among black-and-blue jays of Middle America, as described by Hardy (1974), allofeeding functions prominently as a nonsexual form of social bonding within communal groups. Possibly the scattered allofeedings that I noted among crows could, to a lesser degree, have served in a similar way.

Discussion

Function of shudder calls. Since shudder calls are loud enough to lead one to a nest, it seems likely that they have selective value. Building a nest with crooked sticks that have to be handled and forced into place goes best, in all probability, when one crow is in charge, for there is no room for more than one to work effectively. The growly notes of females plus shudders may serve to warn other crows away. As with American Crows, female Carrion Crows (Picozzi 1975) and Common Ravens (Stiehl 1985) build the baskets of nests.

Mate guarding.   The function of mate guarding is to prevent insemination of a mated female by an outside male. Males of a variety of monogamous species seek extrapair copulations (Ford 1983; Buitron, 1983a), and a resident male needs to be alert during the time that his mate is receptive. Much of what Buitron (1983a) reports for Black-billed Magpies is pertinent to American Crows. The peak of intrusions by male magpies seeking extrapair copulations, she found, was prior to and during egg laying. Magpies, like American Crows, make far-carrying nest calls at this time, and it is likely that neighboring males who hear them know where and when to find a potentially receptive female. Buitron points out that it is advantageous to such males if, due to asynchronous nestings of neighboring pairs, an intruding male is finished guarding his own mate and has time to seek out the mate of a neighbor.

The idea that copulations can be forced on females has been shown only for certain waterfowl. A variety of conditions would have to be met, including time for precopulatory behavior, before a female American Crow would be likely to submit to a strange male. The females that I observed (n = 5) were skillful in taking evasive action.

A more immediate benefit of mate guarding, as Lumpkin (1981) points out for Black-billed Magpies, is to protect a female from troublesome interruptions by outside males in the period after nest building, when she is building up nutritional reserves for egg laying.

7. Cooperative Nesting

Nesting led to a change of pace in watching. In the early breeding season I had to walk a good deal to keep track of the courtship of breeding pairs, the dominance of the breeding males, and other activities that required moving about. With the onset of incubation Jane and I followed activities by sitting in folding chairs as near as we could to a nest and still be able to see over the edge of it. With our sitting by nests seven days a week, the crows became accustomed to us, paying little attention to our walking about if we chose to do so. Sitting is an optimal way of watching. I made some of my better observations of foraging, food storing, and other activities while watching nests.

Special to breeding females were flat, monotonous sounding *caa, caa*s [Fig. 7(B)] that began at or near the time of egg laying and reached a peak when a female began to sit on a nest and give them continuously, either on the nest or, at times, away from it. I have heard these vocalizations in Maryland and New Hampshire as well as in Florida. With females at the ranch (n = 12) the *caa*s came at intervals of three to twelve seconds with the female partly extending her wings with each call. Other crows usually paid no attention to a female giving nest calls away from a nest, although her mate might perch nearby for up to twenty minutes. Once incubation began, the calling became more of a true begging, with the female speeding up calls when a crow brought food. After a few days they dwindled and ceased. Female A2 was exceptional in giving nest calls throughout the first two weeks of the incubation period in two successive years.

Nest Calls

Table 2. Feeding rates for and incubating times (attentiveness) of females in eight cooperatively breeding groups

Year	Group	Total no. in group	No. of helpers Ad.	No. of helpers Yr.	No. of days observations made	Total observation (min.)	Feeding of female rate/hr	Attentiveness of female (percent)
1982	A	9	4	3	19	2981	3.1	88.7
	B	9	4	3	19	1093	4.0	67.0
1983	A	7	5	0	20	2725	3.0	95.1
	B	9	6	1	20	1795	3.4	87.5
1984	A2	8	4	2	19	1885	3.3	90.2
	B	8	6	0	18	2565	2.5	90.0
1985	A2	7	2	3	19	1910	3.8	92.5
	A3	7	3	2	19	1823	3.5	86.0

NOTE: Ad. = adult; Yr. = yearling.

Nest calls are audible at 300 or more meters when at their peak and can be one of the best clues to a nest's location. I found three nests in Florida in this way and three in Maryland. I think nest calls serve to announce that the breeding female, when becoming broody and about to lay eggs, is ready to be fed by her mate and helpers of her cooperative group. In a similar vein, Roskaft and Espmark (1982) believe that the begging calls of the female Rook inform the male of her dependence on him for food. Wittenberg (1968) describes nest calls in Carrion Crows, Warncke (1958) in Common Ravens, and Buitron (1983a) in Black-billed Magpies. Lawton and Lawton (1985) have recently described the whine call of cooperatively breeding Brown Jays. The whine resembles the nest call of American Crows in that it carries well but differs in that it is sustained over a much longer period.

Incubation by the Female

NEST ATTENTIVENESS

The attentiveness of females to incubating and the rates at which they were fed per hour by mate and helpers are given in Table 2. Breeding females were fed three to four times an hour and spent 86 to 90 percent of their time incubating. In 1983 pair A nested for a final time after losing three and pair B after losing two nests. In spite of these delays, attentiveness to incubat-

Table 3. Number of times helpers identified coming to nests A and B of cooperatively breeding American Crows

| Stage of nesting | Nest | No. of days | | Total observation times (min) | Visits to nest | | No. of occasions helpers identified |
		In nesting stage	Nest under observation		Totals	Rate/hr (avg)	
Egg- laying	A	20	19	2981	316	6.00	57
incubation	B	21	17	1093	87	4.50	12
Early nestling	A	14	11	1762	548	19.00	170
(brooding)	B	12	7	660	154	14.00	41
Mid-nestling	A	13	13	1990	319	9.00	62
	B	14	14	1740	322	11.50	56
Last week	A	7	7	1290	123	6.00	6
	B	7	7	780	83	6.25	11
Totals	A + B	55*	50	12,296	1952	9	415

*Length of total nesting period.

ing and the rates of feeding the incubating females remained about the same as for females that, in other years, nested only once. Butler and associates (1984) observed an attentiveness of 86 percent in female Northwestern Crows.

I was able to identify helpers coming to the nest during incubation, as shown in Table 3 for nests A and B in 1982, only at times when two, three, or four crows were at the nest in addition to the incubating female. Stallcup and Woolfenden (1978) noted that yearling Florida Scrub Jays sometimes followed older jays to the nest, with up to five alighting on the rim at a time. Dow (1970), who observed similar gatherings with Noisy Miners, thought that visits of a number at a time might be purely social.

Female crows begged with wings out and fluttering when about to be fed in the first two to three days of incubation, seizing the bills of the incoming crows in their own. We then heard gulping sounds as they swallowed while still calling. Females on a nest are in a poor position to tear up food for themselves. Some crows coming to nests first stopped on the ground to tear up the food they were carrying. When a helper brought one female an entire anole, she flew elsewhere to tear it up. Another helper brought a female a small snake. She seized one end of it, but the other remained stuck in the throat of the helper. The two then had a tug-of-war that ended with both falling to the ground. After swallowing the snake, the female refused the next two feedings.

Breeding males fed their mates infrequently during the first few days of incubation, when they were still busy mate guarding. Later in incubation I noted that the male at one nest was the only one to feed the female for the first hour or more on cold mornings. He did this by taking food from caches in neighboring trees. Crows coming to a nest in the absence of a female might either swallow the food they were carrying and leave, or wait on a branch for a few minutes and feed the female on her return. Females usually took their times off right after being fed. The habit could conceivably reduce the number of feeding visits missed by being absent. Females were seldom fed by other crows when away from nests.

I was surprised to see what looked like nest material brought to one nest on incubation days nine and ten, for I had never seen material added to nests once they were completed. The female flew to her mate thirteen minutes after the second offering and an abortive copulation followed, with both crows falling to the ground. Sticks are sometimes carried in the bill in precopulatory displays, and their being brought to the nest in midincubation could have been sexual.

Behavior of Females

Females flying away from nests rarely made any effort to feed themselves. They spent their time doing leg-wing stretches and preening before returning in one to six minutes. Females also preened while incubating, mostly the breast and belly feathers they could reach without moving. They were generally silent but cawed at times in answer to the cawing of crows in the distance. Female A2 joined her mate in driving an unwelcome crow from the nest tree on one occasion and a Red-shouldered Hawk on another. She also left one morning on a long flight to join in a territorial encounter. Stiehl (1985) observed a female raven leave her eggs to join her mate in attacking other ravens, as well as a Red-tailed Hawk and a Golden Eagle, and Stallcup and Woolfenden (1978) saw incubating or brooding Scrub Jays desert eggs or nestlings to aid in defending boundaries.

Incubation, as watched from the ground, appeared to last about nineteen days (see Table 2). Others, who observed nests by climbing to them, give 18 days for the American Crow (Bent

1946) and 18.3 days for the Northwestern Crow (Butler 1984). Good (1952) states that incubation generally begins with the laying of the last egg, but may at times begin earlier, as indicated by young hatching over a period of one to two days.

Both Good (1952) and I found that only breeding female American Crows incubate, a finding supported by Johnston's (1959) report of an absence of brood patches in a large series of males. While an adult auxiliary or a breeding male might stay by a nest at the ranch for some minutes after a female had left, I never saw one settle down on eggs or young. Stiehl (1985) reports that only female Common Ravens incubate, and Goodwin (1976) reports the same for Carrion Crows and corvids in general.

Hatching and Brooding

A notable event on the day of hatching was a jump in the number of visits paid to a nest. This was especially marked in 1982, when all helpers of inner groups were yearlings. I counted thirty-eight visits in the first hour of my observation by nest A on the day of hatching, the highest number I witnessed in an hour at any nest. It seemed that many of the visits were made out of curiosity, for none of the yearlings appeared to bring food. The female moved aside each time a helper came, giving it a chance to look at the young. Lawton and Lawton (1985) saw up to nine Brown Jays perching on a nest on the day of hatching. Visits to nest A increased from three during incubation to an average of nineteen in the first eleven days of the nestling period and at nest B from an average of four during incubation to fourteen per hour in the first week after hatching.

Female A3 dug mildly into the bottom of her nest on the day of hatching in 1985, then picked up and ate seven or eight pieces of something. When her mate came, she allopreened him, then reached down and ate seven or eight more pieces, three large enough to fill her bill. I have never seen other breeding females feed in this way, and it seemed likely that female A3 was eating a chick that died at the time of hatching. Tom-Tov (1976) found that Carrion Crows, in spite of inhibitions against eating objects in their nests, will eat cracked eggs or dead chicks.

Only female crows brooded in nests I watched, a finding reported for Northwestern Crows by Butler and associates (1984). The extent of brooding of crows at the ranch was apt to vary with the number of young. As shown in Table 4, female B, with five nestlings, brooded for nine days whereas

Table 4. Comparisons of feeding rates and times of brooding and fledging

| Group | NUMBERS | | Time nestlings brooded (days) | FEEDING RATES/HR | | Ages at fledging (days) |
	Crows in Group	Nestlings		For brood	For each nestling	
A3	7	2	21	4.7	2.35	37–38
A2	7	5	9	18.6	3.70	41–42

NOTE: Feeding rates averaged over the first thirty-six days of nesting for two cooperatively breeding groups of crows, one with two young and one with five. Each group consisted of a breeding pair plus five auxiliaries that started nesting within three days of each other in adjacent territories.

female A2 in the same year, with only two young, brooded on and off for twenty-one days. Small broods of various avian species are apt to be brooded longer than large ones, as I have noted for Yellow-bellied Sapsuckers (Kilham 1977) and as Royoma (1966) has for Great Tits. Royoma noted that where there are numbers of young, they tend to keep each other warm by huddling together. Since two young cannot do this effectively, they may need extra brooding on cold or rainy days.

Nestling Period

FEEDING YOUNG

When a crow came to the nest early in the nestling period, the brooding female might seize its bill in her own and get some of the food. She and the other crow might then bend down and feed the nestlings. At other times an incoming crow nudged the female aside and fed the young directly. Of eighteen visits on the third day after hatching at one nest, the female was fed alone in six, both the female and the young in four, and the young alone in eight. Similar events are described by Goodwin (1976) for Rooks. Although nestlings generally shot their heads up and gaped when a crow landed on a nest, they did not always do so in nests occupied by only two nestlings. This may have been because, with the pair and four or five helpers all feeding them, they were not always hungry enough to beg. Crows coming to a nest with food in the nestling period sometimes paused to give a few low *cawk*s, as if to alert nestlings that they were coming. Roskaft and Espmark (1982) refer to comparable vocalizations in the Rook as feeding-young calls, used especially in the nine days after hatching before the nestlings' eyes had opened.

After losing two nests in 1983 (Fig. 9), the B crows built a

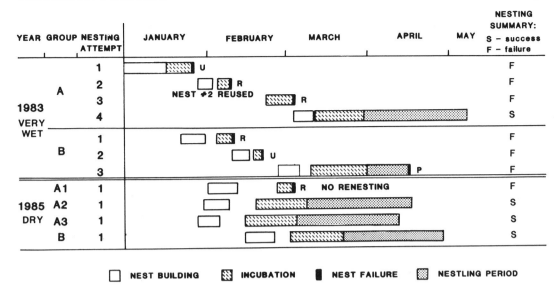

Figure 9. Results of nesting attempts of two cooperatively breeding groups of crows, A and B, in the very wet year of 1983 (El Niño event), and of four groups of crows (A1, A2, A3, and B) that nested in the same area in 1985, a dry year. Causes of nest failures were: R = raccoon (n = 4; see text); U = unknown (n = 2); and P = poorly constructed nest (n = 1).

third one on a single oak limb. This proved to be a poor site, for the nest developed a tilt as nesting progressed. An advantage was that I could see into it while sitting on the ground. When a crow came with food in its antelingual pouch in the first week after hatching, it was apt to put a large amount into the throat of one nestling, then withdraw much of it, before feeding a second one. On a number of occasions a strand of saliva, up to 20 centimeters long hung momentarily between the bill of the adult and that of the first nestling, an indication that substantial amounts of saliva were passed along with food. When nestlings were older, incoming crows fed only one at a visit.

The only account I have found of a *Corvus* species passing saliva is that of Yglesias (1962), telling of a tame female Jackdaw that adopted two young Jackdaws. The Jackdaw did not feed the nestlings, but after Yglesias had fed them, the Jackdaw looked down their gapes, removed some of the food, then dropped in some of her saliva, thus regulating the amount of food given and supplying what may have been essential juices in one operation. One of the difficulties we had in hand raising crows and ravens was to know when one of them had taken too much. It seemed to me from watching at the ranch that incoming crows had a sense of just how much a young nestling should be allowed to retain. If too much was given, some was withdrawn, thus making more efficient use of food brought to the nest. I have encountered no reports of what value saliva from older birds may have to young nestlings. It could conceivably serve multiple needs, from maintaining water balance to providing digestive enzymes, antibodies, or other essentials.

FEEDING RATES

The winter and spring of 1984–85 were unusually dry, and crows feeding nestlings appeared to have limited sources of food. Yet when the seven crows of the A2 group were given fresh road-kills, a surplus of food that was highly attractive, the rates they fed their five nestlings showed no increase over previous or succeeding days (see Table 6 below). The sustained rates of feeding, even in a dry year, suggest that helpers may exert a beneficial effect in keeping a steady supply of food coming in periods when finding food is difficult.

Table 5 compares the rates at which five nestlings were fed in one nest with that of two nestlings in another. The nests were started at about the same time, were in adjacent territories, and were in each case attended by a pair and five helpers. In spite of these similarities, the two A3 nestlings received a third fewer feeding visits per hour than the more numerous nestlings of the A2 nest. These observations run counter to a general finding (Skutch 1976) that parent birds of various species bring less food for each member of a large as compared to a small brood. An important difference between the crows that I observed and the species discussed by Skutch is that crows are cooperative breeders. The begging cries of the five nestlings were, in the aggregate, louder and more sustained than those of the two. Perhaps the louder cries incited the A2 crows to a special effort. Although the crows at both nests came with antelingual pouches loaded with food, a pouch can be moderately full or obviously stuffed. My impression was that the A3 crows, with fewer begging cries to listen to, spent a longer time foraging, but when they did return, they carried more food.

BEHAVIOR OF NESTLINGS

We first heard nestlings four days after they hatched. Their vocalizations, all low, varied from *churr*s to *chee-ap*s, *chee-up*s, *wa-eek*s, and squeaks that burst into a chorus when they were

Table 5. Effect of surplus food (roadkills) on rates that seven cooperatively breeding crows fed their young

| | ROADKILLS | | FEEDING VISITS/HR | | |
Species	Date provided	Age of nestlings (days)	Day roadkill provided	Two previous days (avg)	Two subsequent days
Cottontail rabbit	March 25	17	23	23.5	22.5
Armadillo	April 14	37	26	24.0	26.0

about to be fed. None of the vocalizations sounded like the loud cries made by fledglings. As nestlings became older, they did leg-wing, double wing–back, and straight leg–up stretches and flapped their wings as well.

NEST SANITATION

Crows feeding young up to nine days of age probed among them as if finding and swallowing feces. After this they generally waited on the rim of the nest for thirty to fifty seconds. If a nestling was ready to excrete, it raised its rear end to the level of the nest rim and then, with a shaky motion, extruded its cloaca in releasing a fecal sac. The waiting adult made small biting motions to guide the sac into its bill, positioned sideways to receive the sac. With a few shakes of the head the crows discarded the sacs 20 to 30 meters away from nests, either on the ground or against a branch. This became awkward if a sac broke and excreta ran out of a crow's bill. The white, paintlike liquid then stained the upper or lower mandibles or both and even, at times, the top of a crow's head and back. I mention these details because the white stain, when it persisted for two to four days, provided a way of identifying individuals at a distance. Male A once had a white spot at the base of his right lower mandible that lasted for four days and could be seen from 200 meters.

The staining proved to be an important clue about a group of four crows that remained outside of the territories of those we were following. Having seen little activity, I presumed that these outsiders were not nesting. On throwing corn to them on April 14, 1984, however, I noted that two of them had white on their mandibles. Concluding that they must have been caring for nestlings, I was able to locate their nest within a few minutes.

I have never found fecal spattering on the outside nor on branches adjacent to crow's nests that I have found in Florida (n = 16), or in Maryland or New Hampshire (n = 8). Nestlings, however, excrete over nest rims on occasion. I was watching an auxiliary approaching nest B with a full pouch on April 16, 1984, when it swerved to attack a Crested Caracara. When the caracara left, the crow returned to feed the nestlings. Seemingly still disturbed, the crow left the nest without waiting for a fecal sac. A nestling then sent one over the rim. Nestlings ceased producing fecal sacs two to three days before leaving the nest. Crows attending them, however, continued to wait after feeding, taking small amounts of feces in their bills when young presented. The young expelled feces over the nest rim in these last few days, spattering the ground.

Both Good (1952) and Wittenberg (1968) describe spattering of the outside of nests, adjacent foliage, and the ground below for American and Carrion Crows, respectively. The crows they observed were wary, as they are in most places, so it is conceivable that under these circumstances the attending crows, like the crow that had encountered the caracara, were too disturbed to wait for fecal sacs.

Crows and their nestlings have developed behaviors preventing soiling of nests and surroundings that might betray their location. Removal of sacs should become more effective when helpers as well as parents, undisturbed by human or other intruders, are willing to wait long enough to remove them. As I have noted and Dorn (1972) describes, nests of Common Ravens are heavily soiled. Since ravens are large and powerful birds and are apt to nest in inaccessible places, soiling may not compromise the safety of the nestlings.

Special Behaviors

A peculiarity of male B noted in three years was to fly toward his nest with food, then perch for several minutes before continuing on. Stallcup and Woolfenden (1978) noted a similar type of surveillance, seemingly for predators, in Florida Scrub Jays. After feeding nestlings, male B often came to where I sat to perch over my head for five to twenty minutes of resting and preening. Males B and A2 were the tamest of the crows I watched and were often the first to come for corn.

Females spent varying amounts of time during incubation and nestling periods probing into their nests, with tails uptilted and jiggling. While some females did little probing, others, like female B in 1982, did a great deal. After female B had ceased brooding, she spent periods of up to forty-five minutes, in the mid-nestling period, tending her young and digging into her nest. It is conceivable that probing serves to reduce populations of bloodsucking parasites such as crow flies and blowfly larvae that may be more abundant in some years than others. Probing has been noted for other birds. Stallcup and Woolfenden (1978) describe female Florida Scrub Jays as probing so vigorously that nest bushes were jostled, and Mountfort (1957), female Hawfinches that burrowed into the bottoms of their nests and appeared to eat parasites.

The two A2 nestlings in 1985 left their nests thirty-seven to thirty-eight days after hatching and the five nestlings of the A3 nest in forty-one to forty-three days (see Table 5). Movements to branches up to a meter away and returns were common to both broods for four to five days before final departures. That the smaller brood left sooner than the larger one may have been a matter of space. There being only two nestlings in the A2 nest, each could readily flap its wings and hop from one nest rim to the other, thus developing muscle coordination and an inclination to leave the nest sooner. A factor keeping the nestlings of the larger A3 brood in or by their nest longer was their tendency to stay together, even after several of them appeared ready to leave. With the greatest number of begging cries coming from the nest itself, the nest was the place where they were most likely to get fed. This led fledglings that had moved out on branches to keep returning. Good (1952) described young as leaving nests at twenty-eight to thirty-five days. Since he climbed to nests, which I did not, his birds may have been frightened into leaving sooner.

The juveniles flew to trees as far as 20 meters from their nest trees within three to four days of nest leaving and went to the ground within ten days. The older crows made the same *cawk* feeding-young calls in coming to juveniles that they had used in feeding nestlings. When the five A3 juveniles all begged at once the clamor was considerable, especially when they were together in one or two neighboring trees. Much of the time they were silent, however. The two A2 juveniles, in contrast, made so little noise that it was difficult to find them. Although these juveniles pecked at leaves and twigs as they had done in the nest, they made no effort to feed themselves in the two weeks that I watched them.

Fledging

Renestings

The nests of pairs A and B in 1982 were completed within a day of each other and, after an interval of two weeks, egg laying began at the end of February. The next December was unusually warm, and this may explain why female A was already incubating when we found her nest on January 16, 1983, the earliest of sixteen nests found in Florida. Incubating continued until January 26, when the nest failed for reasons unknown. With little loss of time female A swung on a streamer of Spanish moss to work it loose, picked up sticks, and showed other signs of renesting on the same morning. As Figure 9 indicates, the crows of group A completed their second nest in six days, three days after the crows of group B completed their first one. Both of these nests failed February 9 and 10, when raccoons usurped them.

The crows of both groups renested, but whereas the B crows built a replacement nest, female A relaid in her second nest, thirteen days after the raccoon had occupied it. This third attempt of the A crows at nesting failed on March 4 when a raccoon again occupied it. The B crows had already lost their second nest eight days earlier. In spite of these differences in dates, groups A and B now completed new nests within two days of each other (see Fig. 9). These nestings, the third for the B's and the fourth for the A's, were successful to the extent that they contained nestlings twelve to fifteen days of age on April 15. Nest B, which was poorly located, tilted and slipped from its place on April 16, dumping the nestlings on the ground.

Emlen (1942) noted American Crows re-laying in ten to twelve days in California, and Butler and associates (1984) report Northwestern Crows doing so in thirteen to fourteen days. Wittenberg (1968) describes Carrion Crows as reusing nests after nest failures in six of seventy-six first and in five of sixteen renestings.

Synchronization of Nestings

I followed sixteen nests of A and B crows over four years, and observed that egg layings started within two or three days of each other in twelve of them. Similar synchronizations of nestings are described by Rowley (1975) for Australian Ravens and by Tom-Tov (1975) for Carrion Crows. Tom-Tov, in a belief shared by Charles (1972) and Wittenberg (1968) that Carrion Crows are the chief predators of the eggs and young of their own species, considers synchronizations to be a way of minimizing intraspecific predation. I have no evidence that American Crows prey on each other's nests. The selective value of the synchronizing that I observed was, I think, the social stimulation neighboring groups exerted on each other when nesting at approximately the same time. This so-called Fraser Darling effect (1952) may have had a bearing on the high rate of renestings that I observed in 1983 when both the A and B groups experienced repeated failures (see Fig. 9). In 1984 and 1985 when nest A1 was the only one to fail, no attempts were made at renesting. It is thus conceivable that a pair of crows is more apt to renest if a neighboring pair is doing so at the same time.

The crows that we watched in Florida nested from 200 to 400 meters apart, but these distances did not preclude mutual stimulation. The crows of one group could easily see and hear the activities of their neighbors across terrain that was largely open. They also learned about each other's activities by surveillance flights and intrusions. Five A crows crossed their boundary on February 10 and flew directly to the nest tree of the B crows, then returned with six B crows in pursuit. This was one day after the A crows had lost their second nest to a raccoon and the same day the B crows lost theirs. The intrusion was unusual in that it involved a whole group, possibly because the A and B pairs had lost nests at nearly the same time. Surveillance flights, with one or two crows flying high above a neighboring territory and circling back without being attacked, were another method of gathering information.

Renewal of Courtship

Recrudescence of Early Breeding-Season Behavior

I witnessed a renewal of courtship with the A3 pair that extended from four days before to more than two weeks after their two young were fledged. With only two young to look after and aided by five helpers, pair A3 appeared to have a margin of leisure. On hearing nest calls for the first time in more than seven weeks, I found the pair perched together on April 7, the female elevating her wings slightly as she gave repeated *caa*s. The male spilled the contents of his pouch on the ground, and then both, with heads together, fed on it. Skutch (1976) says that parents of several avian species seem to sense the increasing restlessness of their young toward the end of the nestling period, the emotional state of the parents being revealed by an unusual amount of singing. A similar emotional excitement may have been what led the female A3 crow to renew her nest calling four days before her young were fledged.

Female A3 flew to her mate and perched beside him in a precopulatory pose on April 10. Later that morning, after giving nest calls at a rate of twenty-four per minute, she and her mate squatted close on a limb, exchanging low notes. On other occasions in succeeding weeks the female allopreened her mate, who sometimes solicited by putting his head down.

A THIRD CROW

I saw nothing of trios during the nesting season, when members of pairs were seldom together. From the first days that I saw the A3 pair together at the end of nesting, however, I noticed that they were usually attended by a third bird. The third crow begged from the male at times with bill open and wings extended in the manner of a thwarted female.

Nearly a week after the young had left the nest on April 18, I witnessed the most severe intragroup conflict that I had seen. All I noticed initially was that the third crow kept pushing toward male A3, identifiable by a projecting broken wing feather. The male kept moving from branch to branch of a dead tree as if to get away. A little later, when female A3 was with the third crow on the ground, the male, landing near with "shoulders" out, bowed and gave a *kuck-woo*, a type of aggressive behavior that I had not witnessed for several months. Attacks of male A3 on the begging third crow a little later led to an exhibition of the varied behaviors crows can use in conflict. At one time male A3 caught the third crow by the foot, and I heard distress calls. When female A3 arrived, she attacked the third crow from above. Not long afterward male A3 and the third crow were on the ground, jumping at each other, bill to bill, with wings out. The third crow lay on its back three times with feet moving toward the male. The bout ended with the crows walking away over the grass about 30 centimeters apart, each picking up and dropping bits of turf in what appeared to be displacement activity. After a brief interval in which the two were distracted by a gray squirrel, they fought again and the third crow left. I did not see it with the pair the following week, which was the last one before I left the ranch.

Nesting Success

Although I was unable to make a complete study of nesting success within the limits of times spent at the ranch, the number of yearlings in each group, as found each year in January, was a probable measure of the breeding success of the year before. Of thirteen groups observed in January in five years, seven included yearlings, a total of eighteen (see Table 1), giving 1.4 yearlings as the average survival per group per year. Groups that had no yearlings in January were ones whose nests had failed the year before (n = 4), that were new and had not nested previously (n = 2), or whose earlier experience was unknown (n = 1). Richardson and associates (1985) discuss breeding success in Northwestern Crows.

8. Defense of Nests and
Other Interspecific Interactions

Mammals

RACCOONS

Raccoons were the only cause of nest loss that I was able to recognize. In the wet year of 1983 I found raccoons sleeping in three of six nests by groups A and B. The A crows lost one nest to a raccoon, laid again in the same nest a few weeks later, then had it occupied by a raccoon for a second time. The reaction of the A crows was curious. Female A perched close to her nest the first time, remaining within 30 centimeters of the raccoon for fifty-four minutes. Her mate allopreened her briefly, then perched a little farther back (Fig. 10). Both crows remained silent except for a few nest calls by the female. There was no obvious excitement, and the raccoon appeared to be undisturbed. The B crows reacted in much the same way when a raccoon took over their nest the following morning.

The only time I watched a raccoon occupy a nest was on March 1, 1983. Hearing an outburst of cawing and seeing the A1 crows flying toward their nest on the third day of incubation, I walked over to find a raccoon climbing to it. The four crows of the group clustered about with much cawing, and two swooped several times. But the raccoon came over the rim without pause and, with head down for some minutes, appeared to be eating the eggs. The crows lingered a minute, then flew to chase a territorial intruder. When I left the raccoon was curled up in the nest, a case, seemingly, of "bed and breakfast."

Crows showed little excitement when raccoons came near. Three crows flew toward their nest tree on April 12 when three raccoons walked within 15 meters of the base of it. One crow swooped mildly, then left with another crow. The remaining crow watched quietly until the raccoons were gone. A raccoon on April 13 worked for ninety minutes in a shallow lagoon

Figure 10.   When a raccoon took over the nest of pair A of American Crows, female A rested within 30 centimeters of the raccoon for fifty-four minutes, and her mate, a little farther back.

30 meters from nest A. The crows paid no attention to it until the raccoon, in leaving, passed below the nest tree. Four crows gathered immediately, cawing as they made a few swoops. The raccoon continued on its way and the crows left. In these incidents, as in others, I had an impression that the crows made no more disturbance by a nest than was needed. Giffin (1983) noted that Hawaiian Crows were quiet by their nests, letting pigs, mongooses, and cattle pass near without alarm.

SQUIRRELS

Gray squirrels were very prevalent and a constant threat to crows' nests. Two crows flew at a squirrel silently on March 27, one or the other swooping when the squirrel ran over the ground or exposed itself on a tree trunk. The crows' only vocalizations were a few *kuck-woos*. Crows were especially concerned if a squirrel climbing an adjacent tree reached the level of a nest. Female B was on her nest when a squirrel climbed to her level. She spent the next five minutes driving the squirrel from branch to branch, aided by a second crow. Both crows were silent. The crows left once the squirrel had gone, but, as frequently happened, the squirrel soon returned. Although crows did not appear to guard their nests regularly, one or another of a group always seemed to be on hand when a squirrel came near. Gray squirrels can be a threat to eggs and young. Harthan (1940–41) reported them taking nestling Rooks in three successive years, and Holyoak (1967), in a report on the European Corvidae, states that gray squirrels have accounted "for most of the mammalian predation recorded."

The larger fox squirrels were escorted from the vicinity of nests in the same way as gray squirrels. Fox squirrels, however, ranged farther in their foraging and were around less frequently. When I carried corn in my pockets after feeding crows, I found that fox squirrels could smell it, and one or another of them, depending on where I was, might follow me across several hundred meters of open pasture, then stay close to where I sat watching a crow's nest. Male A perched above me on these occasions as if on guard. When a fox squirrel left me on April 13 to pass under his nest, the male flew low over its head performing a curious "wing-shake," as if to hurry the squirrel along.

The most prolonged attack witnessed was on April 9, 1985, six days before the two nestlings of the A3 crows left their nest. Two crows started attacking when the fox squirrel was 15 meters from the nest tree. The crows continued swooping silently as the squirrel moved across 150 meters of pasture to another oak. Here the crows worked for some minutes to get the squirrel back to the ground, then drove it across 50 meters more of pasture. As with raccoons, I never saw any mobbing in terms of numbers of crows assembling and making much noise in attempts to drive away what could be serious predators.

Black Vultures and Turkey Vultures

Both Black and Turkey Vultures rested in large numbers in the territory of the B crows in most years and frequently soared over the nest trees of both the A and B groups. While the B crows seldom attacked, Jane and I saw the A crows attack Turkey Vultures on many occasions, often making a *weeah* or *ainah* vocalization as they did so. Sometimes three to five crows joined in an attack.

In 1985 I noticed differences between the A2 and the A3 crows in their reactions to Turkey Vultures. The territories of the two groups were adjacent, and I was watching the nesting activities of both for two hours every morning throughout the nesting period. During these mornings the A3 crows drove Turkey Vultures away on four occasions and the A2's on twenty-two. The breeding female made many of the A2 attacks. Female A2 was brooding her young on March 18 when a vulture, blown by the wind, soared close to her nest tree. She flew from her nest, swooping on the vulture and striking it on the tail. On other occasions she attacked Turkey Vultures when they were as far as 100 meters from the nest. She usually did this alone or only briefly attended by another crow. An individual peculiarity was the piteous-sounding cries she made when attacking, ones that I did not hear from other crows.

Other crows of the A2 group also initiated attacks. On February 25 "Hookbill," a yearling with a bill deformity and a missing wing feather, made persistent swoops on a Turkey Vulture. Chamberlain and Cornwell (1971) report an adult crow diving on a Turkey Vulture when near a nest with three fledglings. The crow gave "threat calls" that Chamberlain and Cornwell describe as "screams, cackles, staccato and rattling notes, coos, and other sounds," thus reinforcing my impression that vocalizations used by crows in attacking predators can be highly variable.

Crows seldom attacked Black Vultures sailing by their nests. A possible reason was that Black Vultures were often moving on a straight course, as if going somewhere. The Turkey Vultures, in contrast, soared in lazy circles as if searching trees and ground for carrion or prey. It was this hunting aspect that incited the crows. However, the B crows regularly attacked Black Vultures that came to perch by a cow that died near their nest in 1984.

It is hard to know how much of a threat vultures are to crow nests. Turkey Vultures are not always simple scavengers, for Temple (1961) watched one making repeated visits to a Great Blue Heron rookery to beat the young and make them regurgitate, and Glading and Glading (1970) saw a captive one kill and eat a Curve-billed Thrasher.

Caracaras came to the ranch only occasionally, and, except in the nesting season, the crows generally paid little attention to them. On March 13, 1985, I heard strange vocalizations com-

Crested Caracaras

ing from the sky. It was female A2 making her peculiar cries and flying straight east. Following the direction of her flight, I saw a caracara and a crow, about a meter apart, circling in an irregular mix-up as they fell to the ground. The caracara flew off as female A2 alighted. It is conceivable that the original crow, in trying to drive the caracara away from the vicinity of the nest, had been attacked in turn by the caracara. Myers (1978) describes a Crested Caracara as starting to wheel when pursued by nesting Southern Lapwings, then catching one of its pursuers in its talons. Female A2 had seemingly recognized that one of her group had run into danger when pursuing a caracara and flown to its rescue.

Three B crows swooped on an immature caracara that stood on open ground 20 meters from their nest. The caracara, no more than ducking when a crow passed, continued to look up at the crows' nest, which contained four fledglings. The nest was only seven meters above ground. It was predated four days later, but I had no clue as to the actual predator. A cow had died not far from the base of the nest tree a few weeks earlier, and it seemed likely that, with predators and scavengers attracted to the vicinity, the crow's nest would be found sooner or later.

I once saw a caracara pursuing a crow that had prey in its bill, but the crow escaped into a tree. This was at a time when crows were robbing White Ibis of salamanders. Bent (1936) gives account of three crows pursuing a Northern Harrier with a mouse in its claws. When the harrier dropped the mouse, a crow snatched it and continued on, only to be pursued, in its turn, by a caracara that forced the crow to drop its prize, in a case of what might be termed serial kleptoparasitism.

Red-tailed Hawks

Red-tailed Hawks drew a greater response from crows than any other raptor. The presence of one of them usually drew crows like a magnet, even when the hawk was at a distance. In some attacks (n = 4) Jane and I heard a whack as a crow dived and struck a Red-tailed on a wing. As in the case of conspecific intruders, one crow usually did the attacking while others followed cawing. At other times two crows attacked in alternation, one from one side, its partner from the other, in what Bossema and Benus (1985) refer to, in Carrion Crows, as a pincer movement. When two B crows cooperated in this manner on incubation day eleven, they made many *kwa-aa* calls. Female B was not one of the two, for she remained on her nest.

When a mobbing was down among trees, I frequently heard the screaming of Red-shouldered Hawks mingled with the cawings of the crows. A Red-tailed perched on a bare tree on January 16 attracted a crow and a Red-shouldered almost immediately. When the Red-tailed flew to a second tree, it made a noise like escaping steam. Four crows belonging to a cooperative group of five perched above it, cawing and flicking their wings and tails, but changed to harsh *karr*s as the Red-tailed took flight and they pursued it again.

A mobbing on February 13 was by twenty or more crows, seemingly from three groups whose territories met at the scene of the mobbing. The crows were mostly silent as long as the Red-tailed remained on its perch. But as soon as the hawk flew, their cawing became almost a din. It is difficult, at times, to determine how long an intense mobbing lasts. Morse (1971) watched seven or eight crows in Maine mobbing a Great Horned Owl for ninety minutes.

On the few occasions when I found a Red-tailed coming within 25 meters of a nest, the crows were less noisy. When an immature Red-tailed alighted not far from nest A a few days before egg laying, two crows alighted just above it. One left almost immediately. The other flew back and forth five or six times, making short rattle notes and nearly hitting the hawk on the head. When the hawk flew, the crow dived on it repeatedly. No other crows came near and there was no mobbing.

A Red-tailed Hawk on February 10 worked its way into the newly completed nest of pair A. The two of the pair, one making *cu-koo*s and the other *g-wal-op*s, drove the hawk from the nest. The Red-tailed returned five minutes later. The pair first drove two yearlings down into the tree as if to get them out of the way, then attacked the hawk. When it had left, the pair remained on the nest, leaving the helpers to pursue it. It is conceivable that the Red-tailed came to the empty nest to investigate the possibility of using the nest for its own purposes.

USUAL RELATIONS   *Red-shouldered Hawks*

American Crows I observed in Maryland and Florida nested and foraged in the same general areas as Red-shouldered Hawks did. Under usual conditions the two paid little attention to one another. On December 18, 1957, I watched a Red-shouldered in Maryland perch within three meters of a crow that seemed so little concerned that it continued to preen. A Red-shouldered alighted among several hundred crows a week later without causing any disturbance.

Two pairs of Red-shouldered Hawks nested within the territories of the crows in Florida in five successive years, a pair in one year within 20 meters of a crow's nest. The crows took little notice of their neighbors unless a hawk came close. In 1985 I noticed that crows were indifferent to Red-shouldereds circling and screaming, but attacked on three occasions when one was hunting over open pasture by the nest tree. It thus seemed that the crows, like passerines described by Hamerstrom (1957), were able to distinguish hawks that were hunting and might thus be dangerous from ones that were not. The only severe attack by a crow on a Red-shouldered that I saw was early in the breeding season when a crow dived repeatedly and the hawk, rolling on its back, held its talons toward the crow. The encounter was not near a nest and is difficult to explain.

Joint Mobbing with Crows

On three weekends, from April 10 to 24, in Maryland I watched crows fly from all directions to mob a Barred Owl. The crows sometimes came to within a meter of it. A pair of Red-shouldereds was with the crows on each occasion, the screamings of the hawks and the cawings of the crows intermingling. Both crows and hawks pursued the owl when it flew.

Mobbings of the same type took place at other times of the year. I observed a mobbing on October 14 that was almost identical to those I had watched in April. Although I came to realize that the cawings of crows and the screams of Red-shouldereds meant a joint mobbing, I was never able to ascertain the object of a mobbing unless I could get close. The combined vocalizations came to me nearly every morning one May in New Hampshire. But it was not until May 19 that, working under some hemlocks, I was able to watch twenty or more crows along with a pair of Red-shouldereds mobbing a Great Horned Owl. The owl took three flights, each accompanied by the hawks and a retinue of crows. I saw much the same events in Florida, when crows and Red-shouldereds joined in mobbing Red-tailed Hawks in late winter and early spring. Among observations of others, Good (1952) observed a Red-shouldered

Hawk joining crows mobbing a Great Horned Owl in Ohio and Chamberlain and Cornwell (1971), although they do not mention the Red-shouldered, tape-recorded one screaming among mobbing crows.

My observations suggest that crows distinguish Red-shouldered Hawks from Red-tailed Hawks. A possible reason lies in the kinds of prey sought, Red-taileds preying on large-sized birds, including crows (Baumgras 1945) and pheasants, and Red-shouldereds, when preying on birds, preying on ones of small to medium size (Craighead and Craighead 1956).

Robbing Crows

The Red-shouldered Hawks in Florida foraged in the same pastures and wet places as the crows. In 1981 they robbed crows of fish heads on four occasions, three of them by a water hole where otters were catching walking catfish. The otters never ate the heads, generally leaving them in shallow water, where the crows recovered them. Six to eight crows had retrieved seven heads on January 19 and were removing an eighth when a Red-shouldered Hawk landed among them. The crows, startled, moved back, and the hawk seized the head. Four days later I watched a crow retrieve two heads from the water. It tried to hold both in its bill at the same time, but both fell as a Red-shouldered swooped and seized one. But the hawk made some misjudgments. When an otter, attended by two crows, was walking up a bank, a Red-shouldered landed almost on top of it. There was no fish head and the hawk left.

The crows sometimes cached fish heads in clumps of grass. A crow had pulled a fish head from a clump one morning when a Red-shouldered alighted almost beside it. Other crows flew in, and the hawk, with wings slightly out and tail spread over the grass, looked from one side to the other as the crows surrounded it. Two of the crows had their bills lowered and feathers of head and neck raised as if to attack. But they were wary and came no closer. When the crows started to leave after a few moments, the hawk flew away with its prize.

The Red-shouldereds did not always distinguish what a crow might be carrying. On February 2 I noticed a crow flying with a lump of mud for nest building in its bill and a hawk in pursuit. Ten minutes later I watched two crows in the same area pulling pieces of muddy sod, which they wadded into their bills. They had just taken wing when the hawk attacked as before.

Not long afterward a crow flew into a tree with a piece of sod larger than others. Holding the sod in its feet, it delivered blows as if trying to reduce it in size. The hawk swooped again, this time nearly hitting the crow. The crow, in reducing the sod in size, was behaving in much the same manner as a crow behaves when dismembering prey, and I supposed that was why the hawk attacked. Florida Red-shouldereds use "clumps of grass roots" in their nests, as Nicolson (1930) describes, but the pair of Red-shouldereds by the water hole did not begin building until nearly three weeks later.

The most prolonged encounter between a Red-shouldered and crows that I observed was in 1983 when a crow, after catching a walking catfish at the edge of a swamp, carried it to a dry part of a pasture. It had hardly landed when a Red-shouldered swooped and seized the fish in one of its talons. Four crows gathered immediately, the hawk attacking one, then another. When two crows came behind, the Red-shouldered roughed out its feathers until it looked larger than normal. When the crows left, the hawk carried the fish into the depths of an oak. One crow, returning, perched within a third of a meter of the Red-shouldered and made a barrage of sound — caws and almost every other vocalization that a crow can make — that it kept up for nearly forty minutes. The hawk appeared unfazed but did not start eating until the crow left.

Red-shouldereds were not always successful in robbing crows of prey. When Great Egrets and White Ibis gathered by flooded ditches following a heavy rain, a pair of Red-shouldereds as well as a number of crows stayed close by. The crows were successful in robbing the ibis and egrets of large eel-like salamanders, but the hawks seemed less interested in robbing the water birds than in robbing the crows. I saw them fly at crows with salamanders five times without success, seemingly because they flew from positions too close to the crows. In robbing crows of catfish heads by the water hole, the hawks came on them suddenly with speed attained by flying from a distance.

Bald Eagles,
Barred Owls, and
Other Raptors

The smallest raptors driven away, and ones that seldom came near crows' nests, were Kestrels and a Cooper's Hawk. On a windy day in late January, one of the breeding pair of the A1 crows mounted into the sky, then moved a distance to dive on a Kestrel flying 100 meters away. This was the first indication

I had that the crows had started to build a nest. I watched
a crow on March 11 making wing-tail flicks. I was wondering why it should be doing so when it flew about 30 meters
to drive a Kestrel from a perch about the same distance from
the crow's nest.

Three days after the A1 crows had lost their nest to a raccoon in 1985, they suddenly flew back to it. One was making
sharp, steady caws over my head when a Cooper's Hawk, flying from an adjacent tree, made a mild pass at the crow and
flew on with the crow in pursuit. The cawing continued and
a minute later I saw a repetition of the episode. It would be
interesting to know, in crow–Cooper's Hawk relations, which
species is more apt to attack the other. Mailliard (1908) describes a Cooper's Hawk attacking crows and Norris (1942)
the reverse, of crows knocking down a Cooper's Hawk.

Crows followed Bald Eagles when they came through the
ranch, sometimes swooping on one as it flew, but not coming
closer than a meter. That attacking an eagle can be dangerous
is indicated by Walker's (1983) report of a Golden Eagle catching a mobbing Carrion Crow by rolling in flight.

Although we heard Barred Owls almost daily, I only once
found one in the vicinity of a nest. This was on incubation
day three, when five crows of the B group gathered around
an owl in a cabbage palm. The crows made occasional *kuck-
woos*, but few other vocalizations. Two of them kept biting
and pulling at twigs. When the owl flew, the crows followed,
one of them striking it. Female B continued incubating but
was not fed for the hour that the owl rested within 40 meters
of her nest.

Smaller Birds

Blue Jays were the most strongly attacked of smaller birds coming near nests during incubation and the nestling period. Male
A3 flew so hard at fifteen of them through branches that I feared
he would damage his wing feathers. The A2 crows had a different strategy. Crows flew to their nest tree when jays arrived,
several perching on outer branches while one went to the center and tried to drive the jays out. But the jays were more adept
at moving about among branches than the crow, making it difficult for the crow to reach them. Once the jays left, the crows
pursued them 50 meters to other oaks, taking time to drive them
from these as well.

On January 28 I saw male A3 come from a swamp with a

freshly killed jay in his bill. I had no way of knowing whether he had killed the jay or found it dead or injured.

The only other birds I saw driven from the vicinity of nests, and then only occasionally, were Pileated (n = 3) and Red-bellied (n = 5) Woodpeckers and once a Northern Flicker. Although woodpeckers are not commonly considered to be predators, Conner (1974) describes a Red-bellied preying on nestling Carolina Chickadees and Loftin and Leeds (1981), a Pileated taking a nestling Red-bellied Woodpecker.

Snakes

I never saw crows mobbing snakes. When an indigo snake two meters long moved along the ground 20 meters from a nest tree, a crow walked beside it pecking its tail and sometimes its middle. Neither the snake nor the crow appeared disturbed. After a few minutes the crow perched in a tree along with another crow, both remaining silent as the snake moved on.

I was watching two crows foraging in a pasture in March when both suddenly flew fast and silently to join two others 150 meters from the nest tree. All four followed something in the grass that caused them to jump back. When the crows left after a few minutes, I discovered a diamondback rattlesnake, possibly 1.5 meters in length, coiled and ready to strike. What excited me did not, apparently, rouse more than initial curiosity among the crows.

Mobbing Feathers
on the Ground

On January 28 I heard six to eight crows cawing in a grove of bay trees. The grove was open because cattle pass there, and I could see that the crows were looking at the ground as they cawed or gave harsh *grr* notes. Although I stood within 15 meters, I was unable to perceive any cause for the mobbing. The crows gathered at the same place two mornings later, and I again noted that they were looking at the ground. This time their caws mingled with the screaming of a Red-shouldered Hawk. After the crows and hawk had left I found three piles of feathers from the body, wings, and tail of a Wild Turkey plucked by some predator. The feathers were a dull, dark brown.

Red-shouldered Hawks commonly join crows in mobbing owls and Red-tailed Hawks. I supposed that the Red-shouldered at the grove had joined the crows "by contagion" as Altman (1956) terms it, rather than in any excitement arising from the feathers.

Mobbing versus attacks. Mobbing is when a number of crows caw together in seeming excitement as they pursue, surround, or face either conspecifics in territorial encounters or predators that are a special threat. Mobbing is not limited to the breeding season but may take place in mid-fall with equal intensity, as Slagsvold (1985) has noted for Hooded Crows. Slagsvold found that leaders in mobbings of a stuffed Eagle Owl by Hooded Crows were large adult males. Attacks, in contrast to mobbings, are generally made by only one or two crows and with fewer and lower vocalizations. Nearly all the events of nest defense that I watched were attacks. Although the caws that attend mobbings are easily rocognizable (Chamberlain and Cornwell 1971), I have, when standing close, heard a variety of low vocalizations, ranging from *cu-koo*s and *kuck-woo*s to harsh sounding *kr-aa-ck*s accompanying attacks. Among types of mobbing none is more curious than that of mobbing feathers on the ground.

Mobbing feathers. Mobbing feathers has been described for a number of corvids. Verbeek (1972b) observed Yellow-billed Magpies mobbing a mummified magpie and also on three occasions, black tail feathers, the mobbing being as intense as if they were a predator. Whereas Verbeek found that at least three feathers were needed to induce mobbing in magpies, Lorenz (1970) noted that Jackdaws would react to a single feather. The Jackdaws reacted with similar cries to a pair of black bathing trunks that Lorenz (1952) happened to have hanging from his pocket after a swim in the Danube. I had a similar experience with a hand-raised crow. Surprised at hearing it making angry-sounding caws one afternoon, I went out to find it cawing at a black bathing suit that had been spread on the lawn. Even odder was a friend's pet crow, which attacked people with black hair but not others. It would seem that black objects mean, as Lorenz (1970) suggests, "dead crow" or "dead Jackdaw" and are therefore a cause for alarm. Lorenz (1952) found that he could handle young Jackdaws before they acquired black feathers without setting off rattling cries in adults, but not afterward. Handling one with black feathers meant "Jackdaw in jaws of enemy." The emotion that was induced, Lorenz believed, stamped "an ineradicable picture on the birds' memories" of the handler. Lorenz's experiences, as narrated in *King Solomon's Ring* (1952), were one reason why I have not wanted to climb to nests of crows that I was studying.

Barash (1976), using a replica of a Great Horned Owl, one

of a dead crow, and alternately, a piece of black cloth, substantiated Lorenz's ideas experimentally with the aid of wild American Crows. The owl holding the dead crow or the black cloth elicited more mobbing and more decibels than did the owl alone. Barash concluded that the reactions involved a simple releasing mechanism but was not sure whether they were innate or learned. From the reactions of my hand-raised crow to the black bathing suit, I would think the reactions innate.

Varying responses to predators.   The responses of crows to hawks vary with the time of year, the species of hawk, what the hawks are doing, whether the crows are territorial and nesting or in a wandering flock, and other variables. One of the earlier signs that a pair of crows is nesting or about to nest in a section of woods is to see them driving a hawk or vulture away. Jollie (1976) states that crows are particularly given to mobbing perched hawks. Bildstein (1982) agrees that passerines often mob perched hawks, but he found that they never mob perched harriers, the distinction being that harriers, unlike many hawks, do their hunting on the wing. Like many birds, crows sense when a hawk is alert and potentially dangerous and when it is not. Those at the ranch paid little attention to Red-shouldereds when they were perched at a distance or even when they passed over a nest tree soaring and screaming in courtship. But when one perched on a nest tree or close to it or flew low over a pasture as if searching the ground for prey, one crow or another drove it away. Hamerstrom (1957) made similar observations, noting that small birds mobbed a tame Red-tailed Hawk when it was flying low but not when it was soaring. His perched Red-tailed elicited reactions from small birds when "sharp set" and hungry, but not when well fed. "It is quite plain," he wrote, "that the presence of a hawk does not guarantee a mobbing reaction."

Red-tailed Hawks elicited the most intense mobbing of any predator at the ranch, but this was generally at the periphery of crow territories and only twice by nests. When a Red-tailed came within 20 meters of a nest on one occasion, a single crow attacked it, and when one came onto a just-finished nest, the breeding pair drove it away.

Mobbing can be counterproductive if it attracts attention. Some predators key in on nests by noting where mobbings occur. I have noted this for Common Ravens searching for nests of Common Grackles, as have Thurow and Black (1981) for Gymnogenes and Sordahl (1979) for American Crows looking for chicks of Willets. It is also likely that attacks by a breeding male or female are more effective than mobbings; with a number of individuals involved, the crows may get in each other's way.

There seemed to be little that crows could do to deter raccoons. The same seems to be true for Rooks and Goshawks, Roskaft (1980) observing Rooks leaving the rookery when Goshawks visited.

Parental investment and nest defense.   The idea that parental investment increases as nesting progresses, thus increasing expenditure of effort in nest defense (Trivers 1972), does not appear to hold for all birds. Buitron (1983b) and Knight and Temple (1986) throw doubt on the theory's experimental validity, and I have found no evidence for it in American Crows. Raccoons, which were the most important predators of crows at the ranch, were attacked mildly and Blue Jays, which seemed less of a threat, intensely. One group of crows defended a newly completed nest that contained no eggs against a Red-tailed Hawk and a crow of another group made persistent efforts to drive a Cooper's Hawk from the vicinity of a nest that had been emptied by a raccoon several days before.

Buitron (1983b) noted that Black-billed Magpies attacked crows and red squirrels most vigorously when defending eggs or young nestlings. I wondered whether a similar relation might explain the crows' attacks on Blue Jays. But speculation proved difficult because the Blue Jays, occupied with their own nesting, soon became less prevalent.

Use of sound as a defensive or distractive weapon.   There appear to be few references to birds using sound as a defensive or, on occasion, an offensive weapon. I noticed in Panama that whenever a hawk flew past a tree where Plain Chachalacas were feeding, the chachalacas set up a clamor that was startling to listen to. If hawks count on coming upon their prey unawares, such a noise might be unnerving enough to spoil an attack. Pileated Woodpeckers, when hanging upside down to feed in fruiting trees, give almost continuous loud *cuks*, seemingly for the same reason (Kilham 1976). Among other loud sounds that I have heard in acute situations are those of a Crested Guan when attacked by an Ornate Hawk-Eagle (Kilham 1978) and the caterwauling of a Barred Owl when attacking adult gray squirrels that are at the upper limit of prey size for a Barred Owl (Kilham 1972). Crows also use barrages of sound for special purposes. Among situations noted were the *g-wal-op*s made by a crow to get a Black Vulture to move away from a carcass;

the odd sounds given close to a Red-shouldered Hawk that
had robbed a crow of a catfish; and the extra din crows make
when a Red-tailed Hawk or Great Horned Owl that they are
mobbing takes wing.

Part II. CROWS IN NEW HAMPSHIRE

I hear faintly the cawing of a crow far, far away, echoing from some unseen woodside, as if deadened by the springlike vapor which the sun is drawing from the ground. It mingles with the slight murmur of the village, the sound of children at play, as one stream empties gently into another, and the wild and the tame are one. What a delicious sound! It is not merely crow calling crow, for it speaks to me too. I am part of one creature with him; if he has a voice, I have ears. I can hear what he calls. . . .

H. D. Thoreau, January 12, 1855

Living in Lyme with the elementary school on one side of us and the Record farm backed by woods on the other, thoughts of Thoreau come to me when I walk to the farm to see what the crows are doing. Studying crows in New Hampshire, where they are wary, is more difficult than in Florida. I have to watch them at distances of 200 to 300 meters, and the town of Lyme, being hilly and wooded, makes it impossible to follow them for any distance. But a number of situations are favorable. One is having a study site only a short way across the street. Crows are not always present when I visit the farm, but the owner, Walter Record, who is often out in the fields with his tractor, gives me tips on when and where crows have appeared. Activities of the crows are affected by farm activities. Crows hardly visit the farm at all on some days. They often come when the fields are mowed, manure spread, or dead hens, sheep, or calves dumped at the edge of the woods. My watchings are from the vicinity of sheds and farm buildings that, being on a ridge, furnish an outlook over fields and pasture.

In studying the crows I visited the farm seven days a week

in all weathers and seasons. If no crows were around, I enjoyed views of hills, woods, and pastures, the sight of fifty or more sheep walking single file, black Angus cattle, wild Canada Geese that flew to the farm pond, and a pair of Mute Swans that nested there. Although the crows were not always around, it was surprising on how many days I discovered something. My observations were parts of a puzzle, each serving to bring out a whole picture.

The crows were my bond with nature for the seven years I studied them. They got me up early on winter mornings when I walked across snow-covered fields at sunrise, even at as much as thirty degrees (Fahrenheit) below zero, to tend my feeding station. I was rewarded when I watched and listened to the cawing of the five crows of the resident group as they came flying in over the wintry landscape.

Who can express things better than Thoreau? "What a perfectly New England sound is this voice of the crow!" he wrote. "If you stand perfectly still anywhere in the outskirts of the town and listen . . . this is the sound that you will be most sure to hear."

9. Summer and Fall

Because Jane and I spent the winter and spring in Florida for five years, observations in Lyme were made mostly in the summer and fall. There were two territorial groups, and their common boundary ran through fields that I could easily watch. The boundary in 1981 ran from the woods on the west side toward buildings on the east, a distance of 200 meters, and it had no special features other than two dead elms at the woodland border that the opposing groups used as rallying points. By 1983 the boundary had moved 60 meters to the south. Its best markers were then the positionings of the rival crows when facing each other. I called the crows north of the boundary the N and those south of it, the S crows. In November and December of 1982 there were three N and three S crows. In the summer of 1983, four N and ten S; and in November and December of that year three N and five S crows (Table 6). These numbers were constant once seasonally established, except for a few days when one or two crows were missing.

I watched forty-five territorial encounters between 1981 and 1983. While no two were alike, certain behaviors were observed repeatedly. Cawing, heard in thirty-eight of the territorial encounters consisted of sharp caws corresponding to what Good (1952) refers to as warning calls and Chamberlain and Cornwell (1971) as simple scolding calls. The crows of both groups cawed when flying toward each other from a distance. This was especially so on early mornings when most encounters took place. If one group alighted in the fields and another in trees, the latter did the most cawing. Caws at high intensity were accompanied by cawing displays in which the whole body became involved, with wings moving out at the "shoulders," the

Table 6. Numbers of territorial groups of crows in Lyme, New Hampshire

| | 1982 | | 1983 | | 1984 | | 1985 | |
Season	N	S	N	S	N	S	N	S
Summer	4	?	4	10	7	8	7	8
Fall	3	3	3	5	7	7	5	?*

NOTE: N = north territorial group. S = south territorial group.
*S group moved too far south to be followed reliably.

tail spreading, and the head bowing down and swinging up.

Walking displays (n = 17) varied. In the summer of 1983, the S crows sometimes alighted 20 to 30 meters to their side of the boundary and the N crows, the most aggressive group, close to theirs. The two groups then walked slowly toward each other for ten to fifteen minutes, foraging as they went. When about 15 meters apart, the N crows took wing and swooped on the lead S crows. These sometimes sprawled on the grass as if to evade their attackers, a maneuver that I have observed among American Oystercatchers (Kilham 1980). After a few such attacks, the crows of both groups walked back the way they had come.

A second form of encounter (n = 5) was when a lead N crow alighted 12 to 16 meters inside the S territory while the two others of its group remained at the boundary. The advanced position of the lead crow led either to a clash with a lead S crow or to the latter approaching, then side-stepping away. On December 11 and 15 the N crows occupied their positions for ten to twenty minutes at the start of the day before their rivals appeared. It seemed in these cases as if the N crows were seeking an encounter and were ready to wait for it. The 60-meter shift in the boundary was a result of this greater aggressiveness.

Other forms of behavior included aerial melees (n = 17), bunching (n = 5), and pursuits (n = 5). The melees were spectacular when all members of both groups swirled into the air for three to four seconds, with some swooping on others. On November 19 the N and S crows had five melees in twelve minutes. When about to fly against opponents, crows of either group occasionally bunched before doing so. The S crows on December 8 bunched before flying hard and fast, with repeated diving attacks, at the N crows, a drive that carried them 250 meters north of the boundary. This was one of few times the S crows were more aggressive than their rivals.

Territorial behaviors also included circular flights (n = 11), which carried the crows of one group a short distance over the boundary into their neighbors' territory as if to demonstrate where the boundary lay, and treetop sitting (n = 17). The latter was particularly striking on November 26 when the crows of both groups, after a series of melees, perched on the very tops of their dead elms in full view of each other. In such situations the crows rarely (n = 2) exhibited displacement behavior, for example, exaggerated bill wiping and bark pecking, but wing-tail flicks, which are primarily a sign of alertness or of apprehension, were common in some.

Trespassing and Invasions

The 1983 boundary continued to hold in the two following years. When foraging was good in a field to the north side and the north crows were absent, the S crows moved in to forage for twenty or more minutes at a time. Eight S crows were trespassing there August 23, a morning of heavy fog. When the fog lifted I saw the seven N crows foraging 300 meters to the north. As if aware for the first time that their rivals were trespassing, the N crows flew cawing into trees. The S crows reacted by bunching in midfield with two crows taking advanced positions. As the N crows came flying toward them, the S crows flew farther back and bunched again. A single N crow, leaving the rest of its group, landed among them. There was a sharp conflict, with two crows fighting close to the ground. The single N crow then flew to join its associates while the S crows flew back into their own territory.

Features of the encounter were the way the S crows bunched twice in retreating and the way a single N crow flew among eight of them to fight one, which I presumed to be the dominant male. On the basis of observations made in Florida, it has seemed that leadership and much of the actual fighting in territorial encounters is done by nuclear males. Rowley (1978) noted that when White-winged Choughs (birds that form cooperative groups not unlike those of crows) clashed, it was the dominant males that did the fighting.

A feature of the boundary in 1984 was its stability under unusual circumstances. The S crows foraged almost daily from May until August in a field belonging to the N crows. Since I saw nothing of the N crows, I supposed that they had moved elsewhere to breed and that the S crows were in possession. But when seven N crows returned in August, the groups resumed encounters along the boundary as it had been before.

Territorial Groups

Table 6 shows the numbers of N and S crows in summer and fall months over the course of four years. Both groups had maximum numbers in summer with occasional reductions in the early fall. A phenomenon observed in Florida (see Table 1) was that groups facing each other across boundaries tended to be of the same or about the same size. The numbers of N and S crows were low in 1982 and 1983, and high, with seven or eight members, in 1984 and 1985. Since groups in Florida commonly consisted of seven or eight members, the numbers may be close to an upper limit for territorial groups.

Factors regulating the size of cooperative groups are difficult to assess. When two "outside" crows tried to join eight S crows over a period of several days in August, 1985, a single S crow, which I presumed to be the dominant male, drove them away. It is conceivable, as Rowley (1978) indicates for Whitewinged Choughs, that breeding males play a major role in regulating group sizes.

A Lone Crow

Crows have a strong urge to belong to a group, and there were three crows in each of the groups at the farm in December, 1982. The S crows often came to an elm to preen at the start of a day. Since two perched together and the third one by itself, I believed that the two were the breeding pair and the third one a yearling. The pair disappeared on December 18, but the third crow, which I called Lone Crow or LC, continued to come to the elm. Its behavior had changed, though, for instead of being in conflict with the N crows, it now tried to join them.

Snow was falling on December 20 when I found LC cawing on its elm. The cawing was flat, with the caws evenly spaced and repeated many times in series of up to six. LC raised the pitch and cawed more excitedly when it flew. Its first flight was to the boundary, where it stood motionless, looking north. In the next twenty-eight minutes LC flew to several more places along the boundary, as if waiting for the N crows to come. But the N crows did not appear until the following morning, when they attacked and tried to drive a persistent LC back into its territory. When the N crows chased it around and about over snow-covered fields, LC kept returning to alight among them. After ten minutes the N crows left LC foraging by itself. I now watched some curious behavior. LC had come to a tussock of grass and begun giving low caws as if excited about uncovering what I believed was a piece of turkey cached some weeks before. Instead of feeding on it, LC flew with it to the N crows. Why LC should have brought food to those that had been attacking it was not clear. After a minute the N crows, without paying attention to the food, chased LC even more intensely than before, diving at it in flight while making *krr-aack* vocalizations. By December 22 the N crows were driving LC beyond farm fields into woods beyond.

LC's efforts to join the N crows ceased when the missing S pair returned after a week's absence. LC was thus no longer alone.

IN SMALL GROUPS   *Sentinel Behavior*

Questions that bothered me when I started studying crows included this: "Are one or two crows in a tree there to keep watch for others or are they merely resting there by chance?" And I wondered again, "When no sentinel is in sight, can one still be present, yet hidden from view?" I circumvented some of these difficulties by making observations in the fall, when trees were bare of foliage and the N and S groups consisted of three crows each. On nineteen occasions (Table 7) when I found two of the N crows foraging on the ground, I found the third one in a tree. On eight days when only two N crows were present, I found one of them in a tree on seven. Determining how many crows were present could not always be told at a glance. I sometimes had to wait up to an hour until the group flew to be sure.

The S crows seldom had a sentinel when they came to the farm in 1982. Of ten times (see Table 7) that I saw them in a hayfield on their side of the boundary, one of the three was in a tree acting as a sentinel only twice. Both of these times were when the N crows were away. I thus had an impression that if the N crows had a sentinel, the S crows, in their adjacent field, were less likely to have one.

In periods of twenty to sixty minutes, the longest times that I watched a crow acting as a sentinel, I never saw it relieved. A sentinel might occasionally fly to the ground to join the others of its group, but always flew back to its perch after a few minutes. When on its perch, a sentinel might squat belly-flat on a limb and rest or maintain an alert stance, usually in silence, unless a crow on the ground flew from one place to another or the group as a whole was getting ready to leave. Louder and

Table 7. Summary of observations on sentinel behavior in two territorial groups of crows showing number of times one acted as sentinel while others foraged on ground

Territorial group of crows	No. in group	Sentinel Absent	Sentinels Present	Total times sentinels present (%)
N	3	0	19	100
	2*	1	7	86
S	3	8	2	20

NOTE: Observations (n = 37) made in November and December, 1982, in Lyme, New Hampshire.
*Third crow sometimes missing, leaving only the pair.

sharper cawing was apt to occur when territorial neighbors came in sight, even if 300 to 400 meters away.

BY FEEDING STATIONS

I observed sentinels regularly when I put out chopped suet at the edge of a field from October through November, 1984. Five N crows were present during most of this time. On twenty-seven occasions when they flew to the feeding station, one perched at the top of a high tree while the others went to the ground. After working for five to seven minutes, the crows on the ground began flying away, the white of the suet conspicuous in their bills. Their flights were either to a pasture 200 meters away or to more distant places that involved flying over treetops. The sentinel, in either case, always flew with them. The crows returned from their flights in five to eight minutes, cawing as they came, with one perching on a tree as the others landed.

In August, 1985, I started feeding eight S crows at the far end of the schoolyard next to our house. The eight crows came two or three times a day for the cracked corn, soaked bread, and other items. On eleven occasions when seven crows came to the corn, an eighth one remained in a tree as a sentinel. This eighth one, after two to four minutes, flew to the ground and stood upright at a distance from the others, as if still on guard. On several occasions it drove another crow away before starting to feed. Because the feeding crows were generally peaceful among themselves, the aggressiveness of the sentinel suggested that it was the dominant male. Remaining up in the trees for a few minutes before descending to attack one of the group was a familiar sequence, one that breeding males in Florida had exhibited.

The presence of sentinels seems to depend on circumstances. I never saw sentinels in Florida in the breeding season with the regularity that I saw them in the nonbreeding season in New Hampshire. The only times that crows appeared to be on guard in Florida were when a male dominated his group as they fed on corn; guarded his mate at her peak of sexual activity, or at times, by a nest, if a squirrel or other predator posed a threat.

Foraging

From distances of 200 or more meters I could seldom tell what a crow might be catching. But foraging was best in fields in late March when, as snow melted, I noticed some crows feeding on night crawlers. Crows continued to do much foraging in fields until June, when the grass was tall. After that they came to fields mostly on days when hay had been cut and removed.

When Walter Record was cutting hay on August 21, 1984, by circling a field and working toward the center, the crows waited on trees until the tractor came by, then flew to catch freshly exposed prey. This brought them to within eight to ten meters of the tractor. Since the crows rarely came within less than 200 meters of anyone at the farm, this behavior was a discovery, one that Walter had not seen before. Crows appear to be less afraid of tractors than other kinds of vehicles.

When I started a feeding station on a school soccer field next to our house in the summer of 1985, the crows, after feeding on corn, foraged by hopping about with outstretched wings in an effort to catch flying insects. The crows favored places along the edge of tall grass at the periphery and in a shaded strip, the latter especially on windy days, as if the crows were picking up caterpillars, or other insects blown down with leaves from the trees.

Hayfields became attractive foraging sites in late summer and fall with the annual spreading of manure, which also contained the viscera of hens, afterbirths of cattle, and various dead animals. The carcasses of calves or sheep occasionally dumped out alone were not attractive for foraging because of blowfly larvae, unless coyotes arrived early and tore the carcasses apart before larvae appeared. In the late spring and summer of 1985 such carcasses were monopolized by ravens and the crows stayed away.

Crows fed on various items in the late fall. I noted them feeding on white mushrooms on five occasions between September and November. As the crows seemed to find the mushrooms in trees, they may have been stealing ones stored by red squirrels (Hatt 1929).

Food Storing

I observed the first storing activities of both 1982 and 1983 in November and December, when crows were flying from carcasses of farm animals to other parts of a pasture, making eight trips in ten minutes on one day and twenty in forty-five on another. I was able to check their activities on days of light snow. Tracks of a crow alighting and walking five to eight meters made it easy to locate where it had stopped by a tuft of grass and hidden a scrap of carrion. Two crows on December 13 kept flying 10 to 30 meters from calf remains. Noting that they went to two tufts of thick curly grass, I found a piece of fat in one and a piece of stomach wall in another. Crows were storing in the same areas on the following morning as well as in ones 120 meters farther away. They occasionally (n = 11) carried scraps in their bills but mostly used their antelingual pouches.

I started putting pieces of suet two to three centimeters long at a feeding station in October. The N crows visited the suet for the next few months, following much the same pattern of behavior every day except when robbed by ravens. When storing they spent five to seven minutes loading pouches and bills, then flew to another part of the pasture or continued on long flights over treetops to store in distant locations, returning in five to eight minutes in either case to pick up more suet and fly off as before. It thus seemed that given a surplus of food, the crows concentrated on storing it far and wide, a phenomenon also observed in Florida.

Storing in Trees

The crows often flew among trees along a woodland border, returning in one to two minutes. It seemed that they were lodging food in trees, for I twice watched one fly to a tree, start searching, then feed on a sizable item for five to eight minutes. There were several days of fresh snow in 1985 when I observed storing to better advantage. A crow on December 9 flew with suet to a tiny limb on the trunk of an elm, then leaned down to push it into a furrow of bark. On December 18, after more fresh snow, I watched crows that were flying to dead elms with suet (n = 5), looking into crevices and loose bark, then returning with bills empty.

DEPENDENCE ON COYOTES

Not all days were favorable for feeding and storing. I dragged a dead sheep onto the frozen pasture on November 28, cutting away skin to make abdominal viscera more accessible. But I did not cut enough. Crows visited the carcass for only fifteen minutes on the first day and not at all on the second, but coyotes made a visit on the second night, scattering scraps of viscera over the pasture. With the food thus made more accessible, the crows worked for two and one-half hours on the following morning, flying to storage areas as on other days.

On the third night the coyotes removed almost all traces of the sheep. The crows now spent their time looking for food stored previously and continued to do so for the next three days. On the last of these the pasture was covered with seven to ten centimeters of snow. Would the crows be able to find the stores that they had cached when the ground was bare? Three crows arrived shortly after sunrise. After perching on a tree for a few minutes, one flew directly to one place, dug through the undisturbed snow, and uncovered an item that it fed on for five minutes. A second crow recovered a scrap with equal promptitude. When I visited the places where the crows had dug, I found dry grass and small leaves scattered about on the snow, indicating that they had dug to the ground. Waite (1986) reports a similar case for a Carrion Crow.

RAVENS ROB CACHES OF CROWS

I watched a pair of ravens walking about on December 3 recovering what seemed to be items stored by crows. A few days later, following a light snow, I noticed them doing so again and on inspection found that they had dug in four places where there was a collection of crow tracks. Since I rarely saw ravens storing food, it seemed unlikely that they were recovering stores of their own. The ravens were seemingly attracted by the tracks of the crows. But even without the tracks, it would have been easy for them to have watched the crows flying repeatedly to one area with food.

Fall Breeding Behavior   Marshall and Coombs (1957) and Lincoln and associates (1980) describe Rooks as undergoing an increase in gonad size in the fall and exhibiting changes in behavior. American Crows may undergo a similar change, for I have noted several breeding-type behaviors beginning as early as September.

ALLOPREENING

When crows of a group perched in a dead tree, they were usually scattered, except for two that perched together. I took these to be the nuclear pair. On a few occasions, one allopreened the other, but only briefly. Allopreening became more marked in the late fall. When the two of the S pair were perched side by side after sunrise, one squatted low on a branch, while the other preened the top of its head. December 12, when one crow was preening on a snow-covered field, another flew to it, put its head down, and was allopreened by the first one.

TAIL QUIVERING

An up-and-down quivering of the tail is a precopulatory display that can be used in appeasement or submission. In my observations here, it appeared to be primarily of sexual significance. The crows on the playfield had been feeding on corn on September 7 when one flew a short distance to work on something. A second crow, flying to it, stood upright making wing-tail flicks, behaviors characteristic of a dominant male. The first one squatted belly flat with wings out and tail cocked and quivering. When the first crow walked away, the second one followed. Much the same sequence took place with two crows on November 8. On three other occasions it was the dominant crow that was feeding at a distance with the one that did the tail quiver flying to it.

OTHER BEHAVIORS

On four occasions between November 30 and December 5 one crow walked to another on a field and bowed deeply five or six times. Two of these occasions were when the first crow had found food. In mid-November of both 1982 and 1983 I heard single crows singing with a variety of odd vocalizations. In another manifestation of what I took to be fall breeding behavior, three N crows entered the thick top of a white pine on December 27, as if inspecting a nest site. One crow went in and came out, and then two crows entered while the third waited outside.

In the course of six years I saw sixteen flocks of 11 to 125 crows pass over the farm between mid-September and mid-November, with most of them (n = 11) coming in October. Although many of these crows perched in trees, none alighted on fields to feed. I had no way of telling whether these crows were flocks of local nonbreeders or migratory individuals from farther north. When I maintained a feeding station at the farm in the winter of 1985–86, a winter flock of up to seventy-five came to it daily. In the summer of 1986 the pattern of crows coming to the farm changed markedly. I could no longer distinguish territorial groups. Flocks of up to thirty-five crows came when foraging was favorable, after hay was cut, for example, but few crows came at other times. A similar change took place at a farm 17 kilometers up the valley, with seventy-five to one hundred coming daily all summer, something the owners, who were interested in crows, had never seen before.

Wandering and Other Flocks

The advantages of feeding crows were different in New Hampshire than in Florida. Whereas in Florida I could count on finding the crows I was following almost any day or time, in New Hampshire there were stretches of days, weeks, or even longer when I might see few crows on the farm. The crows were opportunists, and it was usually some special event that attracted them. Feeding stations were a way of observing a number of phenomena, including sentinel behavior, dominance within groups, storage of food, kleptoparasitism by ravens, and responses to predators, that I might otherwise have seen either less well or not at all.

Discussion

Sentinel Behavior.   It is a popular notion that crows "post" sentinels, as though they had a quasi-military organization, but sentinel behavior has not been well studied. Bighorn sheep are thought to post sentinels, but Sheldon (1960), after years of experience, considered the belief a delusion. Dealing with a similar problem, Goodwin (1976) states that when Rooks are feeding, a few, which may be more sated or wanting to rest, are in trees. They may be the first to see danger and their fright may cause the others to fly away, but he does not believe they are deliberately giving information.

Although not every American Crow that perches in a tree while others feed is a sentinel, there are times and places when one member of a group, or more in the case of a flock, appears to be on guard. Montevecchi (1976) noted that one crow perched in a tree while others looked for eggs in a gullery, a caw from it putting the others to flight. Conner and associates (1975) describe four to seven crows posting themselves as sentinels by a landfill in winter before thirty-five to ninety other crows came to feed. It is conceivable that if winter flocks consist, in part, of territorial groups that remain together (Knopf and Knopf 1983), then crows assuming territorial functions could be doing so as members of a group within the flock. But more studies are needed.

One question to be answered is which individuals in a group act as sentinels. Gaston (1978) found in a study of Jungle Babblers that the male or the female of the next season's breeding pair was most likely to do so. A number of observations indicated that the dominant male in a group of crows was the member most likely to be on guard. D'Agostino and associates (1981) concluded from observations on fledging American Crows that sentinels serve to extend parental care.

Storing food.   Hewson's (1982) description of Carrion Crows storing food parallels what I observed in American Crows at the farm. The Carrion Crows pecked at a carcass long enough to get food for a cache, then walked or flew to storage places at a distance, taking only a few seconds to push food into a tuft of grass and conceal it. The total time required to obtain the food and make each cache ranged from one to five minutes. Although Carrion Crows, like American Crows, cover their stores in seconds, the covering can still be effective. Sonerud and Ejeld (1985) watched Carrion Crows conceal eggs of domestic fowl so effectively that they were hard to find.

Carrion Crows (Hewson 1982) and Northwestern Crows (James and Verbeek 1985) walk or fly directly to stores as though finding them was not difficult. Recovery rates for the Northwestern Crows observed by James and Verbeek were as high as 73 percent. For one individual that was fed clams and studied in detail, the rate was 99 percent. The crow cached its clams at distances of nine to ten meters from the nearest crow to prevent their being stolen by other crows. There were survival advantages, it seemed, to scattering food widely and hiding it quickly.

Buitron and Nuechterlein (1985) discovered that Black-billed Magpies can be aided in recovering stores by their sense of smell. Although their olfactory bulbs are not extremely sensitive (Bang 1971), they are apparently keen enough to help at short distances. Caching reaches a peak among corvids in Thick-billed (Swanberg 1951) and Clark's Nutcrackers (Wall 1982), both of which make extensive, long-term stores that they can locate months later.

10. Winter and Spring

Behavior at
Winter Feeding Stations

I fed the crows at the farm for three winters. The station was located 250 meters across snow-covered fields and close to woods. In addition to setting out carcasses of larger farm animals, which sometimes lasted for several months, I placed at the station pieces of chopped suet and steam-rolled corn.

FEAR OF NEW OBJECTS

When I started putting out food in the N territory at the end of November, 1985, only the five crows came until mid-December. Outsiders then began to arrive, until by January and February I was feeding up to seventy-five crows. The crows in the flock were more easily frightened than the local group had been when alone. They lost time in flying up and staying away on what seemed slight provocations. Anything new disturbed them. They were so wary of a dead heifer set out in January that it was three weeks before one came near it or to suet and corn placed within three meters of it. Once accepted and fear dispelled, the heifer became a main attraction.

Crows were especially wary about approaching corn and suet at the start of a day. A few might land three to four meters away and approach slowly, with sixteen to eighteen others trailing behind. Once by the food, the lead crows jumped back several times before taking anything. In a flock that frequently numbered sixty to seventy it seemed that much depended on the boldness or leadership of one or two crows. When I set out a dead quail one day, no crows came near for several hours. One finally walked near, flew away, returned, and then walked around at a distance of a meter as if inspecting, fanning and closing its tail all the while without moving its wings. Two other crows arrived but remained at a distance. After a few minutes they all flew away and the quail remained untouched.

The behavior of the crows in relation to food was seldom predictable. When I put a brown hen chopped in half on the snow in early March, no crows went near, although elsewhere they were busily feeding. When I returned later, all seventy crows were in the woods mobbing something that I could not see. A single crow flew from the woods to the dead hen and fed on it alone, an unusual case of independent behavior.

Writing on bighorn sheep, Sheldon (1960) states that each band comprises individuals that have been attacked at different times. Hence the degree of wariness varied among individuals of a herd, some hardly cautious at all and others continually alert. A few were habitually nervous, never relaxing their efforts to detect an enemy. The increase in wariness that I noted in the flock of crows was due conceivably to similar inequalities of experience, the nervous ones inciting others to flight.

Conflicts

When watching territorial groups in Florida and in New Hampshire, I almost never saw conflicts over food. What a crow found, it kept. But when large numbers of crows were present, conflicts became common. Jump-up fights, with two meeting face to face, occurred mostly at the heifer carcass, where crows crowded close and were in competition. Pursuits in, out, and around trees and out over the snow were a more frequent interaction, occurring on some mornings as often as every three to five minutes when crows were picking up suet. The chases were similar to those of raven versus crow except that I seldom saw one crow succeed in robbing another. Crows flying with suet might fly to the woods or out into the fields away from others to break larger pieces into smaller ones for convenience in eating or storing. On many mornings I observed second crows fly to first ones, either to watch the first crow or supplant it, then pick up bits from the snow. The first crow, in moving away, usually retained the bulk of its food in its bill or pouch. On a few occasions the crow supplanted lay on its back with feet in the air.

Fear of Ravens

A pair of ravens or a pair and an occasional third one came to the feeding station almost daily and, in robbing the crows, contributed to their wariness. The crows were relatively undisturbed when a raven alighted near them on the ground. But when a raven flew low above them chasing a crow or looking for one to chase, all crows on the snow flew up, either to the tops of trees or, on some occasions, on a mass flight away from the farm. On January 23 seventy crows circled into the sky cawing and moving south as a raven flew north with suet in its bill. A pair of ravens followed the crows fleeing the farm on three occasions, flying above, behind, or among them. Since crows sometimes flew with suet in their bills, the ravens may have been looking for them. Over thirty-five crows left on another morning as a raven calling *caw-uk, caw-uk* flew to the feeding station.

Crows have reason to fear the bills and flying abilities of their larger relatives. On January 11 I watched a raven pursue a crow that had no suet in its bill in a roundabout chase that brought the two over my head by the barn and then 250 meters back to the woods. On the return, the raven flew with and behind the crow, appearing to bump into it three times from the rear.

The crows spent considerable time flying into trees or away from the farm. Fly-ups to neighboring trees sometimes occurred every five minutes, and crows that fled ravens on longer flights might perch, silent and motionless, for twenty to thirty minutes before returning. On February 10 thirty-five crows left when the pair of ravens perched in an elm. The ravens left in ten minutes, but the crows did not return to feeding until fifteen minutes after they had gone.

DRINKING AND TAKING GRIT

Half or more of the crows flew one or more times a morning over snow-covered fields to pick up sand along the edge of a main road, but they were seldom able to stay as long as forty seconds before being put to flight by passing cars. Varying numbers continued on to drink at a brook that ran under the road. Nero (1983) describes Common Ravens landing along the edge of a highway in Manitoba to take salt that had become concentrated in one place. Since the sand applied to icy roads in New Hampshire, as in Manitoba, is mixed with salt, it is difficult to say what a bird may be after. But I have watched crows in Florida and Blue Jays in Maryland taking plain sand. Sand may be needed as grit to aid in digestion when crows are feeding on corn.

Storage of Food in the Snow

The N crows regularly stored suet when they had their territory to themselves in November and December of 1984. But
when inundated by outside crows, any crow flying off and
alighting as if to store was almost certain to be watched by some
other crow, and even if an item were hidden, tracks in the snow
would give away its location. Crows spent much time walking
about as if looking for stored bits, which I sometimes saw them
recover. I had good views of one crow robbing the cache of
another on several occasions. A crow on January 22 flew to
the stub of a cornstalk sticking through the snow and poked
food beside it. A second crow, flying over, supplanted the first
one; it put its bill down into the same hole and ate, a scenario
I witnessed again a week later.

I was able to check the storing of crows in more detail on
several occasions. A crow flying with suet in its bill on January 9 dropped into powder snow 30 to 35 centimeters deep and,
without digging, pushed the suet out of sight and left. I went
over and found a walnut-sized piece of suet covered with snow
in the side of the depression where the crow had landed. On
January 14 I again watched a crow fly with suet to snow where
there were no tracks or markers of any kind. The crow landed
on a crust two to three centimeters thick, poked the suet through
with one thrust, and left.

Wariness in a Second Winter

Crows came to the feeding station from December, 1986,
through March, 1987, in the same numbers as the year before.
A difference was that the flock appeared to be less frightened
by the pair of ravens. Their general wariness, however, remained.
After overcoming initial fear of three successive piles of cow
viscera I put out in January and February, they would feed while
the supply lasted. I put out two new piles in March and they
again stayed away, appearing to go hungry rather than touch
the food until four days had passed. I supplied scraps and corn
daily, scattering them in approximately the same place. Yet even
at the end of March the crows of the flock might take an hour
or more to come to feed. On March 28 about forty crows, many
cawing, flew toward the feeding station, landing 15 to 30 meters away. Twenty of those nearest the station gathered together
and started walking toward the food. When they drew near,

they remained close, almost touching each other, but only two or three took corn. Then suddenly all flew up and returned to their starting place. After two or three of these advances and flybacks that occurred for no apparent reason, it seemed on this day, as on previous days, that a large majority of the crows got no food at all. They had had months to get accustomed to the food and the way I set it out but seemed to have made no progress in overcoming their fears. One result of their timidity was that forty to sixty starlings had time to get much of what I provided.

Heinrich (1986) observed similar cautiousness in ravens coming to food in winter. The ravens, he wrote, "form a phalanx, and advance cautiously side by side on foot toward the closer carcass. With pointed beaks and outstretched necks, they continue to advance, until one pecks at the calf. Instantly they all jump and take fright. . . . It seems," he continues, "that all of the ravens want to feed, but none wants to be the first."

The bunching of crows in approaching food reminded me of the bunching of crows in territorial groups prior to territorial encounters. It is conceivable that the crows in both situations derive courage from massing together, as soldiers were trained to do in the eighteenth century and in the American Civil War, as a way of overcoming their fears.

Goshawk Captures a Crow

About forty crows were on the snow feeding on the morning of February 1, with possibly twelve to fifteen more in the woods directly behind. After a half hour of undisturbed feeding, the crows suddenly flew into the air cawing. I saw no cause for the disturbance, and the crows quickly returned to feed as before. But within seconds they whirled up again, and it was then that I saw a Goshawk carrying a crow at snow level out onto the field. With the crow pinned under it, the Goshawk held its head up as the crows, with much cawing, passed 8 to 12 meters above in what appeared to be a panic flight that took them beyond the horizon in seconds (Fig. 11). The Goshawk flew as the crows passed and, surprisingly, so did its victim, seemingly uninjured.

When I inspected the site, I found that the hawk had carried its crow ten meters, so low that the tips of the hawk's primaries and the body of the crow left marks on the snow for the last five meters before the two birds, captor and victim, came to

Figure 11. After capturing a crow at the winter feeding station, a Goshawk holds its head up as other crows pass overhead in a panic flight.

rest. There were no feathers, blood, or signs of struggle. I looked out at the feeding station several times in the next two hours but could not find a single crow. Attempting to reconstruct events, I surmised that the Goshawk had come out of the woods low and fast, caught a crow that flew up after feeding, and continued straight on. The sudden fly-up of the forty to fifty crows that circled without swooping or stopping to mob had, possibly, frightened the Goshawk enough to make it leave. Its victim, seemingly no more than stunned, then flew off.

COYOTE

Responses to Other Predators

A coyote came out of the woods eight times in twenty-five minutes in January to pick up scraps, then loped back to the woods. The crows flew up each time it appeared and returned as soon as it left.

GREAT HORNED OWL

I heard sounds of intense mobbing coming from woods nearest to the farm early in the morning of February 3. The sounds came from various directions as the crows followed something for twenty minutes, and then it grew increasingly quiet. Ninety-six crows then flew from the woods to my feeding station, leaving forty more perched on treetops behind them. This was the largest number of crows that I had ever seen at the farm and the most intensive mobbing. Although I was unable to see what they were mobbing, a Great Horned Owl visited the hen coop that night, taking a duck and leaving behind a severed head plus a wing feather smelling strongly of skunk. Although my evidence for the cause of the mobbing was only circumstantial, the incident showed that the winter flock of crows was capable of intense mobbing on occasion.

RED-TAILED HAWKS

Red-tailed Hawks came to the feeding station at the beginning and end of two winters, primarily to scavenge scraps of meat and suet. When one appeared at the farm on March 26, all of the crows flew into the trees but returned to feeding in less than a minute and remained undisturbed when the hawk came to feed ten meters from them. Almost the same events happened when a Red-tailed appeared on January 4 of the following year. An odd behavior in both years was the way one crow came much closer to the hawk than the others, as if curious about what the hawk was doing. The crow in January walked slowly, with pauses, until it was within 30 centimeters, then jumped back.

Mobbing of Red-tailed Hawks at Onset of Nesting

I have noticed for years that one of the more obvious signs that a pair of crows is getting ready to nest in an area is when one or both of the pair begin attacking hawks, ravens, Turkey Vultures, or other large birds flying over it. But I never had an opportunity to study the situation until March and April, 1987, when a pair of Red-taileds came to a dead elm overlooking my feeding station. The hawks arrived on March 15, and for the first week, when snow and temperatures well below freezing prevailed, they came to feed on the remains of farm animals, which they did for up to thirty minutes at a time. The thirty to sixty crows present continued to feed, paying little attention unless a hawk flew close.

The behavior of the hawks changed when warmer weather left areas of brown grass along edges of the woods and stone walls. Instead of scavenging and then flying to the elm or other tree to rest, the hawks now looked about and, on March 24, made seven low flights along the edge of the woods as if hunting. Their change in behavior did not lead to any in the crows. They might fly up when a hawk flew by, but they quickly returned, and there was no mobbing. I saw the hawks copulating on the elm on March 24 and 27, an indication that they were preparing to nest.

The male hawk came to the elm in the weeks following, as if on hunting rounds. I stopped feeding crows on March 29, but varying numbers of up to forty of them continued to come to the feeding station for the next week. During this time they remained as indifferent to the Red-tailed as previously. This made the behavior of the N group of crows, which, unlike the flock crows, were on their breeding territory, all the more conspicuous.

The large elm above the feeding station where the Red-tailed perched was also a central place for the N crows. They built a nest within 60 to 80 meters of it in 1986 and were building there again between April 6 and 9, 1987. The five attacks on the Red-tailed that I witnessed between March 29 and April 9 started in the vicinity of the elm. In the first two, the five crows of the group followed a Red-tailed circling high over the woods and only one attacked. After four of the group had returned to the elm, what I presumed was the male continued swooping on the hawk for nearly three times as long as it had when with the group. I never saw an auxiliary actually attack or try to attack a Red-tailed. On April 2, when the male Red-tailed, identified during copulations by his smaller size and the narrow band across his lower breast, perched on the tip of a tall white pine, the male N crow made thirteen U-shaped attacks. It rose well above the hawk, dived steeply to within a meter of it, then swung up the other arm of the U to dive again. During these attacks the others of the group remained perched on the elm. By April 6 the three auxiliaries had been driven away, and in two attacks I watched after that time, both on a soaring Red-tailed, the male and female N crows both swooped on it.

In summary, the flock crows, which were nonterritorial when at the farm, paid little attention to the Red-tailed, whether the hawks were feeding on carrion and sated or "sharp set" (Hamerstrom 1957) and hunting. The territorial N crows were equally indifferent, until the approach of nest building. They then began intense attacks every time the hawks appeared.

Spring and a Return to
Small Territorial Groups

REDUCTION OF GROUP SIZE

There were five N crows in the fall of 1985, with infrequent visits by a sixth. When the farm was being visited by up to eighty crows in winter, it was generally impossible to identify the N crows. When I went out at sunrise on some mornings, they were the first to arrive. On February 2 the five were on the top of a bare tree when the sixth one alighted among them. The male left his mate to alight above the intruder, making wing-tail flicks. He then returned to his mate, put his head down, and was allopreened. This was the last mild behavior I observed. Beginning in mid-February the male, sometimes assisted by his mate, persistently attacked and drove away two of the original five crows. On February 16 the pair chased one of them back and forth over the fields and along the edge of the woods. On March 29, the day that snow began to melt and the large flock had ceased coming, the three crows of the final group were together on the ground and separate from a fourth. The pair with heads down and cawing advanced on the fourth one, which kept walking away. When the three flew, the fourth one stayed behind. After this, as territorial behavior reached a peak, I never saw more than three crows in the N group, the same number as in the S crows.

Much the same pattern was observed in the following year. There were six N crows in the fall, but by late February, 1987, the male was trying to drive one away. This left what appeared to be a stable group of five, which moved around together until April 6, when the pair started to build a nest. Both of the pair or, most often, the male then started driving the remaining three auxiliaries away. They kept returning but were tolerated only when the male was trying to drive away the Red-tailed Hawk. By April 13 only the pair remained. It was of interest that the S crows also started nesting as a pair without helpers. I think, on the basis of my observations in Florida, that this was because both pairs failed to nest successfully the year before and thus had no yearlings to serve as auxiliaries in the next breeding season.

PEAK OF TERRITORIAL BEHAVIOR

Since Jane and I went to Florida every winter and spring for five years, it was not until 1986 that I had a chance to observe territorial behavior at the beginning of the breeding season.

The large numbers of outside crows swamped the defenses of the N crows in winter, and I saw no group territorial behavior until the flock began to leave at the end of March. The territorial drive of the N crows was especially notable in 1986. Instead of conflicts along one segment of boundary as in the past, the crows drove intruders from the perimeter of a territory of 60 hectares. The intruders were of three types: flocks of up to forty crows, leftovers from the winter flocks; miscellaneous crows alone or in small groups that happened to be passing through; and the two crows of the N group that had been driven away but kept returning. Of the three types, I saw twenty to forty crows come to tall pines on a ridge above the farm on six occasions. When the N crows flew at them, the flock circled about irregularly and left. The N crows attacked more vigorously on April 12, when one of them rose above the flock three times, closed its wings, and dived. It thus seemed that the N crows, led by what I assumed was the breeding male, were able to prevail against large numbers in a flock. The two N crows that had been driven from the group were persistent in trying to return. They were driven away easily, but it took time and energy to keep them away for any length of time. A third type of intruder was odd crows passing through in small numbers. They kept going in one direction, giving no indication of landing, and the N crows left them alone, a phenomenon also noted in Florida.

The most intense encounters in April were between the N and the S crows. Their common boundary lay in woods beyond the farm so that all I saw were melees (n = 3) above the trees. On April 4 I had a view of two S and the three N crows cawing intensely at each other in a bare tree. One N crow rose in the air twice to swoop down on the S crows. The N crows flew back to the vicinity of their nest tree after most encounters. I noticed that one or two of them used the top spire of a tall hemlock as a lookout on thirty-two occasions, possibly because it gave a view of the entire territory.

NESTING ATTEMPTS

I found the pair of N crows staying in woods behind the winter feeding station on four late afternoons beginning on March 9. On three of the afternoons they attacked other crows, rising above, then diving steeply at them, only to rise and dive again. I began to see them carrying sticks to a site in the same woods three weeks later. The sticks were broken from the tops of dead elms. A second stage of building began on April 4 when a crow flew from a field with a wad of mud and turf. After this the crows carried dry grass. Of seven occasions when the crows flew to the nest, there were six times when only one crow had material in its bill and one time when two crows carried nesting material. I believed, from what I had seen in Florida, that the female was doing most of the building. The nest was built 20 meters above the ground against the trunk of a white pine.

When nests were being built in Florida, the crows of one group might fly high into the territory of another on surveillance flights. In the first week of April I watched the N crows fly over the S territory in this manner on three occasions and the S crows fly into the N territory on two. A curious incident occurred on April 7, when three S crows flew to a field below the woods of the N crows and then walked in a line toward the boundary. One of them filled its bill with dry grass. The three then flew back the way they had come. Their visit showed that both groups consisted of trios and were in the same stage of nest building. The way the S crows walked in a line to pluck grass close to the boundary was unusual. It was as if to demonstrate, while the N crows were watching, that the nest they were building was in its final stages, a demonstration that could have had relevance to synchronization of nestings.

Efforts to witness the nesting of the N crows were short-lived. Nine days after completion of the nest, egg laying began on April 18. The male and the one auxiliary spent much time over the next six days perched on treetops by the nest, driving away an intruder that almost reached the nest on three occasions. The nest failed on April 25 for reasons unknown. The female carried sticks to a new site for several days, then gave up attempts to nest a second time.

Discussion

Responses to Goshawks and other large raptors in winter. I know of no eyewitness accounts of a Goshawk catching a healthy crow of any species. Slagsvold (1982b) saw Goshawks take three Hooded Crows, but they were ones that he had killed or hit when shooting crows that were mobbing a stuffed Eagle Owl. Slagsvold (1985) regards the Eagle Owl, the Eurasian equivalent of the Great Horned Owl, and the Goshawk as being the most serious of predators of adult and juvenile crows. When he used dummies, he noted that Hooded Crows gathered at a greater distance from the Goshawk than from the owl. They repeatedly flew above the hawk in close formation, as Lohrl

(1950) has also described. The crows I watched at the farm flew above the Goshawk that had captured one of them, but their behavior appeared to be an effort to fly away rather than to mob. It would be interesting to know how crows react to the presence of a Goshawk that has not attacked them.

Goshawks are a threat to both Hooded (Slagsvold 1982b) and American Crows as well as to Rooks (Roskaft 1980). Reactions to them may be different than to other raptors. When a Goshawk entered a rookery, Roskaft (1980) noted that the Rooks left their nests, calling loudly and flying 60 to 150 m above. If the Goshawk landed in a tree, the Rooks left the area for some time, not returning until the Goshawk had left. It is of interest that the response of the Rooks and the American Crows at the farm should have been somewhat similar, considering that the Rooks were nesting and the crows were in a winter flock.

Winter is generally a time when little mobbing occurs in the north. The crows' lack of response in New Hamphire to Redtailed Hawks contrasted markedly with their behavior in Florida, where no other raptor roused more intense mobbing. The crows there, however, were living in group territories in their breeding season, whereas the crows in New Hampshire were in nonbreeding, nonterritorial flocks.

Craighead and Craighead (1969) consider Great Horned Owls a major factor limiting crow populations. Hunting at night, they can attack roosting crows at any season and may, in consequence, be subject to more intense mobbing the year round than other predators. Slagsvold (1985) found that Hooded Crows regularly mobbed stuffed Eagle Owls in January and February in Norway. Another of his findings was that mobbings were more intense on mild than on cold days. The temperature on the early morning that I heard 140 crows mobbing what I thought a Great Horned Owl at the farm was 25 degrees above zero (Fahrenheit) in contrast to the much colder weather of previous weeks.

Winter flocks.   A pleasure in winter was the sight of fifty to seventy crows, their bodies jet black against gleaming snow, as they rested by the feeding station in the midmorning sun. Their conspicuousness undoubtedly helps crows find each other and thus form flocks. Good (1952) and Haase (1963) found that flocks are no sudden phenomenon, but consist of small groups that begin combining in the fall. I noted in January and February that, although about seventy-five crows might gather in the first hours of a day, they did not all come at once. A flock of fifteen to twenty, one of thirty, and single individuals or groups of two or three came in from various directions at different times. The majority on any morning spent much time standing away from food, doing nothing. Possibly they were already sated.

An advantage of flocking commonly cited (Morse 1985) is protection against predators. The more eyes, the better the chance of seeing danger approach. This advantage seemed to mean less at the farm, where Red-tailed Hawks and a Bald Eagle were the main raptors seen in two winters. Both species appeared to be more interested in the carrion the crows were feeding on than in the crows themselves. The most serious predator, a Goshawk, appeared only once. It took forty-five feeding crows by surprise and caught one of them.

The benefits of flocking, whatever they may have been, appeared at times to be outweighed by the costs. When five N crows had their territory and the feeding station to themselves, they fed without conflicts and stored food regularly, while one, perched above, acted as a sentinel. Ravens robbed them occasionally, but the crows continued to feed without losing much time. All of this changed with the coming of the large flock. The wariness of a few then appeared to infect the others. Fly-ups that were slow to settle and aggression, which had been absent in the small group, now became common. Physical clashes occurred at carcasses; crows without food tried to rob those that did; and caching, although attempted, appeared to be ineffective with so many crows watching and ready to steal. Added to other interruptions was the excessive wariness of crows in the flock toward any new kind of food I put out or toward old types of food put within meters of it.

Goodwin (1976) suggests that social species like corvids need company most when ill at ease or slightly afraid. Individuals then tend to alight near or feel secure in the presence of one that acts in a confident manner. I saw this daily in winter when one or two crows would advance toward food on the snow while being trailed by fifteen to twenty others that appeared afraid to do so. On other occasions crows walked toward food in a phalanx, as if gaining courage from being close together. Both confidence and fright appeared to be contagious. Knight and Knight (1986) report wintering Bald Eagles as feeding less efficiently in large groups than in small ones.

A difficulty in evaluating the behavior of many species, in terms of selective advantages, is that they live in environments that are continually disrupted by humans. Behavior that once led to selective survival may cease to do so as effects of civilization change even remote areas. It is difficult to see why flocks of seventy to one hundred crows, as I noted in 1986, should be present in the breeding season and summer of 1986 as well as in winter months.

Stress.   Stress can distort the behavior of whatever species a biologist is watching. When studying Red-headed Woodpeckers in the South, I found that when pairs had more space, they went about their breeding quietly and effectively. In areas where snags were largely eliminated, many pairs, in trying to nest where snags were available but in short supply, spent much time fighting over them. Wilson (1975) refers to such situations as scaling of behavior. "At low . . . densities, all aggressive behavior is suspended. At moderate densities, it takes an intermittent form such as intermittent territorial defense. At high densities, territorial defense is sharp, while, if densities are too great, there may be a breakdown into social pathology." The aggressiveness, excessive wariness, and fear of the crows I observed in a winter flock in 1985–86 appeared to be a result of their numbers. Farmlands, the typical habitat of crows, have been declining in New England for a long time. With such long-lived birds, flocks of nonbreeders, many of them adults, could conceivably increase in number as nesting habitats decreased, exposing the crows to increasing degrees of stress.

11. Hand-raised Crows

A profitable way of gaining insight into birds is to live with them and thus augment observations made in the wild. I did this for years with hand-raised woodpeckers and nuthatches, keeping them in aviaries in or attached to the house. They were birds whose requirements I could, to a large extent, meet, and they did relatively well. But crows and ravens are different. Being intelligent, sensitive, and social and hence more like humans, I would hesitate to keep one in a cage unless it was crippled. All of the crows that I have raised, from the first one in 1919 to three many years later with the aid of Jane and the children, were given their freedom when they were old enough to fly. They attached themselves to their caretakers and never wandered far from the yard while we had them, which was never more than three months. The crows were acquired mostly by chance, in years before I began studying crows as a project. As I learned later from our raven, one needs to keep a hand-raised bird at least a year to learn much about it. I did not, however, know the sexes of any of my birds, but for the sake of simplicity I use the masculine pronouns.

A Crow in Lyme

My son removed a crow from a nest in Lyme on May 27, 1966, about ten days before it would have fledged. I would not want to take a healthy bird from its nest now, but the memory of the crow that a policeman had given me when I was eight was strong and I wanted the fun of having a crow again, especially with children to help in raising it. The crow was a success from the start. He opened his red gape in begging for food and made pleasant noises as the food went down. Otherwise he remained silent. After feeding, "Crowsy," as we called him, usually shot his excreta over the rim of his "nest" of towels in a cardboard box. Although his legs were weak at clinging, he performed many wing stretches, including both wings arched up over the back and, seemingly peculiar to young birds, both wings extended down, instead of leg-wing stretches, which he did not perform until later. By June 1 Crowsy was flying in place to exercise his wings. He was also pushing way up with both legs extended and doing a good deal of preening to get rid of remnants of feather sheaths. As I have noticed with nestlings in Florida, Crowsy was generally silent. He did not begin loud begging and clamoring until, fully fledged, he flew to the top of the kitchen door.

I set Crowsy free in the yard when I noticed that he was trying to get out through a window. Once outside, Crowsy began playing with blades of grass and other objects, using his bill like a delicate pair of forceps. He stayed close to the kitchen door. Within a few days he was flying to the roof of a shed from which he would fly down to get fed. When alone, he had the wisdom to perch in a thick spruce and remain silent. These stretches of solitude made him the more eager for our company when we came out of the house.

Crowsy's great interest continued to be playing with pebbles and other objects. One morning he picked up a pebble and, holding it in his bill, did a minuet, taking steps and sideways hops that reminded us of the dances of Crested Cranes we had watched in Africa. He also danced on a stone wall while holding bits of fresh leaves, stems, or flowers. With eyes that were still blue, he suggested, at times, a Satin Bowerbird.

Crowsy was very fond of objects. If I returned from a walk and called, he would leave his spruce limb to alight by my feet, pick a small leaf, dance with it, then lay it by my foot or on my shoe. Years later, in Florida, I watched a yearling pick up a stick, walk around with it, then present it to another yearling. I also observed adults holding or presenting objects in the course of copulatory behavior.

By early July Crowsy was carrying on soliloquies of mixed sounds that sounded like talk or singing, but of a purely crow variety. Although largely an outdoor bird, he liked to come into the kitchen and do his talking there. Numbers of new behaviors appeared about this time. One was his way of greeting us, whether indoors or out, by crouching with wings half extended and tail vibrating up and down. The tail quiver is a precopulatory display in adults, and Lorenz (1970) describes it in ravens, noting that tame ravens of either sex begin using it at a few months of age as an expression of devotion to their keepers. Crowsy greeted me in this way in July. The quiver was not begging, for when he was hungry, his begging had, to our ears, a frantic, desperate sound like "feed me." We would, and then he would gulp and beg "more, more." I heard juvenile crows begging in the wild in the same way at the same time.

Crowsy continued to perform his dances. After greeting me from the roof with a tail quiver on July 8, he picked up a twig and jumped this way and that with wings out, picking up and dropping the twig as Sandhill Cranes do with debris. On the following day he danced by himself on the lawn. Skead (1952) describes a family of Black Crows dancing on the roof of his farmhouse in South Africa. Dances are not restricted to crows, for our hand-raised raven danced and I observed juvenile ravens dancing in June on a dirt field in Lyme.

Crowsy's affection and desire for sociability seemed to be deep. He would pull his head and neck in close to his body when affectionate and push close, making fragmentary low notes, full of understanding, or so it seemed. His love of being close was also shown, if we were walking across the yard, in following at our feet, swinging his body from side to side. Sometimes he would fly a few meters ahead in trying to remain as close as possible. I watched much the same behavior in Florida when "third crows" tried to push in close to breeding pairs.

Seemingly because we fed and looked after him, Crowsy behaved to us much as he would have behaved to his real parents. In this respect he was sensitive to anything we said or did that seemed adverse. When my son poked him one day in play, Crowsy, instead of getting the idea of a mock battle, rolled on his side, then onto his back with both feet up in what appeared to be submission. I saw the same reaction several times in Florida when a yearling was approached by a dominant individual on the ground. On another occasion, when Jane was ironing, Crowsy flew down to the ironing board from the top of a door. When Jane scolded him for getting in the way, he reacted by rolling on his side.

Our hand-raised crows have all been able to recognize us individually and to tell friend from foe or stranger. When a garageman Crowsy had not seen before held out a finger, Crowsy crouched with wings a little out, head feathers raised, and bill turned to the side, a pose I have seen crows assume when facing a Red-shouldered Hawk. And when an acquaintance, a tense individual who never felt at home with a dog or any other animal, tried to be friendly, Crowsy made harsh *grrs* and attacked his ankles, something that we had not seen him do to anyone before. Even on later occasions, when our friend came into the kitchen, Crowsy would raise his head feathers. His greatest antipathy was toward three boys in the neighboring school. One of these had once fired a .22 to frighten him, and the other two had thrown stones. Whenever we heard sudden, excited cawing in the yard, it was apt to be when one of these boys appeared.

Crowsy took fright at objects several times. I was carrying a bucksaw with a curved, tubular frame one day when Crowsy broke out with sudden caws and flew off in fright. Our crows in Maryland appeared to have an innate fear of snakes, and the curved tube of the saw frame may have suggested one. On another occasion, hearing an outburst of cawing, I found Crowsy agitated by a black, fuzzy bathing suit someone had left on the lawn. Lorenz (1970) describes a similar furor set up by his Jackdaws on sighting a pair of black bathing trunks, as discussed in a previous chapter.

Crowsy began a new display in August when, pulling his bill in against his breast, he bowed down, giving a strange concatenation of sounds that included *cok-cok, cok-cok*s as he did so. This was seemingly a rudimentary *cu-koo* performance. From the way yearlings and older auxiliaries in Florida worked at this performance, it seemed to be one that they had to learn by practice. Another behavior of Crowsy's was allopreening my eyebrows, especially when he perched on my shoulder. Having had a female Casqued Hornbill do this to me some years previously, I had no fear. As with Lorenz (1970) and his raven, the bills of crows and hornbills are powerful weapons, but they have inhibitions against using them when performing pair- or social-bonding rituals.

Crowsy liked teasing or provoking other animals. When we adopted two kittens, he sometimes got behind one, pulled its tail, and then jumped to a chair as the kitten turned. As he got older and more independent, Crowsy spent more time at the farm across the street. He was walking among grazing sheep one day when I called to him. He took wing immediately, but swooped on the way to bump a sheep on the rear, as if to see it run.

A problem for anyone who loves to raise wild animals, yet wants to return them to nature when they are ready to take care of themselves, is how to go about doing so. This was, fortunately, a minimal problem with my crows. My first one, the one I had when eight years old, flew about our country place all summer, free to go where he wanted. Both I and my family were his companions, and he never went very far. Then one evening early in September he perched on the porch rail and did a lot of "talking," that is, odd cackles and caws pouring out in a seemingly random fashion. The next morning he was gone. He might, we thought, have been eaten up by a predator except, that a honeymoon couple a kilometer down the road reported that they opened the door on their first morning and were surprised to find a crow on the doorstep. Joe the crow had never gone that far before. It seemed possible, therefore, that he had done so upon feeling an urge to set off on his travels. The last day that we saw Crowsy in Lyme was September 3, almost exactly the same date, and Criddle (1927) relates that four crows he hand-raised in Canada flew away between August 26 and September 6. Conditions, however, may vary north and south. In Florida, where cooperative breeding was strongly developed, juveniles remained in parental territories to become helpers at the nest the following spring.

Two Crows in Maryland

Crowsy behaved well in the country village of Lyme, and we received no complaints from neighbors. The same was not true of two crows that we raised in Maryland, where we had a small yard and neighbors were close. Although I learned much from our crows there, some of our experiences were harrowing.

A newsboy gave us both of the crows, but not at the same time. He had gotten them by climbing to a nest on a golf course when the birds were about to leave. The first one appeared hopeless. His fear reactions had developed and he refused to take food. We had to pry his bill open at first and force food down with a finger. An idea then occurred to me. I had read of a young oriole that had fed from an orange medicine dropper, orange being the color of a parent, but not from ones of other colors. Would black have a similar effect on the crow? I shaped a bill of wood, stained it with India ink, then had Jane, covering her hand with a black cloth and making flapping motions, offer the crow food with the black "bill." Joe, as we called him, responded by opening his bill and begging for the first time. It was a matter, apparently, of getting the right signals. Feeding became easier for the next few days. Then, with a combination of hops and flaps, Joe made his way to the top of a tall tree. He called for food and was still doing so by evening when the newsboy climbed up and brought him down. Joe was now even more responsive. He ate all of the food we offered him, his clamoring interrupted only by gulps as he swallowed. The next morning he was clamoring early and swooped down to the back porch to be fed when I appeared. I was being recognized at last. Then, just as all looked well, Joe disappeared.

Had he flown away? Three days went by. He must, we thought, have gone to seek his own kind. Then came a surprise. A neighbor dropped by to say that he had noticed soot falling into his fireplace for several days and, on looking up, had found a crow sitting above the grate. I imagined that Joe would look terrible, ragged and emaciated after three and a half days without food or water. But nothing of the sort. When our neighbor brought him around he looked bright and well. His delight on seeing us was pathetic to behold. He nestled in Jane's lap, eating a prodigious amount while making contented-sounding noises. From this time on Joe accepted us completely.

The boy who had given us Joe then gave us a sibling that he had been keeping in a cage. He had taken it at an earlier stage, and it had fed readily. But the crow clamored so loudly in the early morning that the boy's parents told him that he would have to give the bird away.

Both of the newsboy's crows loved companionship. If no one was outside, they would fly around the house looking in windows for someone. If I went out to work in the yard, one might alight on one shoulder and one on the other. They ran their bills through my hair, pulled grass from my mouth, or played with sticks I wiggled for them on the lawn. When I sat on the porch they made attacks beginning with my shoestrings. From there one might jump to my arm to loosen my wristwatch, while the other attacked my belt buckle. Anything that was a bit weak and could be torn apart, such as a tear in one's clothing, was a delight, and loose buttons aroused a special interest.

The garden pool was a strong attraction. Although the crows sometimes ducked under the water, their feathers shed water none too well. In hard rains they became so sodden that white skin showed through and they could hardly fly. When tired of playing, one or both of the crows were apt go to a pine to carry on a soliloquy of croaks and caws that sounded not unlike human conversation.

The crows swooped down when our baby was brought out to his playpen by midafternoon. Perching on the rail, they made guttural noises that mixed with the babbling of the infant. All of them, crows and infant, liked bottle tops and a silver bell on a string as playthings. A crow would watch the baby as it played with the bell and string until the baby let go. Then the crow, quick as lightning, would seize the bell and it was the infant's turn to try to get it back. Although able to give blows with their bills, the crows never hurt the baby, in spite of their being occasionally seized by wings or tail. It was not until thirty years later, in Florida, that I discovered the fact that crows belong to cooperative groups, to which the individuals are strongly attached. I think that the crow in Lyme as well as our two in Bethesda regarded Jane, myself, and our five children as being in their family group. They did not alight on or play with other people and were, at times, even hostile. When two bare-legged boys came into our yard one day, the crows drove them out by pecking at their ankles and then swooping on their heads as they ran away.

The crows sometimes gave a *ca-a-a* different from ordinary cawing. It usually meant the approach of a dog. The crows were unusually excited one morning and refused to eat. I could find no cause until I looked down a stairwell and discovered that a black snake I had been keeping had escaped.

A friend warned us that he had had a crow as a boy that had cost him the goodwill of his neighbors. His pet had pulled up seedlings, picked flowers, and removed tops from milk bottles and letters from mail boxes. Our crows did none of these things at first. Troubles began when Jane took the children to our place in New Hampshire for the summer, leaving me alone with the crows. This was a mistake. Since I had to go to work every day, the crows were left unsupervised. They invaded neighbor's yards, tearing up flower beds, pulling clothespins off lines and letting the clothes fall, and attacking the bare legs of children and once, the upholstery of a car. Complaints began to pour in. I was threatened with lawsuits. Yet the crows gave me such a welcome when I came home from work that I hated to give them up. Neighborhood pressure, however, plus a visit from the police finally brought on the inevitable. I had to do something. My first thought was to take the crows out into the country and turn them loose. That evening I drove them to a remote field I knew of by a lonely dirt road. It was not easy to get them to go. I had to push them from the car. All the way back to the house and all that night I was deeply troubled. I knew I had left babes in the wood. I doubted that the crows were old enough to be on their own. I would have to go back, and I was off by sunrise.

Would I be able to find them? It seemed most unlikely. Back on the lonely field where I had "liberated" them the evening before there was not a crow in sight. I went out and called, "Here Joe, here Joe," then listened. From a distance came the thrill of an answering *caw, caw, caw.* In a few moments a crow was flying as fast as it could come to alight on my shoulder.

More calling, more answering *caws*, and the second crow flew to me from another direction. It was pathetic to see how glad they were to be rescued. I got into the car with both of them clinging to me. I was to learn later in Florida and New Hampshire how desperate a yearling can be when, having lost its own group, it tries to join another.

When I reached home with my two crows, I felt that I had reached a dead end. What was I to do next? But hope was in sight. A fellow who worked in my laboratory said that his father, a more or less retired farmer, loved birds and would be glad to have the crows on his farm. The crows adapted to their new situation and, being free to come and go, did well, and as far as I could find out, did well for many years.

Discussion

Fear reactions and imprinting.   Imprinting is easier to understand in geese, where it takes place in a critical period shortly after hatching, than in crows where, as far as is known, it can take place in a period of two to three weeks in the middle or late part of the nestling period. The function of imprinting is to reinforce a bird's innate recognition of its own species (Goodwin 1976). This is especially important in crows that, being all black or nearly so, appear similar to allied species with which they might interbreed. *Corvus* species taken from the nest before they are half-feathered, according by Goodwin, become completely imprinted on man and show no recognition of their own kind later in life. Good (1952), who climbed to nests daily to handle and measure young crows, found that they showed no fear of him until they were two and a half weeks old. Crows taken from the nest after that time were difficult to rear and never became tame. But conditions at crows' nests may vary. When Good visited his nests, he was met by "a barrage of vindictive crow language" that could have hastened the development of a fear reaction in the young. All four of the crows that I raised and one of the ravens were four to five weeks old when taken and were probably within a week or less of fledging. Yet all, with the exception of one crow that was probably older than the others, showed no fear reactions and fed readily.

There was nothing to indicate that we would ever succeed with that first crow. He was afraid of us and seemed to be completely wild. Yet one planned experiment and two unplanned periods of starvation, one for a day, and another, when he was lost, for over three days in a chimney, proved his stubborn phase to be reversible. The ordeals converted him from the wildest to one of the tamest and most dependent of crows we raised. I was interested, in relation to these experiences, to read of Indians in Brazil that tame adult wild animals by putting them "in darkness in a box or under a large bowl for a day or two without food or water, and at the end of that time, if still alive," the animals were "usually prepared to eat and make friends" (Dubos 1955). Our reluctant crow was very ready to eat and make friends with Jane and me after confinement in the dark chimney. Schein (1963) demonstrated an irreversibility of imprinting in Wild Turkeys. But imprinting can seemingly be reversed in some species under drastic conditions.

Strength of affections.   There were several times when I felt the strength of the bonds binding the crows to us. One was when the crow was rescued after the three days in the chimney, the other when I abandoned our two crows in the country and retrieved them the next morning. The social bonds of crows, the need for companionship, can be very strong. How unscientific, I think again, are behaviorists who dismiss feelings in animals as being trivial or anthropomorphic. What is their experience? How do they know? Yglesias (1962) describes raising a young Jackdaw and then releasing it. But the Jackdaw returned, "with open beak and flapping wings, his feathers rising with pleasure and his face expressing intense excitement. . . . He clung frantically to our heads and shoulders as if to make quite sure we were still there. He continued to show his confidence and friendliness towards us, coming in and out of the windows and daily returning for bath and breakfast for over a year; he would often join us in the garden for meals, behaving like one of the family." She continues, "This first instance of a wild bird's trust was a most wonderful experience. 'Wonder' was the right word. We had never dreamt of finding such a beautiful way into another existence." I can believe Yglesias because what she describes, the little details of how the Jackdaw expressed its emotion, rings true. They are much what I have noted and experienced with crows and ravens.

Recognition of people.   Some birds can recognize people individually. Merrit (1984) noted that, in making regular visits to Mockingbird territories to visit nests, he was not attacked until he banded nestlings. After that the male gave alarm calls and followed him whenever he entered the territory, something that the male had not done before. The learned response, Merritt thinks, supports Griffin's thesis (1976) of animal awareness. Crows that Good (1952) visited on a daily basis, became almost frenzied when he climbed to nests. The adults of one pair, in addition to recognizing him, came to recognize his car, as indicated by their circling and scolding as soon as they saw it, something that they did not do to other cars.

Our free-flying crows could distinguish us from strangers and showed us affection that they did not exhibit to other people. The crow in Lyme remembered two boys who had thrown stones at him and attacked them when them came to our yard. Much the same happened some years later with a free-flying crow belonging to a friend of ours at the other end of Lyme. His crow liked to perch on a power line, where he became a target for two boys throwing stones. When the boys rode their bicycles down a hill below the line, the crow, as if seeing his chance, attacked them. The boys' parents complained and the crow had to be deported. This was unfortunate, for it had been coming to the schoolyard, where it mingled with the children in looking for scraps. The children were amused and there were no complaints from them. I was a stranger and the crow would not come to me. Yglesias (1962), in her book on the 116 species of sick and injured birds that she took care of in her hospital in Cornwall, tells of a fledgling Jackdaw that fell down the chimney of a fisherman's cottage. The family cared for him, giving him his freedom once he was ready to fly. "His intelligence," wrote Yglesias, "was amazing. He could recognize the fisherman's two boys, Tom and Ashley, and land on their shoulders, picking them out from all children on the school playground."

Part III. CROW BEHAVIOR IN GENERAL

It takes a very long period of watching to become really familiar with an animal and to attain a deeper understanding of its behavior; and without the love for the animal itself, no observer, however patient, could ever look at it long enough to make valuable observations on its behavior.

KONRAD LORENZ

I presented the behavior of crows in Parts I and II more or less chronologically as it occurred through nesting seasons in Florida and the year round in New Hampshire. In Part III I bring together general attributes and behaviors of crows observed in both states. This has been possible in most cases without repeating. In a few cases, particularly in those involving play and thinking, I have repeated some incidents, enlarging upon them and bringing them together in order to discuss them.

When I first set out to study bird behavior in the early 1950s, one of my first ambitions was to study every detail of the behavior of any bird that I might happen to watch. A benefit of the practice then was that I could always observe something that I could write up when I got home. I now feel that observing a bird's total behavior, as far as possible, is especially important to understanding such problems as play and thinking that have been little studied under natural conditions. To do so adequately presents a considerable challenge. Unfortunately, Jane and I were prevented from returning to Florida for the more prolonged studies we had hoped to make. Crows could make a lifetime study.

12. Miscellaneous Behavior and Attributes

Displacement Activities

BARK PECKING AND BILL WIPING

When I first walked into the A crows' territory in Florida in 1980, six crows alighted on a tree above, looking down and knocking off bits of bark. Since they were all doing it, I thought this must be a common behavior. But I seldom saw it afterward. I was a newcomer who walked about the ranch instead of riding in a vehicle, and I think this made the crows afraid and uncertain. Once they became accustomed to Jane and me, which took only a few days, the bark pecking ceased.

I witnessed bark pecking or twig pulling on other occasions as well, when it seemed to be associated with mobbing predators and territorial encounters. Two of four crows mobbing a Barred Owl near their nest were biting and pulling twigs. At another time three A crows, after flying to a tree by their territorial boundary, pecked at their perches and wiped their bills when their neighbors, the B crows, arrived. I saw the same behavior in New Hampshire on the first days of a series of territorial conflicts, but not subsequently. Among other corvids, pecking and bill wiping as displacement activities have been noted in Rooks and Carrion Crows (Coombs 1978), Hawaiian Crows (Giffin 1983), Common Ravens (Dorn 1972), and Yellow-billed Magpies (Verbeek 1972b).

DISPLACEMENT PREENING

I have seen displacement preening on only a few occasions. A breeding male in January drove first one, then another of two male auxiliaries away from corn. One flew to a fence post and the other to the ground and started preening in a hasty, ineffective way. The two may have resorted to preening because, perched in the open, they had no bark to peck or twigs to pull. Coombs (1978) mentions displacement preening as occurring in Rooks and Carrion Crows.

Wing-tail Flicks

Crows convey impressions of alertness, self-assertion, dominance, readiness to attack, or in some situations, apprehension, by flicking the tips of the wings upward while fanning and closing the tail. A breeding male at a height of his aggressiveness in the early breeding season did more wing-tail flicking and cawing than others of his group. Incubating females commonly paused on a branch to wing-tail flick before settling back on their eggs after being away. One of them cawed and wing-tail flicked on her nest when others of her group flew to attack a Red-tailed Hawk. Four crows, perched above a Red-tailed, did much wing-tail flicking in seeming apprehension.

Crows occasionally open and close their tails without moving their wings. I put a dead quail on the snow by my feeding station in late January in New Hampshire. As usually happened when I put out something new, the crows stayed away. When one individual finally came, it kept opening and shutting its tail as it walked around the quail, keeping about a meter away. The tail fanning appeared to reflect uncertainty—did it dare to feed or not? After four minutes it approached slowly and started to feed.

BEGGING

Appeasement

Begging with bill open and wings out and fluttering may be displayed in two situations in the early breeding season: when an incubating female is about to be fed and when thwarted adult female auxiliaries are close to or about to be driven away by the dominant male. Begging by way of appeasement is especially common with third crows trying to get close to a breeding pair. Begging crows display the pigmentation of the interior of the mouth and throat, which, as illustrated in Good (1952), is pink in juveniles, light in yearlings, and black in adults. The light pigmentation displayed when the younger individuals beg may serve to inhibit attacks from breeding males or other adults.

TAIL QUIVERING

A precopulatory display used by both sexes is squatting and quivering the tail up and down while holding the wings out and letting them droop. The display is also used, as I have seen in late summer, fall, and winter months in New Hampshire, in submission or appeasement ($n = 3$) as well as in begging for food ($n = 3$). When one crow found food in the snow on January 28, a second one approached with head up and making wing-tail flicks. The first one, faced by the dominant behavior of the new arrival, crouched in the snow with wings out and tail quivering for twenty to thirty seconds. On December 28 I saw somewhat the reverse when a crow flew to one that had food and begged by putting its wings out and quivering its tail. Gwinner (1964) noted Common Ravens and Goodwin (1976) Rooks tail quivering in appeasement.

FOOT PUTTING, LYING ON BACK, AND DEEP BOWING

A subordinate and particularly a third crow, when close to the breeding pair, may hold a foot out sideways as if trying to keep from being driven away by the male. Yearlings in submission may lie on their backs or sides with both feet out. A hand-raised juvenile rolled on its back when my son poked at it with a finger, and it did the same when Jane scolded it for getting in her way. I have also seen ($n = 3$) deep bowing, with bill pointed sharply downward, used as if to inhibit an attack, a behavior noted by Goodwin (1976) in Carrion Crows.

Agonistic Behavior

Direct conflicts included jump-up fights in which two crows attacked each other momentarily with beaks and claws, as observed in fights over food in winter, and the grappling in mid-air observed in territorial conflicts. Intragroup aggression was generally mild. A dominant male usually did no more than walk toward an adult auxiliary, strike or pinch it on the foot, or keep supplanting it to drive it away. A more belligerent behavior, seen at the start of a breeding season, was when the two of a pair, with heads down, advanced on an auxiliary that was being forced from their group.

SCRATCHING   *Body Maintenance*

Birds scratch their heads either directly, as woodpeckers do, or indirectly, by lowering a wing and bringing a foot up over it, as is common in passerines. Crows scratch indirectly. I noted an exception when a female flying to her nest with both legs dangling, reached up to scratch directly with one. Simmons (1974) observed the same in a Rook and Crisler (1958) in a Common Raven. American Crows close the nictitans when scratching close to the eye. A special form of scratching is to stretch and expose the membrane at the corner of the mandibles by opening the bill a few centimeters.

STRETCHING

The leg-wing stretch, in which the leg and wing of the same side are stretched down simultaneously, was more frequently observed and the double-wing back stretch, in which both wings are arched momentarily above the back, less frequently observed stretch in American Crows. Advanced nestlings have a special form of stretching — standing as tall as possible with both legs straight.

Erratic flights are a playful way of stretching wings at the start of a day. I have noted the behavior in woodpeckers many times but only once in crows. This was early one morning in December in New Hampshire. A pair were together when a yearling, perched at a distance, circled over a field and returned on a long slanting flight that ended in a series of loops in and out among the trees. Verbeek (1972b) has seen this behavior in young but not in adult Yellow-billed Magpies and thinks that it serves to develop flight as well an ability to escape avian predators. Morse (1975) observed how a European Goldcrest as well as a Treecreeper resorted to erratic flights when pursued by a Sparrow Hawk.

BILL WIPING

Crows may wipe their bills on a branch many times, like stropping a razor, after tearing up prey, feeding nestlings, or removing fecal sacs.

PREENING

Preening is no different in crows than it is in many other birds.
In Florida it was done at greatest length when the sun first came
out from morning mists and the crows' plumages were wet with
dew; on late mornings when crows were resting; or at times
when they had nothing much to do, as during the interim period
between finishing a nest and the start of egg laying. Crows in
New Hampshire preened at special length during and after rains.
Allopreening, though primarily social and pair bonding, is performed in the same manner as autopreening and can be a way
of tending feathers that a crow cannot reach for itself. Brooke
(1985) has demonstrated this combination of functions in penguins, where allopreening in mated pairs reduces parasite loads.

BATHING AND DRINKING

I have seen crows bathing only a few times. One occasion was
when a crow waded into an open, grassy pool in Florida, came
out, preened, then went back for a thorough splashing with
its wings. On coming out it preened, shook itself, then perched
in a tree for five more minutes of preening, body shakes, and
a leg-wing stretch. On another day a crow waded into a similar pool, drank twice, then waded in belly deep to duck its
head and splash water over its back.

I saw the greatest number of crows drinking when I scattered corn by a stream in Florida. Individual crows went to the
water to dip their bills, then raised them to a horizontal or nearly
horizontal position to swallow. Funderburg (1967a) watched
crows in southern Florida skim the surface of a lake on late
afternoons in the manner of swallows drinking. Many observations convinced him that the crows were drinking rather than
feeding on surface organisms. I had a feeling that crows at the
ranch kept away from the shores of some bodies of water, or
approached them gingerly, due to a fear of alligators. This could
conceivably explain Funderburg's (1967a) observations.

When seventy or more crows came to a feeding station in
New Hampshire in winter, groups of them flew to a brook to
drink almost every morning.

BATHING IN SNOW

I watched crows snow bathing in New Hampshire on several
mornings after snowfalls of 8 to 12 centimeters. First one and

then a few other crows came down on the morning of February 5 until a total of nine bathed in one area, as if the impulse to bathe were contagious. The crows ducked their heads and beat their wings in the same manner as when bathing in water, but none preened afterward.

SUNBATHING

The only time I observed sunbathing, as distinct from sunning, in which a bird merely rests in the sun, was when a crow perched on a fence post in Florida, raised its head feathers as it tilted its head back and to one side, and then passed into a trancelike state. It held this position for three to four minutes, opening and closing its white nictitans while holding its bill open and pointed up. This trancelike state is also a feature of anting.

ANTING

I first saw anting in a hand-raised juvenile that flattened itself out with wings extended upon encountering a small column of ants on July 3. It picked up a few and tucked them into its plumage. Some days later it repeated the performance by a small ant hole. I was surprised in both instances at how few ants it took to induce the behavior. I observed anting in a wild crow on September 2 in the schoolyard next to our house. When I first looked out, I saw two crows watching a third writhing on the ground as if injured. The latter, with tail and body flat to the grass, was constantly moving as if trying to get close to the ground. It then stood up to poke items too small for me to see into the underfeathers of its wings. The crow performed four or five rounds of alternately flattening against the earth and standing up in the next three minutes. It then walked away as if nothing had happened.

On May 10, 1986, a warm, sunny day, my son Ben observed a crow anting on an anthill 40 meters distant. The crow behaved in the same manner as the one in the schoolyard that we had observed together. Hendricks (1980) observed two wild crows anting for three minutes by an ant mound in May. There were no ant mounds in the schoolyard, nor could I find any ants when I went searching after the crows had left. I had made my observations from a distance of 220 meters, however, and was not sure that I had located the exact spot.

Potter (1970) found that August, the month when most passerines molt, is also the month when most anting takes place. She further observed that anting is apt to be most intense when it coincides with heavy or prolonged rain. The summer of 1985 was dry in Lyme, but there were several days of rain that ended on the morning of September 2, the day I witnessed the anting. Southern (1963) noted a similar pattern when three species of birds came to feed, bathe, and ant within thirty minutes of his watering a lawn during a drought.

Birds can ant both actively and passively. Those anting actively pick up ants and apply them with their bills. Birds anting passively let the ants run through their plumages. The passive method was the only one observed by Hendricks (1980). The crows that Ben and I watched, in contrast, anted both actively and passively.

There are many theories on the value of anting. Kelso and Nice (1963) and Weisbrod (1971) believe that it controls feather mites, while Whitaker (1957) and Potter (1970) think its value lies in soothing skin irritation. These theories are not irreconcilable. There is no doubt about the forcefulness of the anting impulse. A bird that is anting will persist in the face of danger, as Hendricks (1980) noted when the crows that he observed allowed him to come within seven meters, even though they recognized that he was there. There must, therefore, be some immediate pleasure or satisfaction, such as relief from irritation, to explain this. But this would be only a proximate factor. It is likely that control of feather mites (Acarina, Analgesidae, and allies) (Weisbrod 1971) is the ultimate value, since feather mites can destroy remiges (Kelso and Nice 1963), which are the main feathers attended to in active anting.

Hendricks (1980) and mine are the only accounts, as far as I am aware, of American Crows anting in the wild. Anting by American, Northwestern, and Carrion Crows in captivity is summarized by Whitaker (1957).

Bill Deformities

In our years at the Hendrie ranch I saw four crows with tips of upper mandibles growing sharply downward for a centimeter, giving a hooked appearance. I called these crows "hookbills." The one I watched the most was a yearling. It was able to pick up corn and pull off pieces of carrion as readily as other crows did. I wondered whether it would be able to feed nestlings, but it did so from the beginning, making more visits to the nest than a sibling with a normal bill. Hookbill drove away a Turkey Vulture flying near the nest and, in most activities, did not appear to be different from other crows. But, like other hook-bills, it was unable to preen the feathers of its back. The messy appearance of these feathers plus a missing wing feather made Hookbill easy to identify. A peculiarity was that the breeding female allopreened Hookbill more than any other crow in her group, including her mate. Goodwin (1976) notes that sick captive birds that sit about with feathers fluffed are frequently allopreened by others, including social inferiors.

Hookbills in adult plumage fared less well. One that I watched for three years in the B group would fly to a branch or fence post and caw steadily, as if afraid to come down when others were feeding on corn. It would come down to feed only when the others had flown, reaching in sideways as if still apprehensive. I noticed in 1984 that this individual, although it came near the nest a few times, did not feed the nestlings, possibly fearing to come close to others of its group.

Birds of many species have been found surviving in nature with bill deformities (Pomeroy 1962). Good (1952) collected two American Crows with bills so deformed that it appeared virtually impossible that they could have fed themselves. Yet both were in good flesh, more than two years old, and had full crops. Similarly, Nevin (1962) describes a Rook that was well nourished in spite of having an upper mandible so curved that the tip was embedded in the skin of its breast. It seems likely that such birds are fed by conspecifics, but few observations have been made. Among them are those of Verbeek and Butler (1981), who noted a male Northwestern Crow on many occasions feeding an unmated female with a deformed bill.

Deformities have been described in nestlings of other *Corvus* species. Klapste (1983) observed a Little Raven with crossed mandibles that survived to leave its nest as a healthy fledgling, and Stiehl (1985), two hatchlings, from separate nests of Common Ravens, that had malformed bills and subsequently died. These findings along with mine suggest that some bill deformities could be either genetic or induced by teratogenic agents acting on the embryo or growing chick.

Dead and Injured Crows

I found a crow caught in a barbed-wire fence on a day of strong, gusty winds. The skin of one wing was so entangled that I had difficulty setting the crow free. Other injured crows included two that limped or held one foot up from the ground for several days. One was a female that hung upside down to pull sticks from the bottom of her nest and the other, a breeding male that limped badly on one day in early January and again five weeks later. He also had some broken wing feathers. Being a dominant male, he could conceivably have injured himself flying at other crows through branches of trees, as I observed him doing on several occasions.

At noon on a warm, sunny day in 1985 I found an adult crow lying dead on the grass. It was limp and seemed to have died recently. There were no apparent signs of injury or disease, not even after the bird had been skinned. A peculiarity noted when I picked the bird up was that it had died in the sunbathing posture.

I noticed a crow in New Hampshire on March 24 lying dead on the snow with no other crows paying any attention to it. It appeared to have just died, for the body had not been there an hour before. The crow, its red gape identifying it as a yearling, appeared to be well nourished, in good health, and without signs of injury. Townsend (1923) gives an account of a crow that he found dead in Massachusetts on January 1. He had watched a crow at the top of a birch tree with one foot hopelessly entangled in a piece of string an hour or so before. Another crow swooped within inches of it, both crows cawing violently. The crow in the tree was still tied fast an hour later. A second one, still warm, lay dead on the ground below. Townsend performed a necropsy but could find nothing wrong. He was tempted to say that the crow had died of grief. Konrad Lorenz's (1978) description of the effects of loss of a mate in Graylag Geese lends plausibility to the idea.

Why Are Crows Black?

Although I know of no real studies of the problem, Walsberg's (1982) article entitled "Coat Color, Solar Heat Gain, and Conspicuousness in the Phainopepla" offers ideas that would seem applicable to crows. The black of the Phainopepla makes the bird conspicuous in daylight hours, which is good for social signaling, courtship, and territorial defense, and for inconspicuousness at night or during the day when a bird is resting in the shade.

The mirrorlike specular reflections, which are most conspicuous in dark-colored birds and are sometimes striking in crows, depend on strong angular reflection. Crows coming to a feeding station that lay between me and the sun in the late afternoon looked white or mostly white, when flying or on the ground. It is difficult to know what selective advantage, if any, such a marked color change might have. I have noted, however, that specular reflection can add to the visibility of wing-tail flicks when viewed from a distance.

One might suppose that black would be a handicap in hot climates. But Skead (1952) reports Black Crows in South Africa foraging in the sun when the temperature was 40 degrees Centigrade (104 degrees Fahrenheit) in the shade and all other birds had retired. Walsberg (1982) points out that black does not necessarily mean a greater heat load. It can actually mean less of a load than white, because although the black feathers of Phainopeplas absorb much short-wave radiation, wind and convection readily disperse it.

13. Play and Thinking

Play is a window into the animal mind. When I made initial observations on crows in Florida, I realized that it is not always easy to know, with a new bird, what is play and what is something else. Hence I was content to use the term "play-like." But with more years of watching I feel that many activities of yearlings, particularly in the early breeding season, are as much play as those of a kitten cuffing a ball of yarn or a dog chasing a stick. Provoking animals that were larger or more powerful than themselves to get them to react in some way, was also play in that it had no immediate benefit and seemed to be a way of learning—of learning about animals that were a part of a crow's environment.

Play of Yearlings Early in the Breeding Season

WITH OBJECTS

One of the pleasures of watching crows in Florida was seeing the playfulness of yearlings when the breeding pair were starting to build a nest. In late January three crows came to a tree in which crows would rest and preen in late morning. An adult of the breeding pair perched on a limb while two yearlings moved about between branches and the ground. One swung from a streamer of Spanish moss while hanging upside down. The yearlings next picked up smaller streamers, both pulling on one in a tug-of-war. Their attention was diverted to pecking at sticks held in their toes. One flew into the air a number of times with a stick in its bill, then dropped and caught it with its feet before the stick reached the ground. The two finally perched on either side of the adult, each with a stick in its bill.

I later found a yearling perched on the back of a cow pecking at a stick held between its toes. When the stick fell, the yearling flew to the ground and fetched it back. Then, in wiping its bill, the stick fell again. This time the yearling cached the stick in a tussock, covering it with pieces of cow dung.

Yearlings played with other things. On February 7 I found two of them playing with a weathered raccoon skull. One would play with it for a while, carrying it to the top of a tree stump, pecking at it, then letting it fall. When the first one wandered away, the second one manipulated the skull in its turn. When both crows were about to leave, one of them covered the skull with pieces of dry cow dung, a material much favored for hiding things.

The A1 crows in 1984 consisted of a breeding pair and two yearlings. In the interim between completion of the nest and egg laying I sometimes found the group in trees near the nest or walking on the bank of a nearby canal. One of the yearlings on March 4 picked up a leaf and moved toward the other. When the latter showed no interest, the first one cached the leaf in a tuft of grass. It then hung upside down on a branch. Following the nest's failure on March 24 and the lack of any effort to renest, the crows again seemed to have nothing much to do, especially in the latter part of a morning. One of the yearlings was particularly playful on April 5 in swaying upside down from a loop of Spanish moss for two minutes before dropping to the ground to pick up a stick.

Playing with Vocalizations

The yearlings of a group usually associated with each other when idle, as often happened by midmorning early in the breeding season. At these times I was apt to find them making mixtures of low caws, *cu-koo*s, *g-wal-op*s, and other sounds, as if playing with their voices. Each had its own repertoire, repeated day after day, so established that I could recognize individuals at a distance. A place where I generally found the A1 yearlings was by a series of fence posts in open pasture. I could tell the two yearlings apart because one, usually silent, had a hooked bill and the other a normal bill. I found the latter on several mornings making a continuous stream of vocalizations that I called "many caws" [Fig. 4(E)]. This was in snatches between bouts of playing, once with a large primary from a Turkey Vulture and several times with sticks. It was the mixture of vocalizing and picking up objects that made me believe that both activities were play.

COPULATORY PLAY

At the time when pair A was performing copulations, one of their yearlings picked up a lump of clay, hurried to its companion seven meters away, then lay on its side while still holding the clay. Its companion pecked at the clay mildly. The first yearling then stood with wings out and tail on the ground as the second one came behind and pecked it on the back. The first yearling then assumed an odd posture in throwing its head as far back as it would go while still holding the clay. Breeding females sometimes throw their heads back in this manner when mounted by a male, and either of a pair may hold objects in the bill when copulating. The yearlings could thus conceivably have been playing by copying behavior observed in the breeding pair. This also seemed possible for the yearling lying on its side, a behavior which, curiously, I had noted when male A was close to his mate on the same stretch of canal bank.

Dancing

The crows at the ranch were alert to the activities of animals around them. When a pair of Sandhill Cranes started to dance on February 4, a crow flew to them immediately. The crow moved about in bounces, with wings open, while keeping ahead of and among the cranes, as if the dancing were contagious. I observed similar dancing in one of my hand-raised crows. Seeing me coming when perched on the roof, it partly spread its wings and quivered its tail, then picked up a twig and did a series of jumps, turning to one side and then the other as it did so. On the following afternoon I found it dancing by itself on the lawn. Its turns and leaps with wings out reminded me of the dancing of cranes. Although I have not encountered descriptions of American Crows dancing, Skead (1952) describes the dancing of a family of Black Crows on the roof of his farmhouse in South Africa.

A crow alighted between two carcasses on the farm in Lyme on January 21, one carcass having four or five crows working on it and the other, four meters distant, two or three. The crow did four jump-ups upon alighting, then flew off into the snow, away from either group of other crows, and did sixteen more, bouncing about 15 centimeters into the air each time, wings half-extended as it moved this way and that, like the hand-raised crow that danced on the lawn. None of the other crows that I watched all winter did anything similar. A raven, however, that like other ravens was apprehensive about coming to carcasses, had performed many jump-ups and jump-backs on approaching one of the carcasses a short while before. It thus seemed possible that the crow could have been stimulated by the jumping of the raven, which, against a background of snow, was a striking performance.

WILD TURKEYS

When I scattered corn, wild hen turkeys, which had become even tamer than the crows, often came running to get it. This made little difference in our first years of watching, for the two species were able to feed more or less together. But by 1984 the turkeys had become more aggressive, chasing each other as well as driving the crows away. The crows soon ceased coming. I then noticed that a few of them had begun teasing the turkeys. This was easy to do, even when I had not scattered corn, for the turkeys had come to associate a crow doing something on the ground with feeding on corn. One turkey might even run from a distance to investigate. Male crow MB was making contorted bows on a pasture one morning when a turkey ran toward him. MB picked up some debris and ran with it, picking up and dropping several more items as the turkey pursued. When the turkey got close, MB jumped onto a snag and displayed a stick. When the turkey walked away, the crow walked after it, pecking the ground. The hen then turned and ran at the crow with wings out and tail elevated, in the same way it would have attacked another turkey. MB faced the turkey momentarily, with wings out, then retreated. The interplay, with MB following and provoking the turkey each time it tried to leave, went on for seven minutes. The crow even jumped over the turkey's back on one occasion. In an interlude the crow flew to a fence post 20 meters away with the turkey following to the foot of it. The two then flew back to where they had started, the crow swooping on the turkey on the way.

I was watching a crow working on a cow pie on the following morning when a turkey ran to it. The crow, taking a piece of cow pie in its bill, moved away, the turkey in pursuit. The interplay that followed was much the same as what had occurred the day before. Provoking Wild Turkeys was not limited to the B crows. An A crow repeatedly approached some feeding turkeys on February 18, and a small hen kept chasing it away. Each time the crow was chased, it picked up and dropped debris and made a number of odd vocalizations.

*Provoking
Other Animals*

River Otters

There had been a prolonged drought at the Hendrie ranch when we first began going there in 1981. Walking catfish had concentrated in a water hole, and Jane and I watched otter coming to the pool to catch them. Whenever an otter came running over the pasture, a number of crows gathered to follow it. One of their interests was scavenging heads of catfish that the otter had dropped without eating and another, following the otter as if looking for a chance to pull its tail. We observed tail pulling twenty-eight times. On only one occasion, however, did a crow succeed in getting food. It seemed as if the crows had an inclination to provoke the otter, whether it happened to have food or not. The otter sometimes whirled to face its tormentor, but usually continued with what it was doing as if not greatly concerned.

Tail pulling is common to a number corvids (Goodwin 1976). It is apparently innate in some *Corvus* species, for one of our hand-raised crows pulled the tails of sheep in its first summer and a hand-raised raven the tail of our cat. While the habit can be useful for stealing, it seems to be a source of amusement when food is not involved, as though a crow enjoyed getting an animal or bird larger than itself to react.

Trying to Fool a Red-shouldered Hawk

When the crows scavenged catfish heads, they were sometimes robbed by a Red-shouldered Hawk that perched by the water hole. Three crows were walking on the bank on January 28 when the hawk landed among them. It looked around as if it thought the crows had prey, but finding none, it flew back to its bare tree. One of the crows then picked up a ball of clay and held it up in its bill as if displaying it. Other crows crowded around. A few pecked at the clay mildly. After a minute the first crow and a companion carried the ball to a clump of grass and covered it with three pieces of turf and a piece of cow dung in the way that I had seen crows caching catfish heads. When the crows left, I found that the ball consisted of blue-gray clay, two to three centimeters in diameter, with nothing inside.

While it is impossible to say whether the crow was baiting the hawk to attack, the circumstances did suggest that explanation. Like the Wild Turkeys and corn, catfish heads were, to

Figure 12.   An American Crow pinching the tail of a river otter. The otter drops its fish and whirls around as the crow in front moves in to steal the fish.

the hawk, a probable prize if crows were working on something. It swooped on crows when they had fish heads and on three occasions when they were carrying wads of turf as lining for a nest. Occasionally, such as just before the clay ball incident, the hawk swooped on crows that had nothing but were gathered together as if they did. Curiously, the clay picked up by the crow was not unlike a catfish head in size, rounded contour, and blue-gray color.

One interpretation of the crow's behavior was that it was trying to deceive the hawk. It is conceivable that, if the hawk could be baited into making blank attacks, it might be less likely to attack a crow that really had something. The hawk was one of a pair that nested in the vicinity of the water hole later, and the crows had ample time to become accustomed to it.

That crows can play with a hawk was indicated on January 28, when a yearling, making a mixture of low caws in a kind of vocal play, flew to within three meters of a Red-shouldered. The hawk flew at the crow and the crow retreated. But when the hawk perched, the crow, still vocalizing, approached again. The hawk chased the crow three times in four minutes, each time for three to four meters among the branches of a red maple.

Thinking

We can often tell by look and behavior when someone has a problem and is thinking about it. Similarly, I have said to myself on a few occasions when watching a crow at close range: "That crow is thinking." The selective advantages of crows forming images and thinking consciously are too great to be dismissed by the dodge of anthropomorphism. How much time, I sometimes wonder, have critics using the word spent living with birds as intelligent and generalized as crows, and by living I mean not only with hand-raised individuals but also with ones, such as those in Florida, that allowed a close approach? A number of situations in which I thought crows were thinking, that is, facing alternatives and coming to a decision, are given in the sections that follow.

LEADERSHIP IN TERRITORIAL INVASION

The five crows of group A that had lost their nest to a raccoon were foraging in a pasture 40 meters from their boundary when one of them assumed an upright pose, with head high. Its bill pointed toward the nest tree of the B crows, 200 meters away. The crow held its pose for twenty to thirty seconds, then flew directly toward the nest of its neighbors. The other crows, which had been foraging, followed the lead crow immediately. All I saw in the following minutes was a melee above the B nest tree. My next glimpse was of the five A crows returning the way they had come, with the B crows in pursuit.

Crows of neighboring groups are apt to make intrusions into each others' territories at times of completion of nests, as I have noted for crows in Florida and New Hampshire and as Wittenberg (1968) has for Carrion Crows in Europe. The invasions reflect a curiosity as to the nesting stage of a neighboring group. The nest of the B crows had been taken over by a raccoon on the morning the five A crows intruded. Both groups had thus lost nests within a day of each other and were in much the same situations in regard to renesting, which both did later at about the same time (Fig. 9). The lead A crow, when it assumed its upright position with bill pointed toward the B nest, was, I think, making the decision about invading. Although the others of its group continued foraging, they may have understood what their leader had in mind, for they followed immediately.

I witnessed other intrusions in New Hampshire that seemed to be planned by a lead crow. The three crows of the N group were aggressive in December, 1983, in pushing their boundary with the S crows to the south. The deliberate behavior of the N crows was most striking on December 17, when all three came to the boundary at sunrise. A lead crow landed 30 meters beyond the boundary, then walked 30 meters farther into the S territory before stopping. The two other crows stayed at the boundary. The three N crows held these positions for twenty minutes, as if waiting for arrival of the S crows. When the S crows arrived, the two N crows that had stayed behind joined the lead crow in aerial melees with their neighbors.

If the N crows had not been acting on a preconceived plan, why had they taken a set formation, one that they had used on two previous occasions when the S crows were there, then waited for their rivals to appear? A conceivable reconstruction is that the lead crow expected the S crows to come to the place they had come before, and they did. Having been pushing the boundary south for several years, the lead crow's idea was to keep on doing so, and it was this kind of thinking that kept it waiting. Of course I did not know what went on in the crow's mind, but I had an impression that it had some conscious notion of what it was doing.

The lead crow appeared to exhibit appetitive behavior for aggression in which, as Marler (1952) describes, an "animal searches for rivals because it has learned to expect them . . . at particular places." Those for Chaffinches he was studying, as for the crows at the farm, were "recently contested areas."

Bunching and Leadership

I observed bunching prior to territorial conflicts in Florida and in New Hampshire. When crows of the A and B groups were feeding nestlings in Florida in April, I scattered corn close to their common boundary on the B side. The eight B crows started to fly to it but, seeing their rivals approaching, swerved to alight on a leafless tree. After five minutes of cawing, the B's flew not toward the boundary but 20 meters back into their own territory. There, seven of them bunched on the ground with an eighth, a lead crow, standing two meters in front of the others (see Fig. 3, top). Then all flew at the A crows. There was a mild conflict before the groups separated, the A's to fly back to their territory and the B's to feed on their corn for the first time.

Bunching before an attack was the same in New Hampshire. The formation was suggestive of a football team falling back for a huddle, then launching an offense. It would seem that a leader would be needed in such situations for otherwise, how could the eight crows of the B group have had the same thought at the same time? It is often difficult to detect a leader in the confusion of group movements. Gaston (1977), in studying the problem among cooperatively breeding Jungle Babblers, believed that either the breeding male or female was the initiating bird.

Curiosity and Learning

Two crows that were foraging in Florida suddenly lifted their heads and flew to join two others 150 meters away. All four then followed something in the grass that caused them to jump back. A few low notes were the only vocalizations I heard. The crows left after a few minutes, and walking over, I found a diamondback rattlesnake. Once the crows had had a look, they had nothing more to do with it possibly because of their seemingly innate fear of snakes or because it offered no promise of food.

The incident illustrates the curiosity of crows. Crows spend much time foraging individually, inspecting what another crow has found only when the two happen to be close. But if a crow at a distance finds something unusual the behavior of the finder communicates the news, an indication that crows keep watch on each other even when far apart. A value of this quick curiosity is that members of a group can learn from each other what particular food may be available and where, on a particular day.

Resourcefulness in Relation to Avian Competitors

I witnessed resourcefulness several times when a crow tried to get a larger bird to move away from food. In one incident a Black Vulture alighted by two crows that were feeding on the carcass of a wild hog. When the vulture started to move, one crow jumped over its back several times as if to keep it moving. When this failed, the crow crouched on one side of the vulture and then the other, making loud *g-wal-op, g-wal-op*s. The vulture then flew, pursued for a short way by the crow. The sequence of behaviors revealed not only the crow's resourcefulness in trying one device after another, but also, I think, some comprehension of the psychology of the bird it was trying to move.

Another episode began when a Red-shouldered Hawk robbed a crow of a catfish. Other crows gathered around, but the hawk was not intimidated. It flew into the thick of a live oak and perched there for forty-five minutes, the fish in its talons. One crow kept returning to perch within 35 centimeters of it, making not only loud and varied cawings, but almost every other vocalization a crow can make. It seemed as if the crow were trying to get the hawk to release the fish by bombarding it with sound. The crow was not successful. But it may have learned something about Red-shouldered Hawks by spending so much time close to one. Humphrey (1974) speaks of social primates as being "nature's psychologists" in the way they learn by watching not only animals they exploit in one way or another but also larger birds and mammals with which they compete.

Deciding between Alternatives

Crows that brought food to the incubating female on nest A2 in 1984 consisted of the breeding male and three auxiliaries in adult plumage. All brought food regularly with exception of a male auxiliary, BF, marked by a broken wing feather. BF behaved differently from the other crows on three mornings in flying toward the nest, then swerving to alight on the pasture below as if he had changed his mind. He faced me each time for several minutes in a frozen, semicrouched position, which led me to believe the crow was thinking. Set on one course, he had switched to another. His problem, it seemed, was "Shall I go to the nest with the food I am carrying or, since things do not look just right, shall I fly away and store it?" BF's decision each time was to store the food rather than fly to the nest. He was as tame as the other crows when I scattered corn, but unlike them, he appeared to be hesitant about visiting the nest when I was watching. Hence the need to stop and decide what to do.

Presenting an Idea

I fed the crows at the ranch every morning but later on some mornings than on others. I was walking across a wide stretch of open pasture on January 15 with no crows in sight, when I was surprised to hear a *cu-koo* call behind me. When I turned I found a crow that had alighted eight meters away. It gave five more *cu-koo*s and left. As described in chapter 5, these were the only vocalizations that the crows seemed to address to Jane or me directly. They were also used by crows in greeting each other.

I was crossing the pasture some days later when I again heard *cu-koo*s behind me. This time there were five A crows. They were thickly bunched and making rapid pecking motions as if feeding on corn, although I could see no corn or anything else there. I had never fed the crows in midpasture, so the place had no associations. Jane and I had noticed before, however, that when crows had not been fed, they might go to their regular feeding place and go through a pantomime. It seemed plain to both of us at those times that the crows were telling us what they wanted. What was unusual about the open pasture was that they should have done so well away from wherever I had fed them and that they had used a single call to draw my attention. An interpretation is that the crows looked upon me as an animal that dispensed corn. Wanting me to do so on a morning when I had neglected them, they followed me, caused me to look around, and then all five, acting together, sought to convey the idea of what they wanted.

Crows interacted with various animals at the ranch daily: a cow with lice, which called for one type of approach; an otter another; and a biped with corn something else again. But conveyance of ideas is not all one-way. A feral hog may solicit delousing by lying on its side in front of a crow, or a cow by holding its tail straight out as a perch. Cow and pig present the idea of what they want by soliciting. The crows did the same when, by their pecking motions, they "told" me what they wanted.

Discussion

Thinking and intelligence. Various behaviors have been cited as reflecting intelligence in crows. Tinbergen (1953b) and Griffin (1984) consider the dropping of hard-shell prey on rocks an example of such behavior. But the habit could have been a routine for centuries and even learned from gulls in the first place. A more convincing example is that of Grobecker and Pietsch (1978), who describe American Crows dropping palm nuts on a highway, then waiting for passing cars to crack them. The behavior must have been an adaptation to living in an urban environment. But if one had to find some very special situation to demonstrate crow intelligence and conscious thinking one may, unless favored by chance, have to wait a long time. What I have sought to show is that crows think consciously and make decisions as part of their daily lives.

Dancing and play. In describing activities of crows that seem to have been little noted by others, I have used the terms that have seemed best to me. When I used the term dancing for certain rhythmic motions made by Pileated and other woodpeckers in courtship, I became the target of critics crying "anthropomorphic." After all, these critics seemed to be saying that only humans dance. But how did they learn to dance? Certainly not from chimpanzees or other kin among the primates. Africans refer to certain of their dances as the "hornbill dance" or the "ostrich dance," and in what better way can one describe the leapings and bowings of Sandhill and other cranes? Why should it be regarded as scientific to deny behavioral similarities that exist between man and other animals? Song, dance, play, interest in other animals, and thinking as well as instinct for survival seem to me to be a part of the lives of crows best described in words that we ordinarily use.

Play of types that I have watched appear to be common to other *Corvus* species. McKendry (1973) describes a Carrion Crow playing with a short piece of wood, maneuvering it from bill to feet in the air. Gwinner describes tame (1966) and Murie (1961) and Elliot (1977), wild Common Ravens hanging upside down. Few accounts of play have stated the age of the birds involved. Good (1952) describes a yearling American Crow lying on its back tossing a piece of paper with its bill and feet in March, which is the month of nest building in Ohio.

Behaviors carried out in play are mostly ones that can be functional under other circumstances. Jumping over the back of a vulture can be play, as Jane and I observed on two occasions, but it can also be useful, as when a crow did so in trying to drive a Black Vulture away from a carcass. Swinging upside down is another example. When a pair of crows lost a nest in January, the breeding female, in a move toward starting a new one, swung upside down from a streamer of Spanish moss. The moss, used at the start of nest building for holding sticks in place, is not easy to pull loose and swinging is one way of obtaining it. Hanging upside down can also be a means of escape. I saw a yearling doing so when pushed along a branch by a dominant male, and McIntyre (1953) saw a Carrion Crow doing the same when pursued by another crow.

Provoking larger animals.   These behaviors take varied forms, most of which seem to be play. Smyth (1960) observed a mock battle between three American Crows and a pair of Kestrels, individuals of both species diving with such speed on the other that they were carried way up on the upturn from each dive. Both species appeared to threaten and intimidate without trying to strike. Lorenz (1970) describes, among other corvids, a hand-reared Black-billed Magpie as provoking any mammal or bird it encountered regardless of size, first approaching from behind, hopping sideways, and then, when close, pecking with all its might and jumping away. If its victim fled, the magpie attacked again with increased boldness. Blue Jays are described in Bent (1946) as repeatedly flying into the face of a Sharp-shinned Hawk in the fall and being chased. The behavior appears to be common for I have noted it on several occasions and know of others having noted it as well (unpublished data).

14. Evolutionary Aspects of the American Crow Social System

An early speculation (Gaston 1978) regarding cooperative breeding was that it was a phenomenon of warm temperate, subtropical, or tropical climates. This notion has been invalidated by Verbeek and Butler's (1981) observations on Northwestern Crows, mine (Kilham 1984c) on American Crows in Florida, and June Chamberlain-Auger's ongoing studies (see Table 8 below) of American Crows on Cape Cod, Massachusetts. The cooperative nature of American Crows might have been recognized sooner by a closer reading of earlier authors. Forbush (1927) described three crows building a nest by Commonwealth Avenue in Boston, and Good (1952), three yearlings feeding a female on a nest in Ohio. Good did not seem to appreciate what he was looking at, although he realized that it was something of biologic interest. This was before the phenomenon of "helpers at the nest," described by Skutch (1935, 1961), became widely known.

There are forty-two *Corvus* species in the world, but only the American Crow and the related Northwestern Crow are known to be cooperative breeders, the latter only minimally. In those studied by Verbeek and Butler (1981) no more than a quarter of the pairs had a helper, a yearling, and at only one nest was the helper seen feeding nestlings. Since all pairs of crows that I have observed nesting in Florida (n = 16) had helpers assisting at all stages of nesting, from nest building to feeding the incubating female and then the nestlings and fledglings, the following discussions center on them. But the term cooperative breeders is to some extent limiting, since crows can live as members of groups the year round.

Comparisons with Florida Scrub Jays, the most studied of cooperative breeders in the United States (Woolfenden and Fitzpatrick 1984), bring out some of the problems involved in studying American Crows in many places. The jays are naturally tame, occupy small year-round territories, and are confined to a habitat that is comparatively simple and uniform. American Crows, in contrast, live in territories of up to 90 hectares, are apt to be wary in many areas, and live nationwide in a variety of habitats. They are adaptable in moving into cities, suburbs and other man-made environments. American Crows offer an abundance of research opportunities. As far as is known, in no other avian species north of the Mexican border is cooperative breeding developed to such an extent.

Advantages of Cooperative Breeding

PROLONGED STAYS OF JUVENILES WITH PARENTS

Cooperative groups arose when juveniles began staying with their parents through summer, fall, and winter. Remaining on natal territory gives juveniles and yearlings a chance to learn which predators are most dangerous, where to find food in the various seasons, and other aspects of life important to survival, at less risk than if they were on their own. Benefits to parents are more difficult to assess. Until the next breeding season, benefits would seem to be few other than further protecting offspring that carry their genes. When it came to territorial fights with neighboring conspecifics or driving away a Red-tailed Hawk, as I noted in Florida, the nuclear male or the pair did the attacking, the yearlings seemingly not having the experience to do so safely. They cawed as a mob but stayed at a distance. Numbers alone cannot ensure territorial defense. A group of three in New Hampshire was able to enlarge their territory against a group of five in 1982, and in 1986 a group of three regularly kept away wandering flocks of twenty to fifty individuals at the start of nesting. If juveniles and yearlings are not much help in territorial defense, they may be useful in locating food, acting as extra pairs of eyes in spotting danger, and other ways where numbers might count.

Parental care is prolonged in corvids in general. Thick-billed Nutcrackers (Swanberg 1956) feed their young for 105 days and Blue Jays for four months (Laskey 1958). Times for *Corvus* species vary. Families of Hawaiian Crows (Giffin 1983) consist of parents and juveniles remaining together until the juveniles, as yearlings, are driven away at the onset of the next breeding season. One- and two-year-olds, however, may reunite with parents and younger siblings after the nesting season. Loman (1985) found that juvenile Carrion Crows left their natal territories in July and August and that almost none were left from September on. He noted, however, a few territories with three crows in the next breeding season, and in two of these, the extra birds were yearlings.

Breeding males, while tolerant of yearlings, became aggressive toward adult auxiliaries at the start of the breeding season in Florida. When yearlings were present as helpers, older auxiliaries were driven away. But attacks were seldom severe. Those attacked continued to stay in the territory, although keeping away from the nest until dominant males became less aggressive in the later part of incubation. Gaston (1978) considers selection for tolerance in breeding pairs crucial to cooperative breeding.

BENEFITS TO AUXILIARIES

It takes no special adaptations for crows less than a year old to feed nestlings. The instinct to poke food into a begging gape is so strong that there are many reports of one species of bird feeding nestlings of another (Welty 1982). A Blue Jay raised one year took at once to feeding a nestling Blue Jay that I presented to it in a second year (Kilham 1956b). As described in chapter 7, yearlings in Florida showed immediate interest in nestlings. Some nesting activities in which they participated, however, such as helping to build nests and guarding against predators, may take more time to learn than others.

Crows are long-lived birds. There may be no need for them, in maintaining the population, to breed before they are three or more years of age. By continuing to stay on a group territory, participating in all phases of nesting except copulation, incubation, and brooding, older and younger auxiliaries can continue to gain experience that will make them more successful at transmitting their genes later on. Of benefit to parents, theoretically, is that auxiliaries should have more to contribute as they become older and more experienced.

Devotion of auxiliaries of breeding age to nestlings that are not their own raises the question of altruism. But what would these two- to three- (or more) year-olds be doing if they were not helping? Given a shortage of habitats suitable for nesting, as seems to be the case in Florida and New Hampshire, they would probably be in wandering flocks, gaining experience of some kind, but not in nesting and defending territories. Experienced birds, as Coulson and White (1958) showed for kittiwakes, are the ones most apt to nest successfully.

BENEFITS TO BREEDING PAIR

If parent American Crows had to raise young alone, it is difficult to see how they could do as well as they would if one to five helpers were assisting them. With helpers, parents can devote more time to their special tasks: the female to incubating, brooding, and digging into the bottom of the nest to control parasites; the male to mate guarding during incubation and keeping an eye out for predators. If parents are less occupied in finding food, they will have more time for keeping nest and nestlings under surveillance. Another advantage is that if one parent were killed, the other, aided by auxiliaries, would have a better chance of raising the young. Florida Scrub Jays with helpers have greater nesting success than those without (Woolfenden and Fitzpatrick 1984). American Crows in Florida all had helpers, leaving no pairs to serve as controls. Situations, however, may be different elsewhere.

ADVANTAGES TO NESTLINGS AND FLEDGLINGS

Nestlings get more attention in cooperative groups. Fecal sacs are removed more promptly and, in periods when food is scarce, more helpers may mean that food continues to be brought in. Helpers also mean that when food is plentiful, more will be stored against times such as cold mornings, when prey is less available. Young become especially vulnerable to predation after leaving the nest, when they are clumsy at getting about and attract attention by their begging cries. With up to five helpers as well as parents looking after them, their chances of survival should be better.

ADDITIONAL ADVANTAGES TO DELAYED DISPERSAL

Crows are omnivorous, intelligent, resourceful, and cooperative. While maturing in cooperative groups, individuals gain experience in social interactions with associates that may be older or younger, dominant or subordinate. Such experience is difficult to assess. But this does not mean that it is unimportant to the harmony with which cooperative groups, consisting of as many as nine individuals of varying ages and experience, operate. Social skills are ones that may be learned in play, dominance relations, cooperative foraging, and other activities. Having mature gonads does not mean that a crow is ready to breed. It takes time for an intelligent and social animal, whether a crow or a primate, to learn the complex life of its species. Delayed breeding, with one to three or more years as members of a group, may be of value in providing the time needed to reach a maturity that is more than physical.

I have listed what seem to be the benefits of cooperative breeding as though, on the whole, it were advantageous in crows. But this is far from known. Huels (1981), in studies on Golden-breasted Starlings, suggests that cooperative breeders remain in groups because they are forced to do so, rather than because of any inherent gain. This thought occurred to me in Florida, where the B group had four or five auxiliaries that were all, with one exception, adults in three successive years. Auxiliaries, as Huels (1981) points out, may disrupt the reproductive efficiency of breeding pairs by interfering with nest construction, interrupting copulations and incubation, and attracting predators, the first two of these being disruptions that I noted in crows.

Problems and Complications

Adult auxiliaries were not tolerated by breeding males early in the breeding season. Being older, having similar plumage, black gapes, and, as judged by their behavior, greater degrees of gonadal development, they were more subject to attacks. This led to what appeared to be varying degrees of psychological castration, a suppression of sex that was revealed, according to Brown (1978), when removal of one of a breeding pair leads to assumption of its role by some other, previously nonbreeding member of the same group. The extent of psychological castration doubtless varies. Some of the nonbreeding adults that I watched became "thwarted females." The most persistent of these kept trying from incubation through the nestling period to beg from and get close to the breeding male. One even made repeated attempts to seduce him. Some breeding males devoted considerable time to keeping these females, which appeared to annoy them, away. Adult male auxiliaries also cut into the time and energy budgets of breeding males, but mostly in the limited period when copulatory behavior was at its height.

Woolfenden (1978) postulates that the main contribution of helpers to breeding success in Florida Scrub Jays is in decreasing predation. But with few observations of actual predation and what defenses were used, the statement is difficult to evaluate. Of nine crows' nests lost in Florida, four were lost to raccoons that I saw in the nests. In the case where one raccoon that I watched climbed up and into a nest, the crows, parents plus two auxiliaries, were powerless to do anything. They made a few mild swoops and left. Some of the most dangerous predators may come at night. Craighead and Craighead (1969) consider Great Horned Owls as being the greatest factor limiting crow productivity. As with raccoons, it is difficult to see how much help auxiliaries could be in defending against them. When a Red-tailed Hawk entered a crow's nest that had just been completed, it was the parent crows that attacked it after first driving away two yearlings that seemed to be getting in the way. Where auxiliaries might be helpful is that in feeding and caring for nestlings they give a breeding pair more time to be on guard and keep such predators as gray squirrels at a distance.

Importance of Habitat Saturation

Habitat saturation, as discussed by Brown (1978), Emlen and Vehrencamp (1983), and Zack and Ligon (1985) occurs when all usable habitat in an area is filled by breeding pairs. A consequence is that birds reaching sexual maturity have nowhere to go. Not being able to establish a territory of their own, they remain in their natal area until a vacancy occurs. This seemed to be the case at the ranch where there were as many as five adult auxiliaries in one group in three successive years. The ranch provided a stable habitat, which may have been unusual. Cattle raising is a major industry in Florida, with ranches covering a considerable area. Few of them in the south-central part of the state, however, appeared to be as favorable for crows as the Hendrie ranch. Many ranchers cut down all possible trees to attain a maximum of pasture. The Hendries have been exceptional in preserving groves of live oaks and swampy areas of red maples and bay trees, a diversification that provided forage areas in years of drought as well as of heavy rainfall.

Trios as Starting Points

Trios occur in a variety of *Corvus* species, and it is conceivable that they constitute a step toward development of cooperative breeding, should conditions be favorable. Charles (1972) noted third birds attached to eight of twenty-nine pairs of Carrion Crows between October and April. They came as intruders and were not juveniles of a previous year. "Sheer persistence," he wrote, "appears to be the mechanism which permits a single intruder to be accepted as a third bird in a territory." By allowing a third crow to participate in territorial defense but not in nest building or the feeding of nestlings, Charles suggests, pairs conserved energy that they might have spent defending their territories. But accounts vary. Wittenberg (1968) noted that young Carrion Crows of the year before might stay with their parents, aiding in territorial defense until the following March, when they were driven away. Some, however, stayed until the first eggs were laid. Tompa (1975) observed third crows that stayed with a pair in the breeding season in two of thirty-six territories. Loman (1985) describes juvenile Hooded Crows staying on natal territories throughout the winter and becoming permanent residents. He speculates that they could have served as helpers in defending territory and feeding nestlings, but he made no observations. Taken together, the observations of these authors suggest that Eurasian Crows come close to being or actually are cooperative breeders in some instances.

Trios among Northwestern Crows, although not discussed as such by Verbeek and Butler (1981), represent something of a transitional step between Eurasian Crows and American Crows. Approximately a fifth of 138 pairs of Northwestern Crows observed by Verbeek and Butler were accompanied by a yearling that participated in territorial defense. Two of the yearlings fed nestlings. At one of the nests it was observed to do so only once, and at the other, although the helper made 14 percent of the feedings in one observation period, the parent crows were hostile to it.

Among reports of trios in other *Corvus* species are those of Bijlsma and Meininger (1984) on the regularity with which extra birds attended pairs of House Crows in Suez, of McNair (1985) on an auxiliary attending a mated pair of Fish Crows, and of Ratcliffe (1962) on two nests with eggs of Common Ravens that were visited by third ravens. The phenomenon of trios is not limited to *Corvus* species. Wiley (1975) and Eduardo Santana and associates (1986) describe a male and two female Red-tailed Hawks nesting cooperatively and Mader (1975), trios of Harris Hawks, two males and a female, commonly caring for young and bringing food to nests. Among reasons that groups of three may be more successful in fledging young, Mader suggests, is that with an extra adult, more prey may be brought to a nest in years when prey is scarce. It is also possible that with a third hawk, the primary attending hawk will have more time to guard the nest, and, what may be particularly important, if one parent should perish, the other could probably raise the brood with the aid of the auxiliary. Trios have been noted by Blockstein (1986) in Mourning Doves and by Dow (1970), who noted a "ubiquitous trio" in Noisy Miners.

The phenomenon of trios needs study. Austad and Rabenold (1985) noted that while the presence of a single helper led to a threefold increase in the reproductive success of Bicolored Wrens, additional helpers did not further enhance success. It maybe that trios represent a minimal type of cooperative breeding that, should habitats become saturated, may expand to create groups that are larger but not necessarily more effective.

Competition with Other Corvus Species

Fish Crows, Rooks, and Little Ravens nest in colonies, whereas Eurasian, Pied, and Black Crows and Common Ravens, like the majority of *Corvus* species, nest as individual pairs (Goodwin 1976). Competition among *Corvus* species may have operated in the evolution of these various systems. For European species, Roell (1978) describes Carrion Crows as dominating Rooks, Black-billed Magpies, and Jackdaws in fields. But their main threat to these species appears to be nest predation. Carrion Crows, according to Wittenberg (1968), Charles (1972), and others, are the main egg predators of Carrion Crows. If they are able to do well against each other, they might do even better against magpies and Jackdaws, if these species were open nesters, or against Rooks, if Rooks nested individually. From this point of view Carrion Crows may have been a selection pressure leading magpies to build covered nests, Jackdaws to nest in holes, and Rooks to nest in colonies, where, according to Roskaft (1980), they are relatively well protected. It is also thought (Roell 1978) that Jackdaws, magpies, and Rooks nest close to man as further protection against Carrion Crows, which are wary of human habitations.

Do other *Corvus* species exert pressures on American Crows? Fish Crows appear to be more numerous and more successful than American Crows in some parts of the South. In the vicinity of the Archbold Biological Station they nested on the ridge of scrub that runs through central Florida, and did so later than American Crows that occupied flatlands bordering the ridge. Although Fish Crows flew over the Hendrie ranch at times in hundreds, they almost never landed. How then could they be competitors? As wandering opportunists, Fish Crows are specialists. It is conceivable that wandering flocks of nonbreeding American Crows, which are generalists, could be at a disadvantage in competing with them. Better, then, to stay on a natal territory as an auxiliary until an opportunity to breed arises.

Ravens and American Crows are sympatric in New Hampshire. Competition between them on the farm was mostly for carrion, which can be a major source of food for both in winter. Ravens appear to be more adapted to finding and feeding on it than crows and, being larger and more powerful, are able to drive crows away as well as to rob them in midair. Competition among the various species of a genus is worth keeping in mind, for, as Darwin (1859) wrote, "species of the same genus usually have, though by no means invariably, much similarity in habits and constitution and always in structure, the struggle will generally be more severe between them, if they come into competition with each other, than between species of distinct genera."

Urban Crows

Need for Studies in Differing Habitats

Simply spending time with animals will not of course provide one with understanding of animal behavior. Some places are far more favorable for making observations than others, and selection of an optimal place can be more than half the battle. Unlike my experience in Florida, learning about crows in New Hampshire, where the crows were wary and had to be viewed from a distance, was more difficult. Yet fifteen minutes down the road, in Hanover and on the campus of Dartmouth College, people were walking within three to four meters of crows on commons and along sidewalks. Urban crows offer unique study opportunities for anyone living in a town, as Kuroda (1975) has shown in his studies of Jungle Crows in Tokyo.

Urbanization of crows has been going on worldwide for a long time. Probably no crow is more urbanized than the House Crow, said to be, next to the Common Mynah, the most conspicuous bird in India. "Familiarity with man has made the House Crow bold and thievish to a degree," writes Whistler (1963). "It sidles into rooms, alert and keen, ready to retreat at the least alarm, and with a sudden bounce and dash removes food from the table; it robs the shops in the bazaar, if they are left unattended for a moment; it snatches sweetmeats off the trays of the vendors at railway stations." Australians, fearful that House Crows might invade their country, found that their cities were already occupied by five native *Corvus* species (Bell 1984). Babenko and Barysheva (1982) reported that Carrion Crows were well established in Moscow. Studies of American Crows in urban environments include those of Forbush (1927), Funderburg (1967b), Grobecker and Pietsch (1978),

Houston (1977), and Davis (1983), the last three on college campuses. The only study of the cooperative breeding of American Crows in an urban environment and of nesting success in any environment known to me is the continuing one of June Chamberlain-Auger in Cape Cod, Massachusetts (pers. comm.). As shown in Table 8, the cooperative breeding she has observed there is well developed not only in the urban environment but seemingly more so than on Sandy Neck, a barrier beach on which humans have had relatively little impact.

One of the more basic and interesting questions in studying animals that are cooperative breeders is how social organization and ecology may be related (Altman 1974). Austad and Rabenold (1985) found that two adjacent populations of Bicolored Wrens, which are facultative cooperative breeders, differed markedly. In one population only 15 percent of the groups had helpers and in nearly all of them only one, while in an adjacent population, a majority of the groups had helpers, with half having several. Emlen's (1942) study of American Crows nesting in a colony in California suggests that the social organization of American Crows may differ in different parts of the United States and Canada. Carolee Caffrey (1987), of whose extensive studies of western American Crows I have received only a brief abstract as of this writing, has noted a striking variability in breeding systems. "Pairs," she writes, "may breed (1) unassisted, (2) with one or more yearlings helpers, (3) with an adult helper, or (4) with helpers of both age classes. Not all non-breeding individuals involved with the breeding pair help and a behavioral continuum exists from remaining in the natal area and interacting with the breeding pair, but providing no help, to providing substantial amounts of assistance." All auxiliary birds of known lineage, she found, were offspring of the breeding pair.

Comparisons with Primate Societies

Crows are sometimes referred to as being the most intelligent of birds. The discovery that American Crows live in cooperative groups provides an opportunity to compare them with primates that are among the more adaptable and socially evolved of mammals. As discussed by Washburn and associates (1965) and Jolly (1966), primates of various species live in cooperative groups, defending territories against other groups. Jolly believes that the main bonding elements of groups are "friendly behavior," which includes grooming and play, and attraction to infants, with males doting on them as much as females do. There

Table 8. Average numbers of crows, breeding pair plus auxiliaries, coming to nests, in urban and rural habitats

	URBAN				RURAL			
Year	No. of Nests	Avg. no. crows	Stan. dev.	Range	No. of Nests	Avg. no. crows	Stan. dev.	Range
1983	1	5	0.0	5	1	3	0.0	3
1984	9	3.56	1.13	2–6	4	2.75	0.5	2–3
1985	10	4.60	1.35	2–6	4	3.25	0.5	3–4
1985	10	4.60	1.35	2–6	4	3.25	0.5	3–4
1986	12	5.33	2.02	3–8	4	3.75	1.5	3–6

NOTE: Urban data taken in Barnstable, Mass., and rural data on Sandy Neck, Mass. June Chamberlain-Auger provided the data, from her studies.

is essentially nothing here that does not apply to American Crows. The crows, like many primates, live in cooperative groups within territories, with allopreening, the avian equivalent of grooming, and attraction to the young from the moment they hatch serving as social bonds. In primates the female does all of the feeding alone, others in the group only looking at or handling infants, whereas all members of a group of crows feed and care for nestlings.

Comparing crow and primate societies could be of heuristic value in a number of ways. There have always been varying views on the subject of intelligence. Some humans appear to be intelligent in activities that come naturally to them, and less so in those for which they have no interest. Jolly (1966) points out that most notions of primate intelligence come from laboratory experiments where intelligence is measured by gadgetry. Gadgetry, however, is a forte of man rather than of monkeys or, as I would add, of crows. As Washburn and Hamburg (1965) point out, "Learning is not a generalized ability; animals are able to learn some things with great ease and others only with greatest difficulty." Learning, they believe, is rather "the process of acquiring skills and attitudes that are of evolutionary significance to a species when living in the environment to which it is adapted."

Humphrey (1974), extending an earlier suggestion of Jolly (1966), thinks that consciousness could have arisen when it became important for each group to understand the thoughts, intentions, and feelings of the others. Living in groups tends to make primates "natural psychologists." The same could be said of crows, which, starting out as juveniles, have much to learn socially, not only about the crows among which they grow up, crows of varying sex, age, and status, but also the "psychology" of the animals or birds that are their prey, potential prey, or ones they drive from food or rob. Of equal importance is to understand birds or animals that may steal from them or drive them from food.

Regarding intelligence, Andrew (1962) points out that far more species of animals evolved on large continental land masses than on small ones. More species of prey, preyed on by more species of predators, led to a coevolution of intelligence in predator and prey. It is of survival value for each to observe and understand the other. Crows, being omnivorous and resourceful, are being continually tested for intelligence in interactions with other forms of life, some larger than they are. In competing with them for food, it is important to know how they will react. How can a crow learn this? One way is provoking other animals in play. Pulling the tails of otter and running or flying at or away from Wild Turkeys or Red-shouldered Hawks are examples of ways crows acquire information about animals with which they may have to deal.

A notable step in studying primates (Washburn et al. 1965) was the discovery of how rewarding close field observations can be. The work of Schaller (1963) on mountain gorillas and Goodall (1986) on chimpanzees set new standards. A feature of their studies was the care they took to tame and not to frighten their animals. The lesson is one that cannot be emphasized enough in studying American Crows. If one wishes to understand any animal that is intelligent, sensitive, and capable of conscious thought, it is imperative, I think, to study it in its fearless state. Washburn speaks of needing a thousand hours to become acquainted with baboons. But why not a lot more? With any animal or bird, especially ones living in complex social groups, one might, after four thousand or five thousand hours, get a "second wind," and go on for a few thousand more. Long-term studies at close range are essential to an accurate perception of how animals live.

Part IV. RAVENS IN NEW HAMPSHIRE

*Each time I study a new species I am amazed to find
how much more I see after I have become thoroughly
acquainted with it.*

NIKO TINBERGEN

I did not plan to study ravens. But neither had I planned to
study crows. I have always been an opportunist, and when I
found that ravens came to the farm and that I could watch them
at the same time as the crows, I became interested in them as
well. Studying the two in the same setting provided an opportunity to make comparisons and, additionally, to watch for interactions between the two.

No one knows if Common Ravens were present in New
Hampshire when settlement began three centuries ago. All that
is known is that they became established or reestablished there
in the 1950s. Coyotes arrived at about the same time, and their
joint arrival could have been more than a coincidence. Hope
Ryden (1979) raised the question in her book *God's Dog*. Speak-
ing of western coyotes she writes that,

> The raven . . . has a very special relationship with the coyote.
> Though a coyote may on occasion chase these birds in play or
> in an attempt to drive them off a carcass, he does not prey on
> them. The symbiotic relationship of ravens . . . has been noted
> by even casual observers who have given little thought to the
> mutual benefits each bestows on the other. In summer, when the
> coyote hunts brushy cover in search of rabbits, gophers and
> other rodents, . . . ravens often hover about or perch in nearby
> trees, where they can watch for a chance to pick up left over
> scraps. But in winter, when traveling is difficult for the coyote,
> it is the airborne raven who is likely to discover food, and the
> ensuing circling and squawking of these excited birds alert the

Figure 13.   Is the raven at the top of the avian pyramid in mental attributes?

coyote to the exact location of their find. Thus, the coyote is spared having to make a random search through the deep snow, which could leave him footsore and weary.

The farm where I watched crows and ravens was also a place for coyotes. We have listened to their howls and yippings from a hill above the farm for years, and when animal carcasses were dumped at the edge of woods, I sometimes had a chance to watch the coyotes. They benefit crows and ravens by tearing open carcasses of sheep and cattle, thus making the carrion available to birds unable to penetrate the hides themselves.

Two pairs of ravens have nested in Lyme, one on Holt's Ledge, where Peregrines used to nest, and the other, on a small cliff near Post Pond. The latter and their young were the ones that came to the farm.

My first acquaintance with ravens was not in New Hampshire but in northern Iceland. I have said in the beginning of this book that in many things I have been lucky. In the year after I was graduated from Harvard, I was taken on an expedition to northeastern Greenland, a part of the Arctic that few have had a chance to visit. My job was to collect birds and mammals for the Museum of Comparative Zoology. I do not like to shoot things, but in those days (1933) there was little talk about ecology and conservation. Our last stop before heading for the pack ice was Isafiord, in northern Iceland. About two hundred ravens, tame as chickens, swarmed on a shingle where fish were cleaned. I could not shoot one there with so many people around nor could I elsewhere, for once away from town, the ravens became wild and difficult to approach. Then one morning I seemed to have a chance. I had climbed up the inland plateau and was walking about when a raven came circling overhead. This was it. I lifted my single-barrel, 20-gauge shotgun and fired. One small feather drifted down as the raven continued circling, seemingly undisturbed. I lowered my gun, searched my pocket for another shell, and was reloading when I looked up. The raven was back sooner than I expected. Just as I looked up he took a shot at me. A large, purplish splotch (the raven had been eating crowberries) landed on the front of my hat. I took it off and gazed in astonishment. One can say that it was all fortuitous. But that is not the way it seemed to me. The experience left me with a feeling that ravens, in addition to being sharp mentally, may have a sense of humor.

Had I appreciated the potential of crows and ravens as subjects for a lifetime study, I would have started in on them much earlier. To get at the mind of a crow is a great challenge, but to get at the mind of a raven, as I have found in living with one for a year, is an even greater one. Ravens are, to enthusiasts like myself, at the top of the avian pyramid in mental attributes.

15. Behavior in Lyme

When crows and ravens were coming to the carcass of a cow on October 10, a raven pursued a crow flying skyward with a piece of carrion. The raven was unable to get closer than eight meters in a slanting course that carried the two birds well above the trees. The crow dropped its food at a height of about 70 meters, and the raven, closing its wings, retrieved it in a spectacular dive.

Ravens robbed crows in a sustained fashion when I started a feeding station in November, 1984. Five to seven N crows and a pair of ravens came every morning. The behaviors of the two species varied according to whether they came together or alone. When the crows were alone (n = 7), they filled their pouches and bills with pieces of the chopped suet before flying 30 to 150 meters to store them in clumps of grass. They also carried the suet to nearby woods. When one or both ravens came to the suet alone (n = 4), they poked, then jumped back or up with wings out, repeating their jumps three to five times before seizing a piece and flying away. But when ravens and crows came at the same time (n = 14), the ravens, remaining in the woods, pursued crows that came there with suet in their bills. It was difficult to see among the trees, but on several occasions I observed a raven fly off with suet in its bill and on three, a crow with suet fly into the open with a raven in pursuit. The crow dropped the suet each time, the raven diving and recovering it either in the air or on the ground. The crows continued to come to the feeding station in spite of being robbed. It was only after three weeks that they would land only at a distance, not coming closer if a raven was around. The ravens ceased coming and the crows returned to feed.

I started the feeding station again in November of the following year and continued it through the winter. Instead of

Robbing Crows at a
Winter Feeding Station

just the resident group of N crows coming, forty to seventy additional crows came daily and, as far as I could determine, were robbed every morning by a pair of ravens that stayed in the woods. The robbings upset the crows considerably, leading them to fly into the trees with much cawing. I watched a raven pursuing a crow on twenty-three occasions, on ten of which the crow let its suet fall, the raven picking it up. A number of the chases ($n = 8$) were well above the treetops. Jollie (1976) states that ravens seldom attack crows, which can outclimb and outmaneuver them. But I found the reverse at the farm, where the ravens were able to outmaneuver the crows in woods as well as in the open.

Jump-backs and Wariness

One reason that the ravens spent so much time robbing the crows, it seemed, was their wariness about approaching food on the ground. A sign of this was the way they jumped up or back 30 to 40 centimeters with wings partly extended and tails cocked. When I put hen viscera on the snow on December 7, a raven, coming close, seized a large piece with its feet, jumped into the air, and dropped it, repeating the performance twelve times before carrying the piece 30 meters away to eat.

A raven alighting near a group of crows feeding on a heifer on February 15 was conspicuous in jumping back twelve to fifteen times, its leapings appearing almost like a dance. It flew, then returned to jump as before, finally leaving without once pecking at places where the crows were working. Conner and associates (1975) describe ravens as feeding at a landfill once crows had started to feed, with sentinels in place. None of the ravens alighting in trees above my winter feeding station, in contrast, appeared to gain confidence from seeing crows feeding. Crows occasionally did jump-backs on approaching food, but usually only a few and never as repeatedly or as high as the ravens.

The ravens were equally wary of food that I handled in summer. A coyote killed a lamb on the morning of July 22 but was frightened away before it had a chance to eat. I cut the lamb open, knowing that ravens could not penetrate the hide unless I did so. The family of seven ravens that visited the farm came down but did no more than stand nearby. They did this three times in the course of the morning, without any of them feeding. The carcass remained untouched on the following day, but coyotes ate much of it in the night. The next morning I found nine ravens standing by the carcass, the largest number of ravens I had ever seen at the farm. They approached and jumped back a few times but left without feeding. A little later three ravens alighted at a distance and approached slowly. One started to pull at the carcass. But when a fourth arrived and jumped back, they all left. This happened several times, giving an impression that when one raven jumped, it frightened the others.

Snow aided in locating caches of ravens as it did with crows. There were 18 centimeters of fresh snow on December 17, the last two to three having fallen in the early morning. A raven was the only bird at the feeding station, and I saw it fly with a sizable item to the edge of the wood, drop into the snow, then toss snow aside with swings of its bill. After working a minute with head in the hole, it flew away. I scraped snow from the hollow made by its body and uncovered a chunk of bone and fat six to seven centimeters in diameter.

Storing Food in Snow

A lone raven flew from the feeding station again on the following morning. After working twenty to thirty seconds in one depression, with bill pointed up as if swallowing, it flew to a second one. It worked there a few moments, then flew away. On visiting the depressions, I found in the second one a slab of meat, fat, and ribs measuring roughly 12 by 19 by 3 centimeters. Although crows visited the feeding station daily and coyotes had run across the field several days before, there were no tracks of any kind within ten or more meters of the places where the raven had landed. The sizes and weights of the bones plus suet on both days were greater than anything I had seen a crow attempt to carry.

I set out slabs of pig fat and skin measuring about 8 by 12 by 1.2 centimeters on January 11. These were larger than what I had been supplying, and the pair of ravens, after performing their usual jump-ups, flew off with ten slabs in twenty minutes, flying as far as 300 to 400 meters in the direction of their cliff nest before disappearing among trees. It would have been impossible for them, it seemed to me, to have flown so far, consumed the food, and returned within so short a space of time. It seemed likely that they had left the slabs somewhere before returning. My son Ben, when hunting in December, watched a raven glide through woods to a white birch stump, take out a piece of food, and fly off. Our hand-raised raven used a similar rotten stump for storing when flying free at our woodlot.

Pruk *Vocalizations and Red-tailed Hawks*

Ben and I noted for several years that pairs of ravens became largely silent from the onset of the breeding season until the females finished incubating. Hearing *cawk*s and seeing the two of a pair together again signaled hatching. In 1987 we heard *cawk*s begin again from one pair on April 10 and the other on April 12. The only vocalizations I heard from a raven coming to my feeding station in the silent period were *pruk*s, made when a Red-tailed Hawk was present. A pair of Red-taileds came to the feeding station in the latter part of March and early April. The raven made *pruk*s when one or both hawks were perched on an elm above the feeding station (n = 2) but remained silent when no hawks were present (n = 3). Otherwise, the raven, like the crows, paid no attention to the hawks even when, on some days, they fed on carrion not far from them.

A raven was out on a bare field north of the feeding station on March 30 when I noted a coyote walking toward it. When the coyote was within eight meters, the raven flew away making *pruk*s. The coyote searched the area where the raven had been and then walked back to the woods.

I found two ravens of the Holt's Ledge pair making *gruk, gr-aack* vocalizations in woods below their cliff nest on April 12, the day after their eggs hatched. One of the pair continued making the vocalizations when pursuing a Red-tailed that flew out of the woods. I noted the ravens making the same vocalizations, which were different from *pruk*s, when attacking Red-taileds above their cliff nest in late April of the following year. It thus seemed that *pruk*s may be limited to the "silent" period in ravens before hatching, but more evidence is needed. Goodwin (1976) writes of a female raven making *pruk*s when disturbed at her nest.

Preying on Bird Nests

One or the other of a pair of ravens came through our and other yards in Lyme looking for nests so commonly from April into June that we thought of them as harvesting along a regular egg route. They were unusually bold at these times in allowing us to watch from distances of 8 to 12 meters. When looking about and fending off grackles and Red-winged Blackbirds, they made raspy *hew, hew* calls that I have not heard at other times. Although I could not see what a raven did when it put its head into a nest, I did, on one occasion, see one fly off with a large nestling grackle. My son was amused one day in mid-

May when the owner of a large gravel pit at one end of Lyme wanted to know the name of that large black bird that flew off with small birds in its mouth.

The ravens also appeared to look for crows' nests. When searching a patch of woods for the nest of the S crows on April 18, I had just walked out onto a field when I saw a crow flying into it. I then heard a variety of *cawk*s as a raven moved about among the trees where I had just been. The pair of crows that owned the nest followed the raven about. When the raven flew off after three to four minutes, one crow swooped on it mildly, then turned back. I had an almost identical experience with a raven and the S crows two days later. This time the raven, after leaving the vicinity of the crows' nest, continued on to our yard to circle about some pines as it usually did when looking for grackle nests.

The reactions of ravens to attacks by crows varied. A single crow on May, 1985, dived on a raven along the edge of a wood where I suspected crows nested. The raven did a wing-shake, then alighted on a plowed field with head back and bill open, following the crow. When the raven flew, the crow mounted to treetop height and dived steeply as if to strike, the raven again facing the crow by putting its head back and opening its bill. On another day a raven attacked by crows turned in flight four times and flew with wings held vertically. Two crows made intense attacks on a raven in a grove where I suspected they had well-developed young. They pursued the raven into a tree, swooping on it repeatedly. When the raven flew, the crows dived on it, but instead of leaving, the raven returned and the attacks continued.

The most serious depredation of ravens at the farm occurred on June 9, when a family of five arrived at the farm pond where a female Mute Swan had been incubating five eggs in a nest on an island. Hearing a commotion, Walter Record ran out to see an adult raven fending off the female swan while the other adult and three juveniles smashed the eggs and consumed the nearly hatched cygnets (Fig. 14). The male swan paddled about without attempting to defend mate or nest. A little later Walter found a raven trying to attack a Killdeer's nest in the middle of his barnyard. He had circled the scrape and its four eggs with a sheep fence to protect it from cows, and the raven was putting its head through. Unlike the swans, the female Killdeer stayed by her eggs while her mate, landing on the raven's back, pecked at its head. Three Killdeer chicks hatched successfully on the following day.

Figure 14.   One adult of a pair of ravens fends off a female Mute Swan, while another adult plus three juveniles smash the swan's eggs to consume the five cygnets about to hatch.

Manure Pile Headquarters

Raven Family on the Farm in June and July

The Post Pond pair of ravens, which nested 1.2 kilometers from the farm, brought two to five juveniles to it in late May or early June in four out of five years. Ravens like bare, open places, and one was provided in 1985 by a manure pile extending 15 meters along the edge of a field. A pair of ravens and five juveniles arrived on May 31 and made it their headquarters for the next month. The wailing *qua-aa*s of the young carried for a considerable distance. When the juveniles saw a parent flying toward them, they begged with fluttering wings. Although parents fed by inserting their bills into those of the young, they also laid food on the ground for them to pick up, as noted also by Stiehl (1985).

Three days after the family came to the manure pile I saw the male on top of the female, his tail moving up and down. His wings were down on either side as if holding her. He got off after five seconds and walked away. A week later, when the ravens were on the bare cornfield, what I thought was the female walked to within a meter and a half of her mate and squatted with wings out and drooping and tail quivering. She continued this posturing for two to three minutes, as if soliciting the male. He walked to within less than a meter but came no closer. I think these behaviors represented a post-nesting return of courtship, a phenomenon that I have noted in crows.

The juveniles did not associate with each other equally. Three were often together, but one was a loner, staying apart from the others and giving *quaa*s every ten to fifteen seconds when its siblings were silent. There were mornings when the juveniles, bolder than their parents, came close to buildings to perch on small manure piles or on low trees above a hen yard. The yard enclosed ducks, geese, and pheasants as well as hens, and I was afraid that if the ravens started preying on eggs, they might not be tolerated by the owner. Ben solved the problem with a shotgun, firing blank shells loaded with black powder. The noise scared the young ravens enough to keep them from the hen yard, but they continued to stay by the large manure pile.

The juveniles flew to a bare cornfield near the manure pile to walk about and play. Two might face each other with bills open and heads up, then leap away with wings extended, bouncing and turning this way and that. Sometimes one chased another. I several times saw one lie half on its side, half on its back, as if daring another to attack. The juveniles' interest in walking about was mainly in picking up odd objects, a dried corn leaf, a stick, and so on. Three of them gathered around a piece of crumpled paper, each picking it up and holding it in turn. I found a juvenile one morning working on a length of black hose put out with an idea that, looking like a snake, it might frighten crows from the sprouting corn. But it did not frighten the ravens nor did a dead raven hung up as a scarecrow. Verbeek's (1972b) descriptions of play among Yellow-billed Magpies two months of age are similar to what I observed in the ravens.

The parents tried to drive Turkey Vultures away from carrion that I had placed on the manure pile. One of them, with head feathers sticking out in a thick-head intimidation display (Coombs 1978), rushed at a vulture three times on June 8, first from one side then from the other. But the vulture continued feeding. Two vultures and six of the ravens were by a raccoon carcass on June 21. One raven walked behind a vulture six times, pulling its tail each time. The vulture responded by whirling around with wings raised to chase one raven, then another. Five ravens went to the carcass after the attacks ceased, but when the vulture, attended by the second one, approached, the ravens left. A raven resumed the tail pulling a little later. Although tail pulling does not always work, a crow I was watching used it successfully in robbing a vulture in Florida.

The closest view I had of the family was on July 7, when the seven gathered around the carcass of a lamb killed by a coyote. What I assumed to be the breeding male (by his thick-head displays and the way he drove juveniles away) occupied the center of the carcass. The juveniles begged nonetheless, opening their bills but not extending their wings. They followed the male wherever he went, and he fed them occasionally. The coyote, seemingly the one that had killed the lamb, spent most of the morning in the open looking on, as if afraid to come closer while I was watching.

Behavior in Late Summer and Fall

PERCHING TOGETHER AND ALLOPREENING

I began seeing the pair of ravens perching together in July, and they continued to do so into September. It is difficult to tell from a distance whether a pair of crows or ravens is allopreening unless one is in a position to see between the two birds. The two ravens of the pair were a body's width apart on August 7, with one squatting low on a branch and the other standing tall as it allopreened the feathers of the first one's head and

neck. I heard *kok-uk, kok-uk* and *kok-kok-kok* vocalizations
(see Fig. 17) when one was allopreening the other in August.
Allopreening in ravens is described by Harlow (1922), Gwinner (1964), and Goodwin (1976).

Flying Wing to Wing

On three occasions between October 24 and November 12 and
once on March 19 Ben and I saw a pair of ravens flying wing
tip to wing tip, lazily circling and drifting, rising and falling,
with one sometimes swooping gently on the other. The only
vocalizations we heard were *caw-uk*s or repeated *qu-ak, qu-
ak*s. While watching a pair of ravens returning to a nesting cliff
in early January, Harlow (1922) noted that the two "often soar
high up in the air with wing tips touching, the male always
slightly above the female."

A third raven was following on three of the occasions when
we saw ravens flying wing tip to wing tip. Zirrer (1945) thought
that some pairs of ravens were never without an escort in winter
months, and Ratcliffe (1962) observed two nests with three
ravens present and "in complete harmony."

Flight

Ravens fly about and do stunts in the air at times as if enjoying
themselves. I have watched ravens soaring high up in wide circles
like Buteos, against a blue sky and white clouds. Even more
like play is the way a raven, as if to break up the monotony
of a long flight, closes its wings and drops a short ways in rolling over, repeating the maneuver a number of times. Van Vuren
(1984), who noted hundreds of aerobatic rolls over a windy
island, considered them as being play. Our hand-raised raven,
Raveny, made complete revolutions like a propeller when flying free. Play in flight can take varied forms. Jaeger (1963)
observed ravens dashing in and out of water columns shot into
the air by an irrigating system, the birds interspersing their
dives with interludes of soaring.

A sound particularly noticeable in winter woods is the heavy
"swish, swish" sound ravens sometimes make as they fly over.
Zirrer (1945) compares it to a sudden gust of wind. "A good
part of the folklore and superstition of the northern hemisphere,"
he writes, "is undoubtedly due to this . . . unexpectedly sudden appearance [of ravens]." One day when a raven was flying

overhead, Jane thought that I was saying "shush" to the cat in the backyard. Ravens make the swishes, it would seem, when flying is difficult, as against the wind. Although crows may fly with noisy wing beats, as when they fly off suddenly, their flight is generally silent.

Discussion

Storing food.   Gwinner (1965) describes ravens storing in captivity, and I noted our pet raven doing so innumerable times. I have, however, found no accounts of ravens storing in the wild other than one by Simmons (1970) of a raven storing in Tunisia. Bent (1946), Turcek and Kelso (1968), and Knight and Call (1980) mention storing but give few details.

Gwinner (1965) noted that his captive ravens stored when hungry and before feeding. This could have resulted from numbers of them being caged together. One of the few occasions when I saw wild ravens storing was on July 7, when they had fed for two and a half hours on a lamb. It was only after they were sated and had started to walk about, in contrast to Gwinner's findings, that one of them stored a piece in a clump of grass. My hand-raised raven also stored after feeding.

From watching ravens fly away with food in their bills, it has seemed to me that storing by wild ravens could be overlooked accidentally, especially if, as Lorenz (1970) describes, they are wary about being detected. The raven I observed storing in snow was alone both times I watched it.

Black-billed Magpies (Summers-Smith 1984), Carrion Crows (Waite 1986), and American Crows are, as far as I am aware, the only corvids besides ravens known to cache food in snow. Whereas the magpies and the crows poke food in snow, the raven I watched dug by sweeping with its bill, as I have seen my hand-raised raven do with both dirt and snow.

Robbing crows.   A question that arises is why the ravens at the farm should have robbed the crows so consistently. Birds that rob others (see Brockmann and Barnard 1979) usually do so to save themselves the time and energy of catching it for themselves. Fischer (1985) describes Bald Eagles stealing fish from crows that were pecking through a layer of ice to catch them. It sometimes took a crow twenty minutes peck through the ice to free a fish, only to have it stolen by an eagle.

It would have been easier for the ravens at the farm, one might suppose, to have flown to the snow and taken suet for themselves rather than have crows pick it up for them. My impression was that the ravens were afraid of something that might be on the ground and preferred to let the crows take the chances rather than taking the risk themselves. The risks were not altogether imaginary. Traps were set on the farm every year. I found a crushed trap lying within five meters of the feeding station in 1984 and two others set for coyotes near a carcass the crows fed on in 1985. Both of the latter had, fortunately, been sprung by cattle. Coyotes later killed a sheep halfway between the barn and the feeding station. A trapper ringed the carcass with traps that night, and I found a raven caught in two of them on the next morning. One of its legs was crushed, and the bird died within a few hours in spite of my efforts to save it.

Ravens encounter more traps than do crows in Lyme because of their habit of ranging over woodlands while searching for carrion. Trappers have told me of the speed with which ravens find bait, and two trappers have told of catching a raven by the toes. The phenomenon may be widespread, for Brown (1974) reports that ravens with missing feet or legs are common on a dump in Alaska. It could be that the wariness of the ravens about coming to the ground at the farm was due, in part, to a fear of traps, but one cannot be sure. My hand-raised raven, Raveny, which I had rescued after it fell from its nest prior to fledging and had hence never been exposed to traps, did jump-ups to parts of animals or carcasses that I put in its cage.

Various aspects of raven behavior, including wariness in special situations, are doubtless conditioned by human activities. Ravens living in areas with few people, according to Knight (1984), reacted differently to people approaching their nests than ravens in areas with high human densities and higher levels of persecution.

Feeding habits of ravens.   Various authors have described the versatility of ravens in preying on birds and their nests. Marr and Knight (1985) describe a raven that, flying slowly back and forth along a cliff, alighted by a fissure, pulled a Rock Dove out by its tail, then reached in to remove its eggs. Maser (1975), in an instance of what appeared to be cooperative hunting, observed a pair of ravens flying and diving at Rock Doves along the wall of a canyon. When one dove broke away from the others, the ravens attacked in relays, forcing the dove into a stream, where one killed it with a blow on the head. Once the dove was on shore, both ravens plucked and ate it.

Although ravens are predators (Craighead and Craighead 1969), they are primarily scavengers. In Scotland (Hewson 1981) and in Wales (Newton et al. 1983) they are especially attracted to sheep carcasses. Hewson noted that the ravens he watched in Scotland were usually a territorial pair facing competition from Buzzards and Great Black-backed Gulls. Conner and Adkisson (1976) found ravens in Canada feeding on migrating birds killed by passing vehicles along a highway.

Sentinels.   I have never observed sentinel behavior in foraging ravens. Possibly this was because, when with crows, they could have been using them as sentinels. Conner and associates (1975) noted that ravens would not alight at a landfill until there were four to seven crows acting as sentinels in trees while others fed. It seems probable, however, that sentinel behavior varies. Where ravens are plentiful and crows rare or absent, ravens may have to provide their own lookouts. Ryden (1979) noted in Wyoming that a few ravens in a flock invariably acted as sentinels and that coyotes abandoned carcasses at the sound of their alarm calls.

16. Hand-raised Ravens

Initial Experience

I first acquired a raven in Lyme twenty years before I started any special studies, my interest then being mostly in woodpeckers. A young raven, however, is quite an experience regardless of the circumstances, one that I was able to share with our children, three of whom were a great help in raising it. The raven came from Holt's Ledge, collected by a member of the Dartmouth Outing Club when roping his way down the cliff on May 21.

The nestling was at a maximum pinfeather stage and begged readily. He stretched both wings down in lieu of leg-wing stretches and spent much time preening and removing fine debris from his loosening feather sheaths in his "nest," a cardboard box that we had for him in the kitchen. Ten days after he arrived, and several weeks before fledging, he began making harsh, unpleasant vocalizations in clamoring for food. Nestling crows that we have watched at the same stage have, in contrast, been relatively quiet.

The raven was walking from room to room making *co-ah, co-ah* vocalizations by June 8. Lorenz (1970) describes these as a main vocalization of ravens in Europe, but I have never heard the call from wild ones in New Hampshire nor did I hear them from our second raven. When the raven met the cat for the first time, he ruffled his feathers and made threatening noises. He was friendly with us, putting his head down and making low notes that sounded like talk. We let him go in the yard in the middle of June. One of his first moves was to settle in the birdbath as on a nest and take a long, soaking bath. He was fond of bathing but had a near tragedy when he attempted to bathe in the deep garden pool. Not realizing the danger, he became very frightened and had to be rescued. In a brook Hauri (1956) found three drowned fledgling ravens from a nest of four, and he believed they had been attracted there in a search for water.

A difference between the raven and a hand-raised crow was that the raven had a greater liking for being indoors. He would come in readily if a door was open, then walk to wherever anyone might be. Unlike the crow, which sought high places such as the top of a door, the raven rested readily on low chairs or on the counter by the sink, possibly finding these places more like ledges on a cliff.

Storing food or objects became one of his most constant pastimes. When I held out a handful of pebbles one day, he came to me five times to fill his mouth pouch, then made off with a galloping hop to tuck them in tufts of grass. On another day he filled his pouch with pebbles from the driveway, then carried them into the house for storage. As with other objects, they were pushed under carpets, towels, or piles of laundry. Bits of raw liver or hamburger stored in these places left bloody stains. None of our crows stored with such persistence.

When the cat was feeding from its dish one morning, the raven tried to reach in sideways. But the cat drove him away with a paw. In a maneuver that I have seen ravens perform on Turkey Vultures at the farm, the raven went behind and pulled the cat's tail. Although our crows occasionally attacked children, the raven, with head feathers raised, was rougher and more aggressive. He was especially given to attacking bare feet and legs, which, if none were available close to home, he could find by flying to the schoolyard.

The raven crouched, with wings a little out, on the top of a chair and vibrated its tail up and down for several minutes when two months old. The display was identical with Crowsy's performances at the same age. Lorenz (1970) thought that all of his tame ravens were females when they began making tail quivers, which he considered a female mating invitation. He learned subsequently, however, that juveniles of both sexes squat and quiver their tails as a way of greeting their keepers.

By July our raven was amusing himself by ranging about the village of Lyme. On one occasion he alighted on a roof to pick up nails where carpenters were working; on another he visited an old lady on a porch and played with her thimble. Neither the carpenters nor the old lady seemed to mind. But the raven caused trouble one morning by perching above an auction where his croakings drew the attention of the crowd away from the auctioneer, who became much annoyed. There were other complaints of the raven's doing little things such as pecking at bushes. Fearing a repetition of what we had gone through with our crows in Maryland, we gave the raven to a lady who liked and understood animals. She had to move subsequently, and I am not sure what happened to that raven. But there was a semi-tame one around the remoter parts of Lyme for several years, and some thought it was ours. One of the raven's occupations was visiting a pond and meeting boats when they came ashore with fish. Other than that it was fed by Frank Cutting, who lived below Holt's Ledge. If the raven was indeed our bird, it thus returned to the ledge where it had come from and joined others of its kind.

I started watching a raven's nest on Holt's Ledge in early May, 1986. The nearest view I could get was a mile away (1.6 km). Using 11 x 80 binoculars, I had watched the parents feed their young on May 11 and was following them as they left when I happened to look back. At that very moment a well-feathered nestling, unable to fly, fell out of the nest and tumbled head over heels down the incline of the cliff. That was my first view of Raveny. I hastened over to find that not one but two nestlings had fallen to land among rocks at the bottom of the cliff. One was battered and dying. The other looked to be in surprisingly good shape except for one leg that was dangling. Unable to fly or move about among the rocks, it seemed unlikely that it would survive. I put both young under my shirt and took them to the car. The battered one was dead by the time I arrived. I called the other one Raveny. His leg did not seem to be broken, so I presumed that it had been pulled from catching on something. Fearing that manipulating might make things worse, I decided to leave the leg alone.

A Second Raven from Holt's Ledge, 1986

Ben climbed to the foot of the cliff on the following morning and found that the two remaining young had fledged. It was apparent from a photograph, as well as from observations, that the successful fledglings had longer tails than either of the nestlings that I had picked up, an indication that they were probably older. If two nestlings were older and stronger than the other two, they may have pushed the less developed ones out of the nest in exercising their wings. The nest, built in the crotch of a paper birch growing in a cleft (Fig. 15), provided little room for four nestlings about to fledge. Had it been built on a secure ledge, such as described by Warren (1955), things might have turned out differently.

We kept Raveny in the house for two and a half weeks before setting him free in the yard. I put him to roost in a shed

Figure 15.   Nest on Holt's Ledge, supported by a paper birch growing out of a cleft, with two fledgling ravens. Two others fell from the nest, and, when picked up on the rocks below, one had an injured leg and the other was dying.

at night, thinking that he needed the protection. He was flying into neighboring yards by the end of June. Fearing that this might lead to trouble with our neighbors, we built him a large outdoor cage. Raveny, however, still had considerable freedom, for we took him to our woodlot by Holt's Ledge nearly every day in the summer and fall. Assuming that Raveny would have fledged on May 15, the following is an account of his activities, first about the yard and then, from July on, in his large cage.

Roadkills and Fear Reactions

Raveny took food from the start — raw smelt, liver, and chicken — but backed away from us in his first few days as if still afraid. After three days he accepted us completely. He was able to pick up food for himself in two weeks, but continued to beg when hungry or, at times, in seeking attention. I gave him fresh roadkills as often as I could, thinking to develop his skills as a scavenger. But he was wary. When I presented him with a woodchuck on June 14, one that I had cut open, he was too frightened to come down. I then cut off strips of skin with fur, fat, and muscle. These excited him. He quickly swallowed some, then filled his antelingual pouch with others to store on the roof of the greenhouse. When I presented him with a chipmunk on June 24, he reached in sideways, jumped back, then returned, repeating these maneuvers for three minutes before daring to pull out a string of intestines.

An advantage to roadkills, in addition to roughage afforded by the skin and fur, was that they were something to work on. He would sometimes spend an hour or more nibbling small pieces of meat from a red squirrel I had cut in half; he would shake what remained and move it about. A result of Raveny's feeding on roadkills was that I began finding pellets of fur and bone where he roosted at night. After a week of being exposed to squirrels and learning to accept them, we gave Raveny a naked nestling starling. His fear and wariness were as great as to his first chipmunk. In addition to walking in cautiously and extending his neck as if to touch the starling, then not daring to do so, he three times lifted it with the tip of his bill, then gave a frightened squawk as he jumped back with wings out. As with the chipmunk, it seemed that seeing a dead animal move, even though he had moved it himself, was what frightened him. In between bouts of approaching the starling, Raveny walked about pulling up tufts of grass, a displacement activity, and visited known objects as if to alleviate his fear.

The main food I fed Raveny over several months was a sheep that had died at the farm. After removing the viscera, I froze it and then had Ben cut it in pieces with a band saw. Every morning Raveny received a frozen chunk nailed to a log so that, handicapped as he was by his injured leg, he could work on

Food, Fear Reactions, and Storing

it effectively. He usually began by tearing off tiny pieces as if nibbling. Then, jabbing with his straight lower mandible and sinking the sharp curved tip of his upper one into the frozen meat, he made rapid progress. As the surface thawed he had the advantage of pulling thawed bits from a frozen underlayer. No other activity engaged Raveny's attention so intensely as dismantling a piece of sheep. He might keep at it on and off for hours, pulling snippets of meat, fat, or connective tissue from the underside of the skin or along planes of fascia or bone. He seemed to prefer getting his food in many small bits rapidly obtained than in larger pieces. In between jabs at the flesh, Raveny made little snaps with his bill like those a barber makes with scissors after cutting a lock.

Raveny did not swallow wool but became adept at pulling it from skin. If he was working on a raccoon or squirrel, I visited him from time to time to cut off pieces of skin and fur that he could not pull off for himself. Although the proportion of fur to skin was high in some of these, causing big tufts of fur to stick out on either side of his bill, Raveny swallowed them avidly except for a few that he carried in his pouch so that he could store them elsewhere. The pouch, as described by Bock and associates (1973) for *Corvus* species, is actually a lowering of the floor of the mouth made possible by drawing back the tongue, which I could feel by putting in a finger.

Aggressiveness over Food

Beginning in the first weeks of August, at a time when he had acquired plume feathers on throat and neck due to a molt, Raveny became markedly possessive of food, especially chunks of frozen sheep or roadkills. We soon learned that he was dangerous to approach at these times. Making harsh noises and ruffing out throat, head, and his lower body feathers, like a skirt, he could strike with his bill and draw blood easily. One had to be careful. When he was not guarding something he especially wanted, however, he was as solicitous of our company as ever. Jane and I had much the same experience with a pet leopard in Africa. The leopard was friendly until given a hen or other food. Once he had sunk his teeth into it, he became a wild and ferocious creature, allowing no one to come near.

When I stood holding a frozen Evening Grosbeak at the end of September, one killed when it struck a window, Raveny put on his "ruff-out" display and, making loud, shrill cries, sprang into the air six or seven times. He hovered within a few centimeters of my hand without daring to seize the bird, I supposed because it was something new. When I finally gave it to him, he guarded it with great belligerence. Raveny could also be aggressive about other, non-food objects that he prized. One day in September, making a quick dive on my pocket, he seized my glasses and flew off with them. He defended them in the same way that he did the grosbeak, and I had a hard time getting them back.

STORING

One of Raveny's steadier occupations was storing food and objects. He tried to do so within a few weeks of fledging, but had difficulties finding suitable covering materials. When he poked a piece of liver between two logs, all he could find to cover it was a hopelessly large piece of bark. When I supplied some crumpled green leaves, he tamped them down effectively. He was more proficient by the time he moved to his cage in July. Whether in his cage or in the woods, he spent much time poking into places, picking up a small spruce cone or bits of bark, digging a hole, trying to store them, then going on to something else. When he sang at the same time, or rather, made a conglomeration of odd sounds (Fig. 16), as he sometimes did, he gave an impression of being happily occupied.

The amount of effort he put into caching was related to how much he prized what he carried. Although he stored small objects of brightly colored plastic, as well as spruce cones and pieces of bark, he took particular interest in pieces of roadkill, hopping or flying about with them as if searching for just the right place. If he chose an area of bare earth by a post, he would put his prize in a depression, then cover it with lumps of earth. I noted one day that he picked up pieces of moss but rejected them. He had a sense, it seemed, of camouflage in using materials that blended with surroundings. When he cached in a mossy log, he used moss and in grass, bunches of grass pulled or sheared off with his bill. Lorenz (1970) does not believe recognition of the appropriate object for a particular behavior such as storing to be inherited. There is instead, he thinks, an instinctive tendency to try out objects, the range of which is gradually restricted to appropriate ones. Ravens, he found, gradually restrict their drive to hide all objects to the rational activity of hiding food.

One item that Raveny stored with a seeming lack of under-

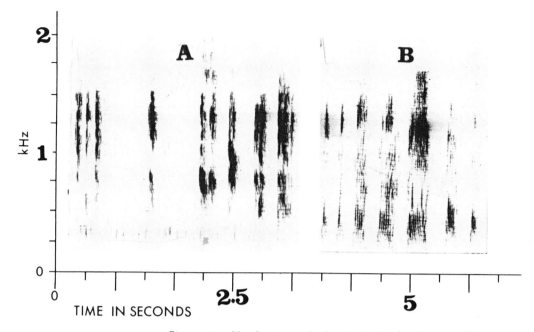

Figure 16.   Vocalizations of a hand-raised juvenile raven: (A) singing; (B) rattling call.

standing was earthworms. I several times watched him pick one up, deposit it, still wriggling, into a depression of earth, then cover it with dirt.

Raveny's cage soon became a place where he had a considerable hoard of treasures cached in odd places. He gave his most convincing appearance of thinking when, with a piece of roadkill in his bill, he went about here and there as if trying to decide into which niche his latest treasure should go. If every place was loaded, as I often suspected it was, he would fly to me with an appraising look. I knew his thought. Alighting on my shoulder, he would touch his bill to my skin, and then, if I wasn't careful, a piece of roadkill would be tucked between my neck and shirt collar.

Carrying Water

We watched Raveny carry about a tablespoon of water in bill and pouch twice in August. The first time, he took the water from a rainwater pool on the flat roof of the school and flew 100 meters to discard it on the roof of our house. A few weeks later he flew from a pool in our woodlot to Ben's truck, throwing water against the windshield. Hauri (1956) watched a parent raven carry water from a pool to its ten-day-old young on a cliff in Switzerland. The raven took the water into its empty pouch on one occasion and on top of food, as though soaking it, on another.

Although Rooks are considered the only *Corvus* species to dig holes regularly (Andrew 1969; Simmons 1970), Raveny dug small sods from under logs, my shoe, or other large objects on the ground. He also dug by picking up lumps of earth and tossing them aside. When rainwater runoff created a hole on the ground inside his cage in October, I filled it with stones the size of a hen's egg and larger. Raveny took immediate interest in digging out the hole, tossing out six or seven stones and many billfuls of dirt from the edge as well as pushing larger stones aside. He was at other times attracted to loose dirt and sand, sweeping it with swings of his bill as I had seen a wild raven do with snow in winter. Noting his interest, I provided him with a pile of sand. Ben, on one occasion, watched him sweep sand aside with a flat piece of wood measuring two by five centimeters, an instance of what might be called tool using.

Digging and Tool Using

Raveny also dug holes in semi-rotten logs in much the same manner as hand-raised woodpeckers that I kept for some years. Both ravens and woodpeckers need to keep their ever-growing bills worn down. We had a rough gauge of the rate that Raveny's bill grew after he accidently nicked his lower mandible one and half centimeters from the tip in midsummer. The tip later broke off but was restored to normal within two months.

DANCING AND ROLLING

Song, Dance, and Play

One of Raveny's more surprising behaviors was to roll on his back, lie like a dead bird for a few moments, then burst into rattling cries as he attacked the foot of his injured leg. After about ten seconds he would roll back onto his feet and go about as if nothing had happened. On two days he repeated the performance twice in five minutes, reminding us of a kitten playing with its tail. As with many activities carried out in play, rolling on the back may have survival advantages. Barnes (1986) witnessed a number of dogfights between Peregrines and a family of ravens. The ravens evaded the Peregrines by rolling over in the air, but one, caught on the ground as a Peregrine passed over, rolled on its back with feet toward the attacker.

Raveny's dances started in the same spontaneous manner as his rolling over. He liked red plastic tops from milk containers and had just taken one from storage when he started leaping this way and that with wings out and head up. It was then for the first time that he rolled over and started playing with his foot. We watched a second episode of dancing five days later when Raveny was playing on the lawn and picked up a small spruce cone. Holding the cone, he sprang a meter into the air with beating wings, four times in succession, all the while making rattles. As when he lay on his back, Raveny seemed to be conducting an imaginary battle. Having watched juvenile ravens in mock fights with each other at the farm, I wondered whether Raveny, having no siblings to play with, had to conjure up "enemies." Although I have not seen adult ravens in jump-up fights or lie on their backs in fights, I have seen both behaviors in fights among crows.

Hanging Behavior

I had supposed that Raveny, having a disabled right leg, would not be able to hang by his feet in the manner described by Gwinner (1964) for his ravens. Raveny, however, started hanging with one or both feet from the netting on the top of his cage in October. A game Ben or I played with him was to pull a trouser pocket inside out. Raveny would then jump up, seize the pocket, and hang by his bill as I once saw him do from a stick he had worked loose in the woods. Thinking that he might like a vertical stick, I hung one by a rope from the top of his cage, the tip about a meter and a half from the ground. Raveny was soon using this in his repertoire, flying to seize the tip in his bill and then swinging back and forth while beating his wings for some moments many times a day. Sometimes when he swallowed my finger I would hold my hand out at arm's length and swing him up, down, and around my head.

Hanging is well known in wild ravens (Murie 1961; Elliot 1977). Elliot was watching six ravens in a dead pine in January when one hung on to an exposed branch by one foot, then "grasped the branch with its bill and released its foot so that the weight of the body was supported by the bill. The wings were partly open but motionless and were not used for support. The bird then gripped the branch with both feet, released its bill and hung by its feet with the wings folded." When the first raven left, a second one flew to the branch and grasped it with its bill. But it was unable to support its weight and flapped its wings. The first raven "then returned, croaking loudly, supplanted the second, and hung expertly by its bill."

Song and Pantomime at a Window

A side of Ben's machine shop, with three large windows, formed one side of Raveny's cage. We put perches by the windows so that Raveny could look in. The light was such that the windows made good mirrors. On some occasions Ben, looking out, saw Raveny stretch his neck, raise his ear tufts, and extend his wings, with bill to the glass, while making odd fragments of vocalizations as if reacting to his reflected image. He also played when no one was around. His high notes, deep guttural sounds, swelling of long neck plumes, and jumps along his perches, flying away and returning, suggested that he was acting out emotional situations. Lorenz (1970) observed the same sort of pantomimes with his tame Jackdaws:

> The song consists partly of imitated sounds, but it also contains (surprisingly) notes taken from the "colloquial language" of the species. The sessile social call-note "kia," the aerial guiding call "kioo," the "Jup"-call and the rattle-call can all be heard in the muddled monologue which the bird utters. Remarkably, the bird adopts the appropriate characteristic posture when uttering sounds with a "communicative" function. For example, the Jackdaw will bend forward and flap its extended wings when rattling, or cower when giving the "Jup"-call. . . . Like an orator, it accompanies its utterances with the appropriate gestures.

Raveny's performances were not limited to his window perches, for he might start rattling and leaping with wings out anywhere, at any time, for no special reason that I could perceive. As Lorenz further observed, "I have repeatedly leapt to the window in order to see what was wrong when a bird uttering a gently undulating song abruptly emitted a loud rattle-call." The windows on one side of our house looked out over Raveny's cage, and I found it hard not to look out many times a day to see what he was doing.

When a fireman from the Hanover Fire Department was watching Raveny perform one afternoon, he remarked that that was what wild crows did almost daily at windows of the fire station. The Hanover Fire Department is at the edge of a golf course, where the crows, being urban, are semi-tame and are regularly about the roof and grounds. "Reflection fighting" before windows has been reported for many smaller birds (Welty 1982). The fighting with them, however, takes place only in the breeding season and is limited to males. Raveny's performances, in contrast, were by a juvenile in the nonbreeding season and only occasionally suggested fighting.

PLAY AND DESTRUCTIVENESS

Much of Raveny's play was destructive. He liked to attack the rubber on windshield wipers, the black plastic seat on a tractor, caps, and many other objects. Young wolves, wrote Rutter and Pimlott (1968), "especially like to take things apart or move anything movable. Anyone working with a litter . . . soon learns to guard such things as shoelaces, hat, and gloves, as these are sure to receive special attention." These remarks applied to Raveny. The destructiveness of young ravens and wolves may seem purposeless, but from watching Raveny's attacks on frozen chunks of roadkills, I suspect that in both cases it could be practice for tearing tough carcasses apart.

Interactions with Other Animals

When a pair of guinea fowl were feeding in the yard on June 10, Raveny kept flying away a few meters while putting out small excreta and keeping his mouth open, both signs of fear that we had noted at other times. Nesting Tree Swallows and Common Grackles aroused his apprehension. When they swooped, Raveny squatted with wings a little out, tail up, and bill open as he made rattling calls (see Fig. 17) and swung his head in facing them. A wild raven at the farm behaved in the same manner when attacked by a crow.

Raveny reacted to our dog in varying ways. Most of the time in June and July he paid little attention to it. On several occasions when the dog went to Ben to be friendly, Raveny flew over and, edging in sideways, pecked or pinched her rear end several times with bill partly open. When the dog ran, Raveny flew after her, hovering above and rattling. These attacks ceased as the two became tolerant of each other. Whenever a strange dog came into the yard, Raveny was usually quick to attack. Four swoops on one large dog were enough to make it leave.

On several occasions when Ben had Raveny on his shoulder and the dog came up to be petted, Raveny gave Ben a pinch on the ear with his bill, something he did at no other time. It may seem curious that Raveny should have directed his aggression toward Ben rather toward the object of his jealousy, the dog, but I had the same experience with a Long-tailed Glossy Starling that I raised in Uganda. I had a small zoo of various animals there, and when I entered it to feed one, the starling was apt to fly to my shoulder and pinch my ear.

Raveny's gentleness toward Ben and me when alighting on a shoulder did not carry over to visitors. He raised his head feathers, then attacked their ankles. If he chose to attack from above, he could be frightening, all too much like a scene from Alfred Hitchcock's movie *The Birds*. Some visitors played with him in spite of the pinches. But there were occasional visitors that Raveny accepted right away. They were, we noted, men that liked animals and knew how to approach in ways that won his confidence.

SMALL TALK   *Bonds of Affection*

One of the most important things about Raveny, recognized early, was his need to receive and reciprocate affection. By learning what he wanted and needed and responding to him, we were supplying the parental and social bonds he would have experienced had he not fallen from his nest. After begging and being fed when we first got him, Raveny liked to push close, making what Gwinner (1964) calls *winseln und gauzen* (tender whimperings) and raising his ear tufts. This later behavior is also described by Lorenz (1970). What is difficult to describe, although Gwinner (1964) does so to some extent, is the expressiveness of a raven's eyes.

As Raveny developed and was free to fly about, he might be busy preening, resting, or poking about for an hour. Then if I came by, his ear tufts would go up and he would beg with mouth open and wings fluttering, even though he had recently fed. We then talked in low whimperings back and forth as I gently poked his bill with a finger. He would also seek intimate sessions at the start of a day and when he went to roost at night. It was at this latter time, at dusk, that Raveny most wanted company. When I entered his cage he sought my shoulder, and with his head against my ear, we talked our small talk together for two to three minutes. At no other time have I felt so much rapport with him. The only parallel that I have encountered is with those who have howled with captive wolves.

"All studies of animal behavior," wrote Rutter and Pimlott (1968), "are impeded by our inability to enter into the animal's world. By howling with wolves it is possible to break down that barrier and, for perhaps half a minute, literally become a wolf." In those last minutes of a day with Raveny, I too had a feeling of kinship. Konrad Lorenz (1978), when asked by a student how she could make geese as tame as possible, replied that she should devote roughly the same care to them as "to a young dog in order to bring it up as a friendly loyal companion. You must take the dog out for walks as often as possible, spend a lot of time talking to it, and if possible allow it to sleep in the same room with you." I took Raveny for walks, spent time talking to him, and though I was not prepared to have him sleep in our bedroom at night, I hoped that the sessions at dusk might be a substitute.

Swallowing a Finger and Allopreening

My sessions with Raveny took a new form in midsummer. When I entered his cage during the day and stood by a perch at eye level, he would fly to me, sometimes with ear tufts raised, and, swallowing my index finger as far as it would go, gradually sink with wings out, while regarding me with a fixed, trance-like stare. I then allopreened him by scratching lightly among the feathers of his throat and the top of his head and around his eyes. These sessions might have gone on a long time if Raveny had had his way. I generally ended them after several minutes by holding his upper mandible as I withdrew my finger. Raveny would have had the fairly constant companionship of others of his kind under natural conditions, and I felt it important to his welfare to give him periodic attention. The location of his cage between the house and Ben's shop, by a path where people were apt to pass, was also helpful in keeping him from being alone for any length of time.

Occasions when Raveny's reactions were especially strong in holding my finger and sometimes sinking low with wings out and tail quivering were ones of emotional stress. On July 9, instead of returning to his cage as I wanted him to, for it was getting late, Raveny flew off to the vegetable garden to attack Jane's tomato plants. Because as he was too interested to respond to usual enticements, I picked him up with wings held lightly against his body as I had done when we first got him. He struggled mildly only just before I set him back in his cage. But when in the cage he appeared to be much disturbed and kept trying to swallow my finger for three minutes. Another event occurred on August 26, when I was nailing something in his cage. I was keeping him away successfully, I thought, when he darted in to get the nail and the hammer knocked a small piece from his lower mandible. Raveny gave a series of short, sharp cries, ones we had never heard before, and flew to nestle down and poke his bill into some long grass. It seemed as if his mandible were as sensitive as a tooth. After resting ten minutes with head feathers ruffed and unresponsive, Raveny flew to a higher perch and, when I approached, raised his ear tufts. He appeared to have an almost desperate need for affection. He also rested on my shoulder, reaching around in an effort to preen my eyebrows. As on other occasions when Raveny had been frightened or upset, he was still solicitous of extra attention on the following morning. If ravens take care of each other when injured, as may be the case for American Crows and other crows, then reversion to fledgling or subordinate behavior may stimulate a care response in conspecifics.

Ravens, like crows, feed nestlings and early fledglings by thrusting their bills into their throats, and males do the same when feeding females in courtship (Gwinner 1964). Raveny, in swallowing my finger, may have been treating it as if it were the bill of a mate or parent. On the other hand, he may have simply swallowed my finger as a way of holding on to me. His leading motivation in soliciting my attention was, I think, neither sexual nor subordinating, but a need of companionship, a fear of being left alone, a need of reassurance. Yearling crows also behave in a seemingly desperate manner when they are isolated and trying to attach themselves to a group. One of the most difficult of all things to endure for a crow, a raven, a wolf, or a human is to feel alone and separated from one's own kind. A sense of belonging is one of the most universal of all feelings.

Allopreening, Molting, and Lice

When Raveny was molting during the summer, we sometimes saw lice on the tips of his head feathers. Having an injured right leg that could not support his weight meant that he was unable to scratch very effectively with either foot in the corvid fashion of leg over wing. Fearing that this might lead to an increase in parasites, we occasionally treated his head feathers with an antilouse preparation. When I allopreened him later, I commonly found twelve to fifteen dead lice coming to the surface. I ceased finding parasites when Raveny stopped molting in September.

Plumage and
Other Changes

A PARTIAL MOLT IN SUMMER

When Raveny's first set of feathers had grown out by late June, I noticed that he was already starting to molt, as indicated by two gunmetal-blue feathers appearing among the black ones on his forehead. These small feathers increased in number, until by early September the whole top of his head was a shiny, iridescent blue. Plumelike feathers, appearing simultaneously on throat and sides of the neck and used in aggressive and other displays, made him look like an adult. Other changes were in the color of his irises, from gray-blue to brown, and of his gape, from bright pink to a dull flesh color with black on inner mandibles and around the end of his tongue. Mouth linings, according to Brown (1974), become entirely black by a raven's fourth year, but Raveny's mouth linings were entirely black by March of his first year. This may have been a result of his having been raised in captivity. Bernd Heinrich (pers. comm.) noted that although the yearling wild ravens that he was banding had pink gapes, two yearlings that he had raised by hand had black ones. This precocity in developing black linings is difficult to explain. It could be related to diet or to hormonal differences.

FEATHERS OF FORTUNE

When Raveny's first set of feathers was still growing, I noticed that those of his median underwing coverts stuck out when he spread his wings or flew. They ceased being conspicuous when fully grown. One or two, however, might protrude when Raveny alighted from a sharp downward or upward flight or was caught in a gust of wind. Keranen and Soikkeli (1985) present photographs showing a male raven "displaying" these feathers to a female in courtship. From observing Raveny, I wonder if the photographer didn't just happen to catch the feathers when they were protruding. Courtship displays are very definite, a function being to prevent birds of similar species from interbreeding. It seems unlikely, therefore, that feathers that can slip in and out of place so easily would be selected for an epigamic display. Keranen and Soikkeli demonstrate that the feathers are inserted into the skin and tendon of the wings in a special way, but it is not clear what the special function is. The authors conclude their note, amusingly, with some Finnish folklore. The raven, it seems, is a bird of ill omen. Hidden below its wing, however, lies a feather of fortune. If a trapper can find it, it is claimed, he will be rewarded by a big catch. I am keeping an eye on Raveny.

17. The Wild and the Tame

Ben owned 30 hectares of woods on the slope of a ridge that ended in Holt's Ledge. He developed the land to the extent of putting in wood roads, clearing a maple sugar orchard of weed trees, building a sap house, and preparing the ground for a pond. The place became Raveny's domain when, almost every afternoon until fall, Ben took him from his cage, perched him on the seat of his truck and drove him to the woodlot. It took a month or two to get the pattern established, but once Raveny got the idea, he took to it as naturally as the dog. When riding he looked about as if taking in the passing scene. He liked to go to the woods, and after some traumatic experiences of getting lost and being alone, he became cooperative about returning. When days became shorter in September, Ben sometimes did not leave until late. On September 30, when darkness came on sooner than expected, Raveny did something that he had not done before. Making little small-talk vocalizations, he took Ben's finger and pulled, as if to say "time to go." Ben lighted the cab of the truck and Raveny got in.

In his car riding Raveny resembled a ninety-pound wolf that I met in our backyard. Its owners had driven up from southern New Hampshire. This was their fourth hand-raised wolf, but they found it useless to try to make it do something that it might not want to, like getting into a car. But if the wolf felt that it was going to be left behind, it would get into the car immediately.

Woods by Holt's Ledge and Wild Ravens

FAMILY OF RAVENS AND THEIR VOCALIZATIONS

Ben had fed the ravens from Holt's Ledge all winter, and I continued feeding the pair by the sap house during the spring and summer. The pair came with their two juveniles in June and early July, and although the nearest glimpses we had of them were at 100 meters, they often settled in trees on the slope above the sap house. At seven in the morning I recorded their vocalizations. The juveniles made *quaa*s [Fig. 17(A)] and *kuck*s [Fig. 17(B)] similar to those of Raveny, and the adults made loud clear calls, some identical to ones heard from ravens at other times of the year.

A call that I believed unique to the pair at this time of year was a strong *cowp, cowp, cowp, -uk* [Fig. 17(C)] that reminded me of the call of a Yellow-billed Cuckoo, a call given as many as twenty times in a row and soon repeated. Sometimes a sharper *kok-uk, kok-uk* [Fig. 17(D)] was interspersed. The vocalizations of the juveniles were mixed and varied, giving an impression that the ravens, scattered among the different trees, were in almost continual communication with each other. On a few occasions I heard a low *er-uk*, a vocalization Raveny gave at our intimate sessions but at no other time.

On June 18 and 21, seeing that the ravens were moving toward Holt's Ledge, I drove to a lookout in time to see them settle on a tree-grown ledge above where they had nested. Once settled, they continued making the loud *cowp, cowp, cowp,-uk*s and other vocalizations that I had heard by the sap house.

Raveny Gets Lost

Raveny was at home in the woods. He stayed wherever Ben worked, flying through clearings in circular flights that brought him back to the vicinity of the sap house. But in his first month or two he was not always cooperative about returning home. Instead of letting Ben put him in the truck on June 17, Raveny flew to a rafter of the sap house. He wanted to roost there and Ben let him stay. Our hope was that this might be a first step in Raveny's return to the wild.

He was close by and engaged in his usual activities on the following morning. Then he disappeared. We searched everywhere, without success. He was definitely not with the wild ravens. Three days had gone by when a friend reported seeing and "talking" to a raven on a fence post by a back road. Ben drove over and found Raveny ready to drive home. He was very glad to see us. What may have happened was suggested by his behavior two days later. When a juvenile raven circled only 20 meters above making *quaaa*s, Raveny talked back in kind. But when an adult went over making harsh *kwack*s [Fig.

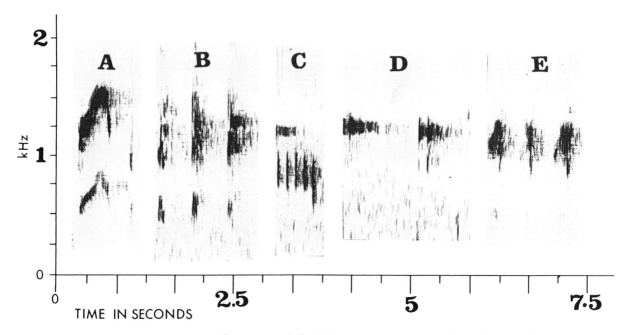

Figure 17.   Calls of a family of wild ravens in June: (A) *quaa*s; (B) *kuck*s of juveniles; (C) *kow, kow, kow-uk*; (D) *kok-uk*; (E) *kwack*s given by the adults.

17(E)], Raveny flew to Ben's shoulder immediately, as if terrified. He reacted in the same way on the following day and on four other occasions in the next few weeks. We wondered whether Raveny's parents, no longer recognizing him, had driven him away.

After his disappearance for three days and development of fear reactions to the adult ravens, the prospects of Raveny's returning to his parents seemed slim. The two wild juveniles continued to come within 20 meters of him, but Raveny showed little interest. One day when he started rattling and rolled over on his back to attack his foot, the two juveniles flew above him immediately.

In the next six weeks the wild ravens seemed to lose interest in Raveny and he in them. Then on August 8 Ben saw two ravens together on the drive. One was Raveny. Raveny flew to Ben, then back to his companion five times in the next hour, both ravens making the same high-pitched *quaa*s. In the next two weeks I saw Raveny fly with a wild raven several times. It seemed as though the wild one was seeking him. Our hopes that Raveny might join his own kind rose again. On August 12 Ben left Raveny with the wild ravens and drove away to climb a cliff with a neighbor. At the top there was not a sign of a raven. Ben then blew a powerful low-pitched dog whistle he had used on Raveny before. A few low *quarck*s came from a mile away almost immediately, then grew louder as Raveny flew in to alight on Ben's shoulder. Raveny's ability to fly about over treetops and find his way encouraged us. It again seemed that he was making progress. He roosted in the woods about twice a week rather than come home, and I noticed that he was becoming less inclined to our intimate sessions. When sitting in the car with Raveny on the roof on August 19, I saw a wild raven perched in a tree overhead, and it sang for ten minutes.

I left Raveny at the woodlot early on August 20 thinking to promote his association with wild companions. I could not find him on a number of return visits. Was Raveny staying with the wild ones? Toward evening I returned for a last look. No Raveny. Then Carl Wing, a neighbor from down the road, drove in. There was Raveny on the front seat, starving and working hard on a piece of meat. He had come to our neighbor in search of food. It seemed possible that, with a leg that dangled when he flew, Raveny was in no condition to keep up with his wild siblings. As on other occasions when he had been lost, injured, or otherwise upset, his devotion to and dependence on Ben and me became stronger than ever. After his day in the wild, Raveny followed one or the other of us more closely than before, riding on Ben's shoulder or mine as if wanting to stay close. If Ben went up the steep slope above the sap house on his three-wheeler, Raveny clung to his shoulder, holding out his wings or seizing Ben's hair to balance himself.

Jane had a remarkable experience with the wild ravens September 21. She was sitting by the sap house when the pair of ravens came to perch not far behind. She heard the *cowp*s that I thought sounded like a Yellow-billed Cuckoo, then sounds she thought similar to spring water gurgling through a tube, so musical that she found it fascinating to listen to.

FLIGHT   *Flying Free*

Raveny and the dog Peewee were always ready to take a walk. When we set out, Raveny flew down the wood road ahead to alight on tree limbs and wait for Peewee and me to catch up. Raveny seldom flew straight for any distance. He wavered and swerved through woods with abandon. If about to hit a tree with a wing, he simply pulled the wing in and passed on. When we came to a pond, the usual destination of our walks, Raveny displayed one of his standard tricks of making complete revolutions in the air, without loss of altitude, as if wings and body had become a propeller. I had wondered the winter before how ravens at the farm managed to rob crows in the woods. Would not the larger raven be clumsy in turning and twisting? But from watching Raveny at the woodlot, it was evident that ravens can be very agile. One day Raveny, seeing a stick hanging perpendicularly from a tree, caught the tip and hung momentarily by his bill before flying on.

Dog and Raven

Peewee and Raveny played with each other on every walk for some weeks. If Raveny alighted on the ground, the dog rushed to put him to flight and within a minute Raveny, seeing his chance, would fly low and silently from behind, letting out a loud *whack* in passing within centimeters of the dog's head. After some weeks Raveny lost interest, although Peewee, a bird dog, continued to flush him from the ground.

A dachshund brought by a neighbor became a steadier attraction. When it first arrived, it rushed at Raveny, barking and barking. Raveny kept alighting just ahead as if to keep it doing so. When the dachshund began to lose interest after repeated encounters, Raveny advanced head-on, as if to peck its nose. After several weeks the dachshund stayed away. But the dachshund had a tail, an appendage Peewee lacked. By pulling it Raveny got the dachshund rushing about and barking again. His seeming delight in provoking dogs was similar to much of what I have observed in crows provoking other animals.

Foraging

Although opportunities were few, Raveny was adept at catching prey when he had a chance. When I dug a hole one day, he quickly found and swallowed a dozen small earthworms. He picked up beetles and small prey when swishing away leaves with his bill, and upon encountering a grasshopper, he snipped off legs and wings, then carried the body about as if looking for a place to cache it. After a few minutes he returned to pick up the appendages and swallow them.

Ben rescued a live meadow mouse from the cat on August 18. Raveny made a rattle, jumped back, then seized the mouse by the head. He killed it with a few shakes and then cached it where I could not find it. The next day I watched him recover the mouse and swallow it whole.

Ben uncovered a number of mice when clearing away brush piles. Raveny was quick to catch and kill a white-footed mouse, which he tore to pieces before eating. An hour and a half later he put up a pellet of mouse fur. When Peewee pointed at a half-grown red-backed vole, Raveny flew down and seized and ate it right away. But he stored a medium-sized frog caught at about the same time. Although Ben watched and thought he knew where the frog was hidden, he searched for it in vain. When Raveny arrived the next morning he went straight to the frog and uncovered and ate it.

With the fall of leaves in late October, Raveny flew off and got lost several times. Each time, hunger drove him to visit some isolated house looking for food. On the last occasion he attacked an old lady, flying at her head and driving her into the house. When a man working on the place tried to ward him off, Raveny bit him on the ear. The lady called for help at the farm next door, where, fortunately, the farmer was able to catch the raven with a pair of gloves and shut him in a milk house until I arrived. It was now apparent that Raveny, with his powerful bill, could be hazardous to other people, and for a while we ceased taking him to the woodlot.

Onset of Winter

REACTION TO SNOW

How would Raveny take to snow and cold? With the onset of winter he roosted in a part of a shed that opened into his cage. The first snow fell on November 6. Raveny, always cautious about anything new, would have nothing to do with it. He perched, quiet and subdued in his shed, refusing to come out. I cleared areas of ground and built a snow pile, to no avail. Then at midday Raveny caught on. He suddenly found that the snow made a wonderful playground. The first glimpse I had of him was putting his head down and doing a somersault down the snow pile, then making a descent by lying on his side and taking a roll. He could not seem to get enough of the white stuff. He squatted in it, lay on his side or back, revolved around and around or tumbled about for minutes at a time, all the while biting at the snow and filling his bill. His bill was caked with snow so frequently that he began to look like a white-billed raven.

I was watching a wild raven at the farm on March 26 as it fed on a scrap of meat. After storing what remained, the raven walked about on granular snow four to five centimeters deep and melting. It was a dark day with occasional squalls of light rain. When a squall started, the raven began pushing its breast against the snow, putting his head well down into it, taking snow in its bill, lying on its side with both feet in the air, and at the end of each bout, resting on its lower belly with neck, head, and bill stretched upward. These bouts went on for five minutes, many of the positions being the same as those I had seen with Raveny. The performances might be called snow bathing except that there were no movements of the wings as if to get snow into the plumage. In two winters of feeding hundreds of crows I never saw one of them behave in a similar manner. On the one occasion I saw crows bathing in winter the snow was light and deep after a recent snowfall, and they made the same motions with their wings as crows do when bathing in water.

Water

I wondered how Raveny could get water to drink when his water bath froze. But I need not have worried. When I offered him water during the winter, even on days when everything was frozen, he took no interest. As far as I could determine snow alone, even when there was not much of it, seemed to be enough.

Raveny had no aversion to icy water. When Ben took him to the woodlot on a cold, windy afternoon, Raveny took a bath in an ice-rimmed brook, then in a box with running water 30 centimeters deep where, supported by his wings, he took a thorough soaking. When he emerged he was shaking ice crystals from his plumage. After this I filled his water bath several times a week and, regardless of the temperature, he always bathed, which then led to an hour or so of preening.

We were surprised to see Raveny bathe in water 30 centimeters deep. Stainton (1986) reports that when watering troughs 75 centimeters deep and two meters across were set out in Kent, she rarely saw Jackdaws, Rooks, and Carrion Crows bathe anywhere else.

PROLONGED FRIGHT AND JUMP-UPS

Wild ravens were exceedingly shy about coming to food at winter feeding stations. I saw no long-lasting fear in Raveny until, with a week of warmer weather at the end of November, several skunks ran along the edge of his cage at night trying to get in. This did not disturb him. But when a skunk dug a hole that came up inside his cage, a hole that may have been used by a rat as well, Raveny became terrified and remained in his shed, refusing to come out for nearly five days. This was in spite of my having box-trapped the skunk and filled in its hole. The hole, located at the juncture of Raveny's alcove in the shed and his cage, formed a zone Raveny was scared to cross. If pushed into his outdoor cage he alighted on only a few perches, jumping repeatedly on each as if getting electric shocks. During these days he ceased almost all usual activities and ate little. By the sixth day he was doing better and on the seventh he resumed his usual activities, in spite of finding it difficult to cross the skunk zone to reach his roosting place. His behavior reminded me of the way horses retain memories of where they were once frightened.

ABILITY TO FLY IN THE DARK

Raveny flew off one evening in the late fall, and Ben, unable to find him, started home without him. He had driven a mile when he stopped to chat at a friend's house. Happening to look up he saw Raveny flying well above the trees. He called and Raveny came down to the truck but refused to get in. Ben got in and drove to the sap house in the dark with Raveny following. Raveny then entered the cab and rode home. A time I especially noted Raveny's ability to see in the dark was when I went in to see him at or after roosting time in winter. On most nights I stepped out to visit Raveny an hour after sunset. If Raveny was still out in his cage, as he sometimes was, he would fly to me making his low *er-uk* vocalizations, take my finger, and be allopreened. Although I could not see him, he had no difficulty flying to my shoulder and then to his roost perch. According to Tansley (1964), numbers of birds normally diurnal, including pigeons and starlings, can adapt to the dark, although not as rapidly as man. Since ravens are among a relatively few avian species able to winter in the high Arctic with its months of darkness, one might suppose that some degree of night vision would be important.

Vocal Mimicry

Raveny was able to imitate three vocalizations by late fall — one of a small dog barking, one of crows cawing, and a third of Canada Geese, all being vocalizations that he could hear from his cage. I have read no descriptions of ravens mimicking vocalizations of other animals in the wild. Goodwin (1976) intimates that they do not. It is not easy, however, to know whether a vocalization one hears in the wild is real or mimicked. As I was standing on the farm on December 24, a raven flew over giving *cawk* vocalizations. After it had disappeared, I heard what I thought was a second raven coming over. I was surprised, on looking up, to see a Blue Jay overhead making *cawk*s indistinguishable from those of a raven. I have been unable to find accounts of Blue Jays mimicking ravens, and had I not been in just the right place I might never have discovered that they can.

By the end of the winter Raveny was making two new kinds of vocalizations. One was a mimicking of words that I used in talking to him, such as "Old Raveny" or "Hi, Raveny." Perching with his neck ruff bulging forward, Raveny vocalized to himself in stretches of up to twenty minutes when alone, but he would stop if he spied me looking at him from a window. The other set of vocalizations that Raveny developed in late winter were the common *cawk, cawk, cawk*s of adult wild ravens. Since wild ravens sometimes came to the yard or flew overhead, I could not tell whether he learned the vocalizations from them or developed them spontaneously.

Nesting of Wild Ravens on Holt's Ledge, 1987

Storing Food near the Nest

The pair of ravens that nested on Holt's Ledge built their nest in 1987 in an alcove, using for support a small tree growing within a cleft. There was no way of viewing the nest at close range. I could a get a good view, however, from across the valley by using 11 x 80 binoculars along with a 40-power telescope. This was in the morning when I had the sun behind me. Although I had no complete evidence, observations made from May 7 to 21, the day after the young fledged, suggested that the ravens stored food in places about the cliff as they fed them. The places were either small rocky ledges or, more frequently, patches of grass isolated here and there on the face of the ledge, all within 80 to 90 meters of the nest. On the morning of May 7 one of the ravens spent thirty-five minutes perched on trees not far from the nest. During this time it fed the two well-grown young four times, finding food in one grassy place three times, and once, after some searching, in another place. On the next morning a parent fed the young three times in twenty-five minutes from one crevice high on the cliff. Later in the morning, finding food appeared to be more difficult. A raven staying by the young had to visit five places on the cliff before finding food in one search and seven times in another. Ravens continued to find food in special places without flying away to forage on May 9 and 10, but on May 13 a raven staying by the young had to spend some time searching before recovering food. On May 14 all of the five times that I saw the young being fed were by a raven flying in from a distance, and no time was spent searching the cliff.

Ben's woodlot sloped, the last part steeply, to the portion of Holt's Ledge where the ravens nested. Ben dumped a considerable pile of trimmings and viscera from a cow in his woods at the end of April, and the pair of ravens fed on them daily, making flights to and from the cliff, seemingly to cache some of the surplus. Coyotes and other scavengers had largely consumed the remains by early May. This may have explained why the ravens ceased feeding their young on stored food by the middle of the month. When I began at this time setting out food every morning, they began feeding their young from special places on the ledge as before.

An advantage to storing, it seemed, was that a parent could stay on guard for up to an hour or more without having to fly away to forage. This concern of the adults for their young as fledging approached may have been due, in part, to fear of a pair of Red-tailed Hawks that nested not far from the cliff top. Of the two pairs of ravens that nested in Lyme in 1987, each fledged two young, one pair on May 20, forty days after the estimated day of hatching, and the other on May 21, thirty-nine days after hatching.

Discussion

Provoking other animals.   Provoking animals into attacks that can be dodged or escaped, as seen with Raveny and the dachshund, is a behavior well developed in crows, Black-billed Magpies (Lorenz 1970), and ravens. A magpie, wrote Lorenz (1970), will approach a victim from behind, hopping sideways with a characteristic crouched posture indicating preparation to fly away if need be. Then, if it can get close enough, it will peck

with all its might and simultaneously give a rapid wing beat
and retire, attacking immediately and with increased boldness
if the victim flees. Such attacks, carried on as play by a number of corvids, can be functional. Lawrence (1986) describes
ravens as attacking young wolves, wolves that had not yet
learned that if they charged one raven, others would steal their
unguarded meat. Zirrer (1945) observed a similar phenomenon in the woods of Wisconsin when watching a tomcat with
a meadow mouse. "Suddenly," he wrote, "I heard the familiar
swish of the wings [of ravens] and saw, like a bolt of lightning,
a big black object diving down at the cat's head, which caused
the surprised animal to drop the mouse and jump three to four
feet high and out of the way. At the same moment another black
object dived at the mouse and in a second or two both birds
vanished among the trees."

Not all attacks by ravens have any apparent practical objective, some seemingly spurred by sheer deviltry. Both Schaller
(1964) and Fossey (1983) describe White-necked Ravens swooping on mountain gorillas. The gorillas Schaller was watching
ducked when a pair of ravens flew over. The ravens turned and
swooped on the gorillas again and again, provoking the males
to greater anger than Schaller had ever seen in them. Fossey
observed similar attacks in the same area twenty years later.
She noted how a large male sat rigid with fear as ravens dive-
bombed his head. In both sets of observations the gorillas
seemed powerless against attacks from the air. Wolves swooped
on by Common Ravens leaped at their attackers as if joining
in play (Mech 1970).

Play.   Ravens have a strong sense of play. Moffett (1984) photo-
graphed one that rolled on its back, slid down a snowbank head-
first, then returned to do so again. Its mate slid in the same
way. Playfulness in young ravens reflects not only curiosity
about what they can do with their bills, wings, and bodies but
also with all manner of objects. Our raven investigated almost
everything from pieces of bark, to dirt in a gravel bank, shoelaces, and windshield wipers. Ravens are what Lorenz (1970)
calls "specialists in non-specialization." Such animals, having
a wide-ranging curiosity, treat everything at first as if it were
of biological importance. In terms of natural selection the
species-preserving aspect, according to Lorenz, is that a raven
constructs its environment for itself.

Tool using.   When Janes (1976) was coming from a raven's nest
in a cleft extending from the top to the bottom of a cliff, the

pair made an extremely vociferous attack, then took a position at the top of the cleft. Janes, on looking up, saw one of them toss a rock at him with a flip of its head. The ravens then tossed six more. Bonnet (1986) describes a similar defense near a nest in a crumbling cliff. When he walked below, a raven, much excited, started a small avalanche by tearing out pieces of loose rock. Ravens can toss objects in other contexts. Montevecchi (1978) watched one that was looking for eggs drop tufts of grass on an incubating kittiwake. Having seen Raveny toss stones, dig in gravel banks, and pull up tufts of grass at random, it seems likely that ravens, wild or tame, may gain experience in manipulating objects before they need to use some of them to advantage.

Returning a hand-raised raven to the wild.   It can be extremely difficult to return a hand-raised wild animal to its own kind. A few things, however, appeared to be favorable in Raveny's case. He had left his nest close to the time of fledging and, thanks to the nearness of Ben's woodlot to the nesting cliff, he had a chance to fly about in woods visited daily by his parents and siblings. He did not associate with them in his first two months, but he did have a chance to hear their vocalizations, and such vocalizations, given within a family of ravens, may be important in keeping them together. Harlow (1922) found striking individuality in males and females of breeding pairs. "Nearly every raven I have met," he wrote, "has some note that is distinctive." Roskaft and Espmark (1984) found that sibling Rooks can recognize each other even after being separated for ten months. Siblings that can recognize each other vocally, they speculate, may be more tolerant of each other than of nonsiblings, a tolerance that might be advantageous in feeding situations.

Our raven became imprinted on us even though taken within only a few days of fledging. A question is whether a raven imprinted on a human would ever be able to mate with one of his own kind. Gwinner (1964), who reared numbers of ravens taken in the mid-nestling period, found that females courted him on reaching sexual maturity. One of them performed nesting behavior with him in spite of having a male that courted her. But when Gwinner withdrew and left her with the male, she paired with him. Thus it seems that the effects of early imprinting with humans may not persist in ravens unless there is continued contact.

Vocalizations of wolves and ravens.   I find it fascinating to read of the bonds that can exist between ravens and wolves.

The two associate in feeding on carcasses, and ravens can seemingly locate kills by the howling of wolves (Harrington 1978). But food is not the full extent of their relationship. Each, according to Lawrence (1986), appears to be fascinated by the other. "Nothing is more haunting, spiritual, and primitive than the calls of ravens and wolves coming at the same time from the same location, a wild concert not infrequently heard during the breeding season of wolves and after a pack has made a kill." When the wolves howl and "the ravens respond, perhaps a dozen or more of them spread around a pack, each uttering its own particular repertoire of gurgling notes, bell-like sounds, and slurred chatter that to my ears is akin to human language." Lawrence heard seven of these concerts in the Yukon. When he and his wife raised two wolf cubs and kept them in a large cage, nine ravens perched by it every afternoon. The wolves then sang with the ravens for three minutes, with the ravens continuing to talk to each other for another half hour. As Mech (1970) expresses it, "Perhaps in some way individuals of each species have included members of the other in their social group and have formed bonds with them, much as wolves raised with humans are able to form social bonds with them."

Epilogue

My remarks are the result of many years' observation; and are I trust true in the whole, though I do not pretend to say that they are perfectly void of mistakes, or that a more nice observer might not make many additions, since subjects of this kind are inexhaustible.

Gilbert White

When I started studying crows on a bleak day at the Hendrie ranch in Florida, I had no idea where my studies would lead. All I knew was that I had loved crows for a long time and studying them was a project that I could continue for years. Making discoveries is one of the greater joys known to humankind. A marvel to me over the last forty years that I have been studying bird behavior is that so much remains to be discovered about even our commonest birds.

One of the pleasing aspects of studying crows and having a tame raven in a small town is the interest that people of country and farm backgrounds take in them. They are people who, whether hunting, fishing, farming, working in the woods, mowing the golf course, or operating the skiway, take pleasure in noting what crows, ravens, and other wild animals they happen to see are doing. The great amusement of the man mowing the golf course in Hanover, as I witnessed by going to watch him, is to buy English muffins and toss pieces of them to the crows that follow him as gulls do a ship. He thinks crows are intelligent and gives me examples. He has noted, without the aid of university courses, that the crows on the golf course live in groups and have territories. What continually impresses me about these native-born New Hampshirites is their enthusiasm. I love crows and ravens and find it gratifying that these birds occupy a special place in the minds of so many ordinary people.

"Among the numerous reasons for wishing to preserve nature," observes Griffin (1984), "are our perception of kinship with other animals and our deep curiosity about their feelings and thoughts. . . . Are these attitudes holdovers from an earlier stage of human history when hunting and protection against predators, and other interactions with the natural world were of crucial importance for human activities?" I think the attitudes are holdovers and ones to be cultivated, as I have tried to bring out in this book by portraying crows and ravens as I saw them — namely, as sentient, intelligent beings, well worth a lifetime of study.

Appendix: Scientific Names

Alligator, *Alligator mississippiensis*
Amphiuma, Two-toed, *Amphiuma means*
Anole, Green, *Anolis carolinensis*
Armadillo, *Dasypus novemcinctus*
Babbler, Gray-crowned, *Pomatostomus temporalis*
Bear, Polar, *Thalarctos maritimus*
Bobcat, *Lynx rufus*
Calfbird, *Perissocephalus tricolor*
Caracara, Crested, *Caracara plancus*
Catfish, Walking, *Clarias batrachus*
Chachalaca, Plain, *Ortalis garrula*
Chimpanzee, *Pan troglodytes*
Cooter, Peninsula, *Chrysemys floridana peninsularis*
Cormorant, Double-crested, *Phalocrocorax auritus*
          Pelagic, *P. pelagicus*
Crane, Sandhill, *Grus canadensis*
Crow, American, *Corvus brachyrhynchos*
      Black, *C. capensis*
      Caledonian, *C. moneduloides*
      Carrion, *C. corone*
      Fish, *C. ossifragus*
      Hawaiian, *C. tropicus*
      Hooded, *C. corone cornix*
      House, *C. splendens*
      Jungle, *C. macrorhynchos*
      Mariana, *C. kubaryi*
      Northwestern, *C. caurinus*
      Pied, *C. albus*
Deer, Black-tailed, *Odocoileus hemionus*
     Mule, *O. hemionus*
     Virginia, *O. virginianus*
Eagle, Bald, *Haliaeetus leucocephalus*
     Golden, *Aquila chrysaetos*

Egret, Cattle, *Bubulcus ibis*
    Great, *Casmerodius albus*
Elk, *Cervus canadensis*
Finch, Zebra, *Taeniopygia guttata*
Fox, Bat-eared, *Otocyon megalotis*
Goose, Canada, *Branta canadensis*
Goshawk, *Accipiter gentilis*
Guan, Crested, *Penelope purpurascens*
Gull, Great Black-backed, *Larus marinus*
    Laughing, *L. atricilla*
Harrier, Northern, *Circus cyaneus*
Hawk-Eagle, Ornate, *Spizaetus ornatus*
    Red-shouldered, *Buteo lineatus*
    Red-tailed, *B. jamaicensis*
Heron, Gray, *Ardea cinerea*
    Great Blue, *A. herodius*
Hog, Feral, *Sus scrofa*
Hornbill, Casqued, *Bycanistes subcylindricus*
Ibis, White, *Eudocimus albus*
Jackdaw, *Corvus monedula*
Jaeger, Parasitic, *Stercorarius parasiticus*
Jay, Beechey, *Cyanocorax beecheii*
    Blue, *Cyanocitta cristata*
    Brown, *Psilorhinus morio*
    European, *Garrulus glandularus*
    Florida Scrub, *Apelocoma c. coerulescens*
    Green, *Cyanocorax yncas*
    Pinon, *Gymnorhinus cyanocephalus*
Killdeer, *Charadrius vociferous*
Kite, Swallow-tailed, *Elanoides forficatus*
Lapwing, Southern, *Vanellus chilensis*
    V. vanellus
Magpie, Black-billed, *Pica pica*
    Yellow-billed, *P. nuttalli*
Mallard, *Anas platyrhynchos*
Miner, Noisy, *Myzantha melanocephalus*
Mouse, White-footed, *Peromyscus leucopus*
Nutcracker, Clark's *Nucifraga columbiana*
    Thick-billed, *N. caryocactes*
Otter, River, *Lutra canadensis*
Owl, Barred, *Strix varia*
    Common Screech, *Otus asio*
    Great Horned, *Bubo virginianus*
Oystercatcher, American, *Haematopus palliatus*
Partridge, Chukor, *Alectoris grecae*
Ptarmigan, Willow, *Lagopus lagopus*
Puffin, *Fratercula arctica*
Quail, Japanese, *Coturnix c. japonica*

Rabbit, Cottontail, *Sylvilagus palustris*
Raccoon, *Procyon lotor*
Rat, Cotton, *Sigmodon hispidus*
Rattlesnake, Diamondback, *Crotalus adamanteus*
Raven, Australian, *Corvus coronoides*
      Common, *C. corax*
      Little, *C. mellori*
      White-necked, *C. albicollis*
Rhino, White, *Ceratotherium simum*
Robin, American, *Turdus migratorius*
Rook, *Corvus frugilegus*
Sandpiper, Spotted, *Actitis macularia*
Siren, Greater, *Siren lacertina*
Skua, *Stercorarius parasiticus*
Squirrel, Fox, *Sciurus niger*
      Gray, *S. carolinensis*
Starling, Common, *Sturnus vulgaris*
      Golden-breasted, *Cosmopsarus regius*
      Long-tailed Glossy, *Lamprotornis purpuropterus*
Stork, Wood, *Mycteria americana*
Thrasher, Curve-billed, *Toxostoma curvirostra*
Tit, Marsh, *Parus palustris*
Tortoise, Gopher, *Gopherus polyphemus*
Toucan, Chestnut-mandibled, *Ramphastos swainsonii*
Turkey, Wild, *Meleagris gallopavo*
Vole, Red-backed, *Clethrionomys gapperi*
Vulture, Black, *Coragyps atratus*
      Egyptian, *Nephron percnopterus*
      Turkey, *Cathartes aura*
Walrus, *Odobenus rosmarus*
Willet, *Catoptrophorus semipalmatus*
Wolf, *Canis lupus*
Woodchuck, *Marmota monax*
Woodpecker, Chestnut-colored, *Celeus castaneous*
      Pileated, *Dryocopus pileatus*
      Red-headed, *Melanerpes erythrocephalus*
Wren, Bicolored, *Campylorhynchus griseus*
      Stripe-backed, *C. nuchalis*
Yellowlegs, Lesser, *Totanus flavipes*

Invertebrates

Beetle, Dung, *Scarabaeidae*
      Long-horned, *Cerambycidae*
Blowfly, *Protocaliphora* spp.
Crab, Horseshoe, *Limulus polythemus*
Dragonfly, *Anisoptera*
Flea, Crow, *Ceratophyllus rossitensis*

Katydid, *Pseudophyllinae*
Louse, Hog, *Haematopinus suis*
    Red, *Damalinia bovis*
Moth, Polyphemus, *Antheraea polyphemus*
Tick, Black-legged, *Ixodes* spp.
Whelk, *Thais lamellosa*

Plants

Bay trees, *Persea* spp.
Moss, Ball, *Tillandsia recurvata*
    Spanish, *T. usenoides*
Myrtle, Wax, *Myrica cerifera*
Oak, Live, *Quercus virginiana*
Palm, Cabbage, *Sabal palmetto*
Pokeberry, *Phytolacca americana*
Winterberry, Smooth, *Ilex laevigata*

References

Altman, S. A. 1956. Avian mobbing behavior and predator recognition. *Condor* 58:241–53.

———. 1974. Baboons, space, time, and energy. *Am. Zool.* 1: 221–48.

Amadon, D. 1944. A preliminary life history study of the Florida Scrub Jay, *Cyanocitta c. coerulescens. Am. Mus. Novit.* 1252: 1–22.

Andrew, D. G. 1969. Food-hiding by Rooks. *Brit. Birds* 62:334–36.

Andrew, R. J. 1962. Evolution of intelligence and vocal mimicking. *Science* 137:585–89.

Arbor, A. 1954. *The mind and the eye.* Cambridge: Cambridge Univ. Press.

Austad, S. N., and K. N. Rabenold. 1985. Reproductive enhancement by helpers and an experimental inquiry into its mechanism. *Behav. Ecol. Sociobiol.* 17:19–27.

Babenko, V. G., and I. K. Barysheva. 1982. Numbers and some ecological features of synanthropic populations of Corvidae. *Zool. Zh.* 51:1837–45 [review, *J. Field Ornithol.* 55 (1984): 275].

Bacchus, J. C. 1943. Song of Carrion Crow. *Brit. Birds* 37:38.

Baeyens, G. 1979. Description of the social behavior of the Magpie (*Pica pica*). *Ardea* 67:28–41.

Baker, D. W., and J. G. Morris. 1980. Florida Scrub Jays foraging from feral hogs. *Auk* 97:202.

Bang, B. G. 1971. Functional anatomy of the olfactory system of 23 orders of birds. *Acta Anat. Suppl.* 58:1–76.

Barash, D. P. 1976. Mobbing behavior by crows: the effect of the "crow-in-distress" model. *Condor* 78:120.

Barnes, J. 1986. Raven rolling on the ground to avoid Peregrine. *Brit. Birds* 9:252.

Bateson, P. 1979. Sexual imprinting and optimal outbreeding. *Nature* 273:659–60.

Baumgras, P. 1945. Crow killed by Red-tailed Hawk. *Wilson Bull.* 57:129.

Bell, H. 1984. The House Crow is coming. *RAOU Newsletter* 60:5.

Bent, A. C. 1937. *Life histories of North American birds of prey.* Part 1. U.S. Nat. Mus. Bull. 167.

———. 1938. *Life histories of North American birds of prey.* Part 2. U.S. Nat. Mus. Bull. 170.

———. 1946. Life histories of North American jays, crows, and titmice. U.S. Nat. Mus. Bull. 191.

Bijlsma, R. G., and P. L. Meininger. 1984. Behaviour of the House Crow *Corvus splendens* and additional notes on its distribution. *Le Gerfaut* 74:3–13.

Bildstein, K. L. 1982. Responses of Northern Harriers to mobbing passerines. *J. Field Ornithol.* 53:7–14.

Bird, J., J. Alcock, and W. J. Erickmann. 1973. Starlings stealing worms from robins. *Wilson Bull.* 85:480–82.

Blockstein, D. E. 1986. Nesting trios of Mourning Doves. *Wilson Bull.* 98:309–11.

Bock, W. J., R. P. Balda, and S. B. Vander Wall. 1973. Morphology of sublingual pouch and tongue musculature in Clark's Nutcracker. *Auk* 90:491–519.

Bonnet, J. 1986. Comportement curieux d'un Grand Corbeau à son site de nidification. *Alauda* 54:71.

Bossema, I., and R. F. Benus. 1985. Territorial defence and intrapair cooperation in the Carrion Crow (*Corvus corone*). *Behav. Ecol. Sociobiol.* 16:99–104.

Brockmann, H. J., and C. J. Barnard. 1979. Kleptoparasitism in birds. *Anim. Behav.* 27:487–514.

Brooke, M. de L. 1985. The effect of allopreening on tick burdens of molting Eudyptid Penguins. *Auk* 102:893–95.

Brown, E. D. 1985. The role of song among Common Crows (*Corvus brachyrhynchos*). *Z. Tierpsychol.* 68:115–36.

Brown, J. L. 1978. Avian communal breeding systems. *Ann. Rev. Ecol. Syst.* 9:123–55.

Brown, R. N. 1974. Aspects of vocal behavior of the raven (*Corvus corax*) in interior Alaska. M.S. thesis, Univ. Alaska, Fairbanks.

Buitron, D. 1983a. Extra-pair courtship in Black-billed Magpies. *Anim. Behav.* 31:211–20.

———. 1983b. Variability in the responses of Black-billed Magpies to natural predators. *Behaviour* 87:209–36.

Buitron, D., and G. L. Nuechterlein. 1985. Experiments on olfactory detection of food caches by Black-billed Magpies. *Condor* 87:92–95.

Burley, N. 1985. Leg-band color and mortality patterns in captive breeding populations of Zebra Finches. *Auk* 102:647–51.

Butler, R. W., N. A. M. Verbeek, and H. Richardson. 1984. Breeding biology of the Northwestern Crow. *Wilson Bull.* 96:408–18.

Caffrey, C. 1987. To help or not to help. Not so straightforward in American Crows. Paper presented at 105th AOU meeting, San Francisco. Abst. No. 230.

Carr, A. 1983. Life lines. Triple-clutchers. *Anim. Kingdom* 86: 46–49.

Chadwick, D. H. 1983. Etosha: Namibia's kingdom of animals. *Natl. Geog.* 163:344–85.

Chamberlain, D. R., and G. W. Cornwell. 1971. Selected vocalizations of the Common Crow. *Auk* 88:613–34.

Charles, J. K. 1972. Territorial behavior and the limitation of population size in the crow, *Corvus corone* and *Corvus cornix*. Ph.D. diss., Aberdeen Univ.

Christian, K. A. 1980. Cleaning/feeding symbioses between birds and reptiles of the Galapagos Islands: new observations of inter-island variability. *Auk* 97:887–89.

Conant, J. B. 1964. *Two modes of thought*. New York: Trident Press.

Conner, R. N. 1974. Red-bellied Woodpecker predation on nestling Carolina Chickadee. *Auk* 91:836.

Conner, R. N., and C. S. Adkisson. 1976. Concentration of foraging Common Ravens along the Trans-Canada Highway. *Can. Field-Nat.* 90:496–97.

Conner, R. N., I. D. Prather, and C. S. Adkisson. 1975. Common Raven and Starling reliance on sentinel Common Crows. *Condor* 77:517.

Coombs, F. 1978. *The crows*. London: B. T. Batsford.

Coulson, J. C., and E. White. 1958. The effect of age on the breeding biology of the Kittiwake *Rissa tridactyla*. *Ibis* 100: 40–51.

Craighead, J. J., and F. C. Craighead, Jr. 1969. *Hawks, owls, and wildlife*. New York: Dover Publications.

Criddle, N. 1927. A tale of four crows. *Can. Field-Nat.* 41:179–83.

Crisler, L. 1958. *Arctic wild*. New York: Harper & Brothers.

Croze, H. 1970. Searching image in Carrion Crow. *Z. Tierpsychol.* (Suppl.) 5:1–86.

D'Agostino, G. M., L. E. Giovinazzo, and S. W. Eaton. 1981. The sentinel crow as an extension of parental care. *Wilson Bull.* 93:394–95.

Darling, F. F. 1952. Social behavior and survival. *Auk* 69:183–91.

Darwin, C. 1859. *On the origin of species by means of natural selection, or the preservation of favoured races in the struggle for life*. London: John Murray.

Davis, W. H. 1983. Behavior of crows (*Corvus brachyrhynchos*) in Lexington. *Kentucky Warbler* 59:33–34.

Dean, W. R. J., and I. A. W. MacDonald. 1981. A review of African birds feeding in association with mammals. *Ostrich* 52: 135–55.

Dhindsa, M. S., and P. S. Sandhu. 1984. Morphometric variation in a population of the House Crow, *Corvus splendens*. *Le Gerfaut* 74:139–144.

Dorn, J. L. 1972. The Common Raven in Jackson Hole, Wyoming. M.S. thesis, Univ. Wyoming, Laramie.

Dow, D. D. 1970. Communal behavior of nesting Noisey Miners. *Emu* 70:131–34.

Dubos, R. 1965. *Man adapting*. New Haven, Conn.: Yale Univ. Press.

Dunn, P. J. 1985. Feeding methods of coastal Carrion Crows. *Brit. Birds* 78:151–52.

Dwight, J., Jr. 1975. The sequence of plumages and molts of the passerine birds of New York. *Ann. N.Y. Acad. Sci.* 13:73–360.

Eduardo Santana, C., R. L. Knight, and S. A. Temple. 1986. Parental care at Red-tailed Hawk nest tended by three adults. *Condor* 88:110–11.

Elliot, R. D. 1977. Hanging behavior in Common Ravens. *Auk* 94:777–78.

Ellison, L. N., and L. Cleary. 1978. Effects of human disturbance on breeding of Double-crested Cormorants. *Auk* 95:510–17.

Emlen, J. T., Jr. 1936. Age determination of the American Crow. *Condor* 38:99–102.

———. 1942. Notes on a nesting colony of Western Crows. *Birdbanding* 13:143–54.

Emlen, S. T., and S. L. Vehrencamp. 1983. Cooperative breeding strategies among birds. In *Perspectives in ornithology*, ed. A. H. Brush and G. A. Clark, Jr. Cambridge: Cambridge Univ. Press.

Erikstad, K. E., R. Blom, and S. Myrberget. 1982. Territorial Hooded Crows as predators of Willow Ptarmigan nests. *J. Wildlife Man.* 46:109–14.

Erpino, M. J. 1968. Nest-related activities of Black-billed Magpies. *Condor* 70:154–65.

Erskine, A. J. 1968. Encounters between Bald Eagles and other birds in winter. *Auk* 85:681–83.

———. 1980. A House Sparrow die-off. *Nova Scotia Bird Society Newsletter* 22:183–84.

Fischer, D. L. 1985. Piracy behavior of wintering Bald Eagles. *Condor* 87:246–51.

Forbush, E. H. 1927. *Birds of Massachusetts and other New England States*. Vol. 2. Boston: Commonwealth of Massachusetts.

Ford, N. L. 1983. Variation in mate fidelity in monogamous birds. *Current Ornithol.* 1:329–56.

Fossey, D. 1983. *Gorillas in the mist*. Boston: Houghton Mifflin.

Funderburg, J. B. 1967a. Common Crows drinking in flight. *Fla. Nat.* 40:66–67.

———. 1967b. Common Crows preying on feral pigeons. *Fla. Nat.* 40:67.

Gaston, A. J. 1977. Social behavior within groups of Jungle Bab-blers *Turdoides striatus*. *Anim. Behav.* 25:828–48.

———. 1978. The evolution of group territorial behavior and co-operative breeding. *Am. Nat.* 112:1091–1100.

Gent, C. J. 1949. Coition of Carrion Crow on ground. *Brit. Birds* 42:242.

George, W. G., and T. Kimmel. 1977. A slaughter of mice by Com-mon Crows. *Auk* 94:782–83.

Giffin, J. G. 1983. Alala investigation. Final report. State of Ha-waii, Dept. of Land and Nat. Res., Div. Forestry and Wildlife, pp. 1–51.

Glading, B., and C. H. Glading. 1970. An instance of a captive Turkey Vulture killing prey. *Condor* 72:244–45.

Gladstone, D. E. 1979. Promiscuity in monogamous colonial birds. *Am. Nat.* 114:545–57.

Good, E. E. 1952. The life history of the American Crow *Corvus brachyrhynchos* Brehm. Ph.D. diss., Ohio State Univ.

Goodall, J. 1965. Chimpanzees of the Gombe Stream Reserve. Pp. 425–47 in *Primate behavior*, ed. I. DeVore. New York: Holt, Rinehart and Winston.

———. 1986. *The chimpanzees of Gombe*. Cambridge, Mass.: Belknap Press, Harvard Univ.

Goodwin, D. 1976. *Crows of the world*. Ithaca, N.Y.: Comstock Publishing Assoc.

Grant, P. R. 1971. Interactive behavior of puffins (*Fratercula arc-tica*) and skuas (*Stercorarius parasiticus*). *Behaviour* 40:263–81.

Greenslet, F. 1946. *The Lowells and their seven worlds*. Boston: Houghton Mifflin.

Griffin, D. R. 1976. *The question of animal awareness*. New York: Rockefeller Univ. Press.

———. 1984. *Animal thinking*. Cambridge, Mass.: Harvard Univ. Press.

Grobecker, D. B., and T. W. Pietsch. 1978. Crows' use of auto-mobiles as nutcrackers. *Auk* 95:760–61.

Gwinner, E. 1964. Untersuchungen über das Ausdrucks und So-zialverhalten des Kolkraben (*Corvus corax*). *Z. Tierpsychol.* 21:657–748.

———. 1965. Über den Einfluss des Hungers und anderer Fak-toren auf die Versteck-Activitat des Kolkraben (*Corvus corax*). *Vogelwarte* 23:1–4.

———. 1966. Über einige Bewegungsspiele des Kolkraben (*Cor-vus corax*). *Z. Tierpsychol.* 23:28–36.

Haase, B. L. 1963. The winter flocking behavior of the Common Crow (*Corvus brachyrhynchos* Brehm). *Ohio J. Sci.* 63:145–51.

Hamas, M. J. 1984. Crow predation on Spotted Sandpipers. *J. Field Ornithol.* 55:117–18.

Hamerstrom, F. 1957. The influence of a hawk's appetite on mob-bing. *Condor* 59:192–94.

Hanford, D. M. 1969. Carrion Crow persistently stooping at swallows. *Brit. Birds* 62:158.

Hardy, J. W. 1974. Behavior and its evolution in neotropical jays (*Cissilopha*). *Bird-banding* 45:253–68.

Harlow, R. C. 1922. The breeding habits of Northern Ravens in Pennsylvania. *Auk* 39:399–410.

Harrington, F. H. 1978. Ravens attracted to wolf howling. *Condor* 80:236–37.

Harrison, C. J. O. 1965. Allopreening as agonistic behavior. *Behavior* 24:161–209.

Harthan, A. J. 1940–41. Grey squirrels taking young Rooks. *Brit. Birds* 34:94.

Hartman, F. A. 1955. Heart weight in birds. *Condor* 57:221–38.

Hatch, J. J. 1975. Piracy of Laughing Gulls *Larus atricilla*, an example of the selfish group. *Ibis* 117:357–65.

Hatt, R. T. 1929. The red squirrel; its life history and habits. *Roosevelt Wild Life Annals* 2:7–146.

Hauri, R. 1956. Beitrage zur Biologie des Kolkraben (*Corvus corax*). *Ornith. Beobachtungen* 53:28–35.

Henrich, B. 1986. Ravens on my mind. *Audubon* 88:74–77.

Hendricks, P. 1980. Anting by Common Crows. *J. Field Ornithol.* 51:177–78.

Hess, G. K. 1978. Possible food storing by a Common Crow. *Delmarva Ornithol.* 13:21.

Hewson, R. 1981. Scavenging of mammal carcasses by birds in West Scotland. *J. Zool. Lond.* 194:525–37.

———. 1982. Hoarding of carrion by Carrion Crow. *Brit. Birds* 74:509–12.

Hicks, L. E., and C. A. Dambach. 1935. Sex ratios and weights in wintering crows. *Bird-banding* 6:65–66.

Hoglund, J. 1985. Foraging success of Rooks *Corvus frugilegus* in mixed species flocks. *Ornis Fennica* 62:19–22.

Holyoak, D. 1967. Breeding biology of the Corvidae. *Bird Study* 14:153–68.

———. 1970. Sex differences in feeding behavior and size in the Carrion Crow. *Ibis* 112:397–400.

Houston, C. S. 1977. Changing patterns of Corvidae on the prairies. *Blue Jay* 35:149–55.

Huels, T. R. 1981. Cooperative breeding in the Golden-breasted Starling (*Cosmopsarus regius*). *Ibis* 123:539–42.

Hughes, J. 1976. Carrion Crows submerging to catch fish. *Brit. Birds* 69:273.

Humphrey, N. K. 1974. Nature's psychologists. *New Scientist* 78: 900–903.

Imler, R. H., and F. B. McMurray. 1939. Sex ratio and weights of crows wintering in Oklahoma. *Wilson Bull.* 51:244.

Isenhart, F. R., and D. F. DeSante. 1985. Observations of Scrub

Jays cleaning ectoparasites from Black-tailed Deer. *Condor* 87: 145–49.

Jaeger, E. C. 1963. Aerial bathing of ravens. *Condor* 65:246.

James, P. C. 1981. Attempted predation of juvenile Starlings by Northwestern Crows. *Can. Field Nat.* 95:473–74.

———. 1984. Reverse mounting in the Northwestern Crow. *J. Field Ornithol.* 54:418–19.

James, P. C., and N. A. M. Verbeek. 1983. The food storage behavior of the Northwestern Crow. *Behaviour* 85:276–91.

———. 1984. Temporal and energetic aspects of food storage in Northwestern Crows. *Ardea* 72:207–215.

———. 1985. Clam storage in a Northwestern Crow (*Corvus caurinus*): dispersion and sequencing. *Can. J. Zool.* 63:857–60.

Janes, S. W. 1976. The apparent use of rocks by a Raven in nest defense. *Condor* 78:409.

Johnston, D. W. 1959. The incubation patch and related breeding data of crows. *Murrelet* 40:6.

———. 1961. *The biosystematics of American Crows.* Seattle: Univ. Washington Press.

Jollet, A. 1984. Variations saisonières du régime alimentaire de la Corneille noire (*Corvus corone*) dans le bocage limousin. *L'Oiseau et Rev.-Française d'Ornithol.* 54:109–30.

Jollie, M. 1976. Species interrelationships of three corvids. *Biologist* 58:89–111.

Jolly, A. 1966. Lemur social behavior and primate intelligence. *Science* 153:501–506.

Kelso, L., and M. M. Nice. 1963. A Russian contribution to anting and feather mites. *Wilson Bull.* 75:23–26.

Keranen, S., and M. Soikkeli. 1985. The feather of fortune in the courtship of the raven. *Ornis Fennica* 62:23–24.

Kilham, L. 1953. Behavior of two young crows. *Atl. Nat.* 8:189–93.

———. 1954. Territorial behavior of red squirrel. *J. Mammal.* 35:252–53.

———. 1956a. Breeding and other habits of Casqued Hornbills (*Bycanistes subcylindricus*). *Smithsonian Misc. Coll.* 131 (9): vi, 1–45.

———. 1956b. Notes on courtship behavior of wild and tame Blue Jays. *Auk* 75:128–29.

———. 1958. Territorial behavior in pikas. *J. Mammal.* 39:307.

———. 1959. Territorial behavior of wintering Red-hooded Woodpeckers. *Wilson Bull.* 70:347–58.

———. 1960. Eating of sand by Blue Jays. *Condor* 62:295–96.

———. 1964. Interspecific relations of crows and Red-shouldered Hawks in mobbing behavior. *Condor* 66:247–48.

———. 1972. Caterwauling of the Barred Owl: a speculation. *New Hampshire Audubon Quart.* 25:93–94.

———. 1975. Breeding of Red-breasted Nuthatches in captivity. *Avicult. Mag.* 81:144–47.

————. 1976. Winter foraging and associated behavior of Pileated Woodpeckers in Georgia and Florida. *Auk* 96:15–24.

————. 1977. Nesting behavior of Yellow-bellied Sapsuckers. *Wilson Bull.* 89:310–24.

————. 1978. Alarm call of Crested Guan when attacked by Ornate Hawk-Eagle. *Condor* 80:347–48.

————. 1979. Courtship of Common Caracaras in Costa Rica. *Raptor Res.* 13:17–19.

————. 1980. Cocked-tail display and evasive behavior of American Oystercatcher. *Auk* 97:205.

————. 1982a. Behavior of river otters by a water hole in a drought year. *Fla. Field Nat.* 10:60–61.

————. 1982b. Florida Red-shouldered Hawk robs American Crows. *Wilson Bull.* 94:566–67.

————. 1982c. Common Crows pulling the tail and stealing food from a river otter. *Fla. Field Nat.* 10:39–40.

————. 1982d. Cleaning/feeding symbioses of Common Crows and feral hogs. *J. Field Ornithol.* 53:275–76.

————. 1983. *Life history studies of the woodpeckers of eastern North America.* Nuttall Ornithol. Club Publication No. 20.

————. 1984a. Play-like behavior of American Crows. *Fla. Field Nat.* 12:33–36.

————. 1984b. Foraging and food-storing of American Crows in Florida. *Fla. Field Nat.* 12:25–31.

————. 1984c. Cooperative breeding of American Crows. *J. Field Ornithol.* 55:349–56.

————. 1984d. Intra- and extrapair copulatory behavior of American Crows. *Wilson Bull.* 96:716–17.

————. 1984e. American Crows feeding on and storing the dung of river otters. *Fla. Field Nat.* 12:103–104.

————. 1984f. American Crows rob Great Egrets and White Ibis of large eel-like salamanders. *Col. Waterbirds* 7:143–45.

————. 1985a. Common Raven, *Corvus corax*, robs American Crows, *Corvus brachyrhynchos*, in aerial chase. *Can. Field-Nat.* 99:372.

————. 1985b. Sustained robbing of American Crows by Common Ravens at a feeding station. *J. Field Ornithol.* 56:425–26.

————. 1985c. Attacks on fawns, pigs, and other young or weakened mammals by American Crows. *Fla. Field Nat.* 13: 17–18.

————. 1985d. Food storage by American Crows in winter. *Conn. Warbler* 5:8–9.

————. 1985e. Behavior of American Crows in the early part of the breeding cycle. *Fla. Field Nat.* 13:25–31.

————. 1985f. Territorial behavior of American Crows. *Wilson Bull.* 97:389–90.

————. 1985g. Some breeding season vocalizations of American Crows in Florida. *Fla. Field Nat.* 13:49–57.

———. 1985h. American Crows provoking reactions from Wild Turkeys and Red-shouldered Hawks. *Fla. Field Nat.* 13:94–95.

———. 1986a. Renestings of American Crow in Florida and predation by raccoons. *Fla. Field Nat.* 14:21–23.

———. 1986b. Vocalizations by female American Crows early in the nesting period. *J. Field Ornithol.* 57:309–10.

Klapste, J. 1983. Little Raven *Corvus mellori* with abnormal bill. *Australian Bird Watcher* 10:25–26.

Knight, R. L. 1984. Responses of nesting Ravens to people in areas of different human densities. *Condor* 86:345–46.

Knight, R. L., and M. W. Call. 1980. *The Common Raven.* U.S. Dept. Interior, Bureau of Land Management. Tech. Note No. 344, pp. 1–61.

Knight, R. L., and S. A. Temple. 1986. Why does intensity of avian nest defense increase during the nesting cycle? *Auk* 103:318–27.

Knight, S. K., and R. L. Knight. 1986. Vigilance patterns of Bald Eagles feeding in groups. *Auk* 103:263–72.

Knopf, F. L., and B. A. Knopf. 1983. Flocking pattern of foraging American Crows in Oklahoma. *Wilson Bull.* 95:153–55.

Kuroda, N. 1975. Observations of territorial life in breeding season of a pair of Jungle Crows in city Tokyo. *Misc. Rep. Yamashima Inst. for Ornithol.* 44:1–34.

Kushlan, J. A. 1978. Nonrigorous foraging by robbing egrets. *Ecology* 59:649–53.

Lamm, D. W. 1958. A nesting study of the Pied Crow at Accra, Ghana. *Ostrich* 29:59–70.

Laskey, A. 1958. Blue Jays at Nashville, Tennessee: movements, nesting, age. *Bird-banding* 29:211–18.

Lawick-Goodall, J. van. 1967. *My friends the wild chimpanzees.* Washington, D.C.: Natl. Geog. Soc.

Lawrence, R. D. 1986. *In praise of wolves.* New York: Henry Holt.

Lawton, M. F., and R. O. Lawton. 1985. The breeding biology of the Brown Jay in Monteverde, Costa Rica. *Condor* 87:192–204.

Lincoln, G. A., P. A. Racey, P. A. Sharp, and P. J. Klangford. 1980. Endocrine changes in the Rook (*Corvus frugilegus*) associated with spring and autumn. *J. Zool.* (Lond.), 190:137–53.

Linsdale, J. M. 1946. American Magpie (*Pica pica hudsonia*). Pp. 133–55 in A. C. Bent, *Life histories of North American jays, crows and titmice.* U.S. Nat. Mus. Bull. 191.

Lockie, J. D. 1955. The feeding and breeding of Jackdaws and Rooks with notes on Carrion Crows and other Corvidae. *Ibis* 97: 341–69.

———. 1956. Habitat selection, flocking and feeding behavior of Hooded Crows *Corvus corone.* *Ornis Fennica* 60:105–11.

Loftin, R. W., and J. Leeds. 1981. Pileated Woodpecker takes Red-bellied Woodpecker nestling. *Fla. Field Nat.* 9:41.

Lohrl, H. 1950. Verhalten der Rabenkrahe (*Corvus c. corone*) gegenüber dem Habicht. *Z. Tierpsychol.* 7:130–33.

Loman, J. 1984. Breeding success in relation to parent size and experience in a population of the Hooded Crow. *Ornis Scand.* 15:183–87.

———. 1985. Social organization in a population of the Hooded Crow. *Ardea* 73:61–75.

Lorenz, K. 1952. *King Solomon's ring.* New York: Thomas Y. Crowell.

———. 1970. *Studies in animal and human behavior 1.* Cambridge, Mass.: Harvard Univ. Press.

Lumpkin, S. 1981. Avoidance of cuckoldry in birds: the role of the female. *Anim. Behav.* 29:303–304.

McIntyre, N. 1953. Curious behaviour of Carrion Crow. *Brit. Birds* 46:377–78.

McKendry, W. G. 1973. Carrion Crow persistently "playing" with object. *Brit. Birds* 66:400.

McNair, D. B. 1985. An auxiliary with a mated pair and food-caching in the Fish Crow. *Wilson Bull.* 97:123–25.

Mader, W. J. 1975. Extra adults at Harris' Hawk nests. *Condor* 77:482–85.

Mailliard, J. 1908. Cooper's Hawk attacking crows. *Condor* 10:129.

Marler, P. 1952. Studies of fighting in Chaffinches (4) Appetitive and consummatory behaviour. *Brit. J. Anim. Behav.* 5:29–37.

Marr, V., and R. L. Knight. 1985. Raven predation on feral Rock Dove eggs. *Murrelet* 63:25.

Marshall, A. J., and C. J. F. Coombs. 1957. The interaction of environmental, internal and behavioural factors in the Rook. *Proc. Zool. Soc. London* 128:545–89.

Maser, C. 1975. Predation by Common Ravens on feral Rock Doves. *Wilson Bull.* 87:552–53.

Mech, L. D. 1970. *The wolf.* New York: Nat. Hist. Press.

Meinertzhagen, R. 1959. *Pirates and predators.* London: Oliver and Boyd.

Merritt, P. G. 1984. Observer recognition by the Northern Mockingbird. *J. Field Ornithol.* 55:252–53.

Miller, D. B. 1979. Long term recognition of father's song by female Zebra Finches. *Nature* 280:389–91.

Moffett, A. T. 1984. Raven sliding in snow. *Brit. Brids* 77:321–22.

Moller, A. P. 1983. Habitat selection, flocking and feeding behavior of Hooded Crows *Corvus corone. Ornis Fennica* 60:105–11.

Montevecchi, W. A. 1976. Egg size and the egg predatory behavior of crows. *Behaviour* 57:307–20.

———. 1978. Corvids using objects to displace gulls from nests. *Condor* 80:349.

Morse, D. H. 1971. Great Horned Owls and nesting seabirds. *Auk* 88:426–27.

———. 1975. Erratic flights of Goldcrests *Regulus regulus* and Treecreepers *Certhia familiaris. Ibis* 117:379–82.

————. 1980. *Behavioral mechanisms in ecology.* Cambridge, Mass.: Harvard Univ. Press.

————. 1985. Flocking. Pp. 226–28 in *A dictionary of birds,* ed. B. Campbell and E. Lack. Vermilion, S.D.: Buteo Books.

Mountfort, G. 1957. *The Hawfinch.* London: Collins.

Murie, A. 1961. *A naturalist in Alaska.* New York: Devin-Adair.

Murie, O. J. 1962. Why do birds sing? *Wilson Bull.* 74:177–82.

Myers, J. P. 1978. One deleterious effect of mobbing in the Southern Lapwing (*Vanellus chilensis*). *Auk* 95:419–20.

Nero, R. W. 1983. Ravens eating salt? *Blue Jay* 41:211–12.

Nevin, W. S. 1962. Rook with unusual bill deformity. *Brit. Birds* 55:46.

Newton, I., P. E. Davis, and J. E. Davis. 1983. Ravens and buzzards in relation to sheep farming and forestry in Wales. *J. App. Ecol.* 19:681–706.

Nicolson, D. J. 1930. Habits of the Florida Red-shouldered Hawk. *Wilson Bull.* 42:32–35.

Norris, R. T. 1942. Cooper's Hawk knocked down by crows. *Murrelet* 38:37.

Picozzi, N. 1975. A study of the Carrion/Hooded Crow in northeast Scotland. *Brit. Birds* 68:409–19.

Polanyi, M. 1959. *The study of man.* Chicago: Univ. Chicago Press, Phoenix Books.

Pomeroy, D. E. 1962. Birds with abnormal bills. *Brit. Birds* 55:49–72.

Potter, E. F. 1970. Anting in wild birds, its frequency and probable purpose. *Auk* 87:692–713.

Preston, F. W. 1957. The look-out perch as a factor in predation by crows. *Wilson Bull.* 69:368–70.

Purchas, T. P. G. 1980. Feeding ecology of Rooks (*Corvus frugilegus*) on Heretaunga Plains, Hawke's Bay, New Zealand. *N.Z. J. Zool.* 7:557–78.

Radford, A. P. 1970. Carrion Crows stooping at swallows. *Brit. Birds* 63:428–29.

Raitt, R. J., and J. W. Hardy. 1979. Social behavior, habitat, and food of the Beechey Jay. *Wilson Bull.* 91:1–15.

Ratcliffe, D. A. 1962. Breeding density in the Peregrine Falcon, *Falco peregrinus,* and the raven, *Corvus corax. Ibis* 104:13–39.

Rebecca, G. W. 1985. High density breeding and ground nesting of Carrion Crows. *Scottish Birds* 13:188.

Richards, D. B., and N. S. Thompson. 1978. Critical properties of the assembly call of the Common American Crow. *Behaviour* 64:184–203.

Richards, P. R. 1976. Pair formation and the pair bond in captive Rooks. *Bird Study* 23:207–208.

Richardson, H., N. A. M. Verbeek, and R. W. Butler. 1985. Breeding success and the question of clutch size of Northwestern Crows (*Corvus caurinus*). *Ibis* 127:174–83.

Roell, A. 1978. Social behavior of the Jackdaw, *Corvus monedula*, in relation to its niche. *Behaviour* 64:1–124.

Roskaft, E. 1980. Reactions of Rooks *Corvus frugilegus* during the breeding season to intrusions by other birds and mammals. *Fauna norv. Ser. C. Cinclus* 3:56–59.

———. 1983. Male promiscuity and female adultery by the Rook *Corvus frugilegus*. *Ornis Scand.* 14:175–79.

Roskaft, E., and Y. Espmark. 1982. Vocal communication by the Rook *Corvus frugilegus* during the breeding season. *Ornis Scand.* 13:38–46.

———. 1984. Sibling recognition in the Rook (*Corvus frugilegus*). *Behavioural Processes* 9:223–30.

Rothschild, M., and B. Ford. 1964. Breeding of the rabbit flea (*Spilopsyllus cuniculi* Dale) controlled by reproductive hormones of the host. *Nature* 201:103–104.

Rowley, I. 1967. Sympatry in Australian Ravens. *Proc. Ecol. Soc. Aust.* 2:107–15.

———. 1970. Lamb predation in Australia: incidence, predisposing conditions, and the identifications of wounds. *CSIRU Wild. Res.* 15:79–123.

———. 1974. Display situations in two Australian ravens. *Emu* 74:47–52.

———. 1975. The Australian Raven. In *Bird Life*. London: The Australian Naturalist Library, Collins.

———. 1978. Communal activities among White-winged Choughs *Corcocorax melanorhamphus*. *Ibis* 120:178–97.

Royoma, T. 1966. Factors governing feeding rate, food requirement and brood size of nesting Great Tits (*Parus major*). *Ibis* 108:313–47.

Rutter, R. J., and D. H. Pimlott. 1968. *The world of the wolf.* New York: J. B. Lippincott.

Ryden, H. 1979. *God's dog.* New York: Penguin Books.

Sakai, H. F., C. J. Ralph, and C. D. Jenkins. 1986. Foraging ecology of the Hawaiian Crow, an endangered generalist. *Condor* 88:211–19.

Schaller, G. 1963. *The mountain gorilla: ecology and behavior.* Chicago: Univ. Chicago Press.

———. 1964. *The year of the gorilla.* Chicago: Univ. Chicago Press.

Schein, M. 1963. On the irreversibility of imprinting. *Z. Tierpsychol.* 20:462–73.

Schoener, T. 1971. On the theory of feeding strategies. *Ann. Rev. Ecol. Syst.* 2:369–404.

Serpell, J. 1986. *In the company of animals.* New York: Basil Blackwell.

Sheldon, C. 1960. *The wilderness of Denali.* New York: Charles Scribner's Sons.

Shepherd, J. D., and J. Mathews, Sr. 1983. Fish Crow behavior. *Conn. Warbler* 3:15–16.

Simmons, K. E. L. 1970. Further observations on food hiding in the Corvidae. *Brit. Birds* 63:175–77.

———. 1974. Direct head-scratching by Rook in flight. *Brit. Birds* 67:243.

———. 1983. Starlings eating dog feces. *Brit. Birds* 76:411.

Skead, C. J. 1952. A study of the Black Crow *Corvus capensis*. *Ibis* 94:434–51.

Skutch, A. F. 1935. Helpers at the nest. *Auk* 52:257–73.

———. 1961. Helpers among birds. *Condor* 63:198–226.

———. 1976. *Parent birds and their young*. Austin: Univ. Texas Press.

Slagsvold, T. 1982a. Sex, size, and natural selection in the Hooded Crow *Corvus corone cornix*. *Ornis Scand.* 13:165–75.

———. 1982b. Mobbing: Goshawk attacking stuffed Eagle Owl. *Brit. Birds* 75:330–33.

———. 1985. Mobbing behavior of the Hooded Crow *Corvus corone cornix* in relation to age, sex, size, season, temperature and kind of enemy. *Fauna norv. Ser. C. Cinclus* 8:9–17.

Smyth, T. 1960. An avian air battle. *Auk* 77:355–56.

Snow, D. W. 1976. *The web of adaptation*. New York: New York Times Book Co.

Sonerud, G. A., and P. E. Ejeld. 1985. Searching and caching behaviour in Hooded Crows — an experiment with artificial nests. *Fauna norv. Ser. C. Cinclus* 8:18–23.

Sordahl, T. A. 1979. Vocalizations and behaviour of the Willet. *Wilson Bull.* 91:551–52.

Southern, L. K. and W. E. Southern. 1985. Some effects of wing tags on breeding Ring-billed Gulls. *Auk* 102:38–42.

Southern, W. E. 1963. Three species observed anting on a wet lawn. *Wilson Bull.* 75:275–76.

Ståhl, A. 1985. Fishing by Hooded Crows (*Corvus corone cornix*). *Vår Fagelvärld* 44:486.

Stainton, J. M. 1986. Birds bathing in deep water. *Brit. Birds* 79:593–94.

Stallcup, J. A., and G. E. Woolfenden. 1978. Family status and contribution to breeding by Florida Scrub Jays. *Anim. Behav.* 26:1144–56.

Stiehl, R. B. 1985. Brood chronology of the Common Raven. *Wilson Bull.* 97:78–87.

Stoddard, H. L. 1978. Birds of Grady County, Georgia. *Bull. Tall Timbers Res. Sta.* 21:1–175.

Stokes, D. W. 1979. *A guide to the behavior of common birds*. Boston: Little, Brown.

Stutterheim, C. J. 1980. Cleaning symbioses involving crows and white rhino. *Lammergeyer* 30:61.

Summers-Smith, D. 1983. Magpies eating dog faeces. *Brit. Birds* 76:411.

———. 1984. Magpies hiding food in snow. *Brit. Birds* 77:25–26.

Swanberg, O. 1951. Food storage, territory and song in the Thick-billed Nutcracker. *Proc. Ornithol. Cong.* 10:545–53.

———. 1956. Territory in the Thick-billed Nutcracker *Nucifraga caryoctactes. Ibis* 98:412–19.

Tansley, K. 1964. Vision. In *A new dictionary of birds*, ed. A. L. Thompson. New York: McGraw-Hill.

Temple, S. A. 1961. A case of Turkey Vulture piracy on Great Blue Herons. *Wilson Bull.* 81:94.

Thompson, N. S. 1969. Individual identification and temporal patterning in the cawing of Common Crows. *Comm. Behav. Biol.* 4:29–33.

Thoreau, H. D. 1893. *Walden.* Boston: Houghton Mifflin.

Thurow, T. L., and H. L. Black. 1981. Ecology and behavior of the Gymnogene. *Ostrich* 52:25–35.

Tinbergen, N. 1953a. Carrion Crow striking Lapwing in the air. *Brit. Birds* 46:377.

———. 1953b. *The Herring Gull's world.* London: Collins.

Tomback, D. F. 1986. Observations on the behavior and ecology of the Mariana Crow. *Condor* 88:398–401.

Tompa, F. S. 1975. A preliminary investigation of the Carrion Crow *Corvus corone* problem in Switzerland. *Ornith. Beobachtungen* 72:181–98.

Tom-Tov, Y. 1975. Synchronization of breeding and intraspecific interference in the Carrion Crow. *Auk* 92:778–895.

———. 1976. Recognition of eggs and young by the Carrion Crow *(Corvus corone). Behaviour* 59:247–51.

Townsend, C. W. 1923. *Beach grass.* Boston: Marshall Jones.

———. 1927. Notes on the courtship of the Lesser Scaup, Everglade Kite, crow, and Boat-tailed and Great-tailed Grackles. *Auk* 44:549–54.

Trivers, R. L. 1972. Parental investment and sexual selection. Pp. 136–79 in *Sexual selection and the descent of man*, ed. B. Campbell. Chicago: Aldine Publishing.

Turcek, F. J., and L. Kelso. 1968. Ecological aspects of food transportation and storage in the Corvidae. *Commun. Behav. Biol.* (Part A), 1:277–97.

Van Vuren, D. 1984. Aerobatic rolls by ravens on Santa Cruz Island, California. *Auk* 101:620–21.

Verbeek, N. A. M. 1972a. The exploitation system of the Yellow-billed Magpie. *Univ. Calif. Publ. Zool.* 76:1–58.

———. 1972b. Comparison of displays of the Yellow-billed Magpie *(Pica nuttalli)* and other corvids. *J. Orn.* 113:297–314.

———. 1982. Egg predation by Northwestern Crows: its association with human disturbance and Bald Eagle activity. *Auk* 99: 347–52.

Verbeek, N. A. M., and R. W. Butler. 1981. Cooperative breeding of the Northwestern Crow *Corvus caurinus* in British Columbia. *Ibis* 123:183–89.

Waite, R. K. 1984. Sympatric corvidae: effect of social behavior, aggression and avoidance on feeding. *Behav. Ecol. Sociobiol.* 15:55–59.

———. 1985. Food caching and recovery by farmland corvids. *Bird Study* 32:45–49.

———. 1986. Carrion Crow recovering bread from beneath snow. *Brit. Birds* 79:659–60.

Walker, D. G. 1983. Golden Eagle killing mobbing Carrion Crow. *Brit Birds* 76:312.

Walker, M. C. 1974. Crow kills and eats Sparrow Hawk. *Oriole* 39:13–14.

Wall S. V. 1982. An experimental analysis of cache recovery in Clark's Nutcracker. *Anim. Behav.* 30:84–94.

Walsberg, G. E. 1982. Coat color, solar heat gain, and conspicuousness in the Phainopepla. *Auk* 99:495–502.

Walters, G. J. 1983. Carrion Crows causing death of Grey Heron. *Brit. Birds* 76:459.

Warncke, K. 1958. Legeruf des Kolkraben. *Vogelwelt* 79:186.

Warren, E. F. 1955. Fledging of a brood of ravens. *Brit. Birds* 48:172–75.

Warren, R. B. 1969. Carrion Crow taking Starling in the air. *Brit. Birds* 62:237–38.

Washburn, S. L., and D. A. Hamburg. 1965. The study of primate behavior. In *Primate behavior,* ed. E. DeVore. New York: Holt, Rinehart and Winston.

Washburn, S. L., P. C. Jay, and J. B. Lancaster. 1965. Field studies of old world monkeys and apes. *Science* 150:1541–45.

Weisbrod, A. R. 1971. Grooming behavior of the Blue Jay. *Living Bird* 10:271–84.

Welty, J. C. 1982. *The life of birds.* New York: Saunders College Publishing.

Whistler, H. 1983. *Popular handbook of Indian birds.* London: Oliver & Boyd.

Whitaker, L. M. 1957. Anting in birds. *Wilson Bull.* 69:195–262.

Wiley, J. W. 1975. Three adult Red-tailed Hawks tending a nest. *Condor* 77:480–82.

Wilson, D. S. 1975. The adequacy of body size as a niche difference. *Am. Nat.* 109:769–984.

Wilson, E. O. 1975. *Sociobiology: the new synthesis.* Cambridge, Mass.: Harvard Univ. Press.

Wittenberg, J. 1968. Freilanduntersuchungen zu Brütbiologie und Verhalten der Rabenkrahe (*Corvus c. corone*). *Zool. Jb. Syst.* 95:16–146.

Woolfenden, G. E. 1973. Nesting and survival in a population of Florida Scrub Jays. *Living Bird* 12:25–49.

———. 1978. Growth and survival of young Florida Scrub Jays. *Wilson Bull.* 90:1–18.

Woolfenden, G. E., and J. W. Fitzpatrick. 1977. Dominance in the Florida Scrub Jay. *Condor* 79:1–12.

———. 1984. *The Florida Scrub Jay.* Princeton, N.J.: Princeton Univ. Press.

Yapp, W. B. 1975. Carrion Crow taking House Martin. *Brit. Birds* 68:342.

Yglesias, D. 1962. *The cry of a bird.* London: William Kimber.

Zack, R. 1979. Shell dropping: decision making and optimal foraging in Northwestern Crows. *Behaviour* 68:106–107.

Zack, R., and J. D. Ligon. 1985. Cooperative breeding in *Lanius* shrikes. 1. Habitat and demography of two sympatric species. *Auk* 102:754–65.

Zirrer, F. 1945. The raven. *Passenger Pigeon* 7:60–67.

Index

The American Crow and the Common Raven was composed into type on a Compugraphic digital phototypesetter in eleven point Palatino with two points of spacing between the lines. Palatino was also selected for display. The book was designed by Jim Billingsley, typeset by Metricomp, Inc., printed offset by Thomson-Shore, Inc., and bound by John H. Dekker & Sons. The paper on which the book is printed is designed for an effective life of at least three hundred years.

TEXAS A&M UNIVERSITY PRESS : COLLEGE STATION